WOMEN'S WORK AND LIVES IN RURAL GREECE

T0300425

To my mum Alexandra, to my Freddie and to my wonderful friends in Leicester

Women's Work and Lives in Rural Greece
Appearances and Realities

GABRIELLA LAZARIDIS
University of Leicester, UK

Routledge
Taylor & Francis Group

LONDON AND NEW YORK

First published 2009 by Ashgate Publishing

2 Park Square, Milton Park, Abingdon, Oxon OX14 4RN
711 Third Avenue, New York, NY 10017, USA

Routledge is an imprint of the Taylor & Francis Group, an informa business

First issued in paperback 2016

British Library Cataloguing in Publication Data
Lazaridis, Gabriella
  Women's work and lives in rural Greece : appearances and
  realities
  1. Rural women - Greece - Social conditions 2. Rural women
  - Greece - Economic conditions 3. Sex role in the work
  environment - Greece 4. Greece - Rural conditions
  I. Title
  305.4'2'09495'091734

Library of Congress Cataloging-in-Publication Data
Lazaridis, Gabriella.
  Women's work and lives in rural Greece : appearances and realities / by Gabriella Lazaridis.
    p. cm.
  Includes bibliographical references and index.
  ISBN 978-0-7546-1212-4
  1. Rural women--Employment--Greece--Crete--History--20th century. 2. Women in agriculture--Greece--Crete--History--20th century. 3. Women--Greece--Crete--Social conditions--20th century. I. Title.

  HD6181.83.Z6C744 2009
  331.409495'091734--dc22

                                                                    2008040169

Transferred to Digital Printing 2014

ISBN 978-0-7546-1212-4 (hbk)
ISBN 978-1-138-27305-4 (pbk)

Contents

Contents

List of Figures and Tables

Figures

Tables

Acknowledgements

This book has been long in the making and the debts I have accumulated are many. I received hospitality, friendship and intellectual support from Jackie West in Bristol, to whom I remain deeply grateful.

To the people of Nohia and Platanos, let me express my profound gratitude for their hospitality and for having given of their precious time to answer my questions and share with me their way of life. Without their cooperation and understanding, this study would have been impossible.

I am indebted to Katerina Grenda-Christodoulaki for introducing me to the villagers and hence facilitating their acceptance of me. The invaluable help of the various officials working in the Orthodox Academy of Crete in Kolymbari, in the local government offices and cooperatives in Nohia and Platanos and in the offices of the Agricultural Bank of Greece and the Local Departments of the Ministry of Agriculture situated in Kastelli, Kolymbari and Chania, in giving me access to records and information is greatly appreciated.

The preparation of the final manuscript for publication has been assisted by Jo Morgan. Thank you, Jo. Many thanks to Nick James for preparing the index efficiently.

Many thanks to Taylor and Francis for letting me reproduce the paper 'Sexuality and its Cultural Construction in Rural Greece', published in the *Journal of Gender Studies*, 1995, Vol. 4, No. 3, http://informaworld.com.

I would also like to thank the Malta University Publishers Ltd for letting me reproduce parts of the papers 'Market Gardening and Women's Work in Greece' and 'Aspects of Greek and Cretan Rural Development'; both appeared in the *Journal of Mediterranean Studies*, 1995, Vol. 2, and Vol. 5 respectively.

My debt to Nick James, Tristram Hooley and Veronica Moore, whose unceasing encouragement sustained me during the difficult times, is enormous.

Over the last five difficult, rainy years, my beloved Freddie and my loving friends in Leicester have always been there for me, supported me and encouraged me to keep going on. It is to them and to my mother Alexandra that I dedicate this book.

Glossary

Agrotis (m.), *agrotissa* (f.), *agrotes* (plural)	used as a generic term in the Greek literature referring both to those who, with the help of their families, work the land, own their means of production and land and can dispose of it and its products, and to those who engage in agricultural wage-labour
ATE	Agricultural Bank of Greece
Cafeneion	Coffee shop
CAP	Common Agricultural Policy
EEC	European Economic Community
EU	European Union
EOMMEX	Hellenic Organization for Small and Medium-size Industries, Handicrafts
EOT	Greek Tourist Board
FEOGA	Fonds Europeen d' Orientation et de Garantie Agricole
GDP	Gross domestic product
IMPs (in Greek, MOPs)	Integrated Mediterranean Programmes
KEPE	Centre for Planning and Economic Development
KKE	Greek Communist Party
Koukouli/koukoulia	Cocoon/cocoons
NELE	County Council Committee for Popular Education
Nomos	Prefecture, county
OAK	Orthodox Academy of Crete
OGA	Organization for Agricultural Insurance
PASOK	Panhellenic Socialist Party
Stremma	0.25 acres or 0.10 hectares

Have women in rural Greece been empowered by economic development?

This book explores the limits and the possibilities of economic change in transforming the lives of women in rural Greece at a time of great economic and political change. The book's detailed analysis is of the period from 1970 to 1988, from the regime of the Colonels, to the rise of PASOK and Greek membership of the EU, with many additional references to the period thereafter. It is based on ethnographic research conducted in two communities of Western Crete: Nohia and Platanos. Lazaridis concentrates on three activities women are involved in: handcrafts in Nohia, market-gardening in Platanos, and olive-growing which is common to both villages. She further draws on a wealth of statistical and demographic data from Greek government and state archives, on contemporary government and other reports and on interviews with government agencies, agricultural scientists and women's organizations.

The result is a rich and fascinating account of the changing dynamics of rural life in a still-remote part of Europe. Gabriella Lazaridis is interested in the socio-cultural influences of economic development. How do the communities she studies differ in their views on women's identity and role? Are they able to move beyond traditional and religious ideals to address the needs of local women and how is this related to their different economic development? In addressing these questions Lazaridis offers an important contribution to social anthropology, rural sociology and to the literature on gender and development.

Introduction

This is a study of the limits and possibilities of economic change in transforming women's lives in two villages, Nohia and Platanos, both located in the region of Kisamos in Western Crete, between 1970 and 1988. My association with Crete began in June 1987 when I first visited the island. A three-week visit to the western part of the island provided an invaluable opportunity to get familiar with the area, which, in turn, helped me formulate a more precise research plan. During this initial visit, contacts were made with people living in six villages in the province of Kisamos and one in the province of Selinon, as well as with official agencies in the respective villages and in Chania. At this time efforts were concentrated on identifying the different work situations for women in the villages. The decision as to which villages to visit in the first place and which ones to select for the research was, to a great extent, based on the invaluable intimate knowledge of the area of an ex-social worker, whom I met in the field and who introduced me to the villagers. This, and the fact that I am of Greek origin, speak Greek fluently and had insights into some basic rules, values and meaning contexts related to Greek culture, facilitated my entry in and acceptance by the respective communities and helped to gradually create an atmosphere of friendship, mutual respect and trust. They enjoyed pointing out to me differences in the dialect they used from what they called 'Athenian Greek' and to highlight differences in customs, food, music. It took time for me to explain to them what exactly I was doing and for them to believe that I was not a tax-officer or government official in disguise. Many were, at least in the beginning, reluctant to give information on their income or *periousia* (wealth); the same holds true for political beliefs, but not to the extent described by anthropologists who did fieldwork in Greece during the 1960s and early 1970s, a period during which Greece was ruled by the Junta (dictatorship) and anyone who openly discussed his/her political beliefs, or was labelled as a political opponent of the government, ran the risk of being arrested and subjected to interrogation and torture. My nickname in Platanos was *kataskopos*, the Greek word for a spy, whereas in Nohia they called me *kopelia*, that is young girl and joked about my name, which is an unusual one in Greece. Although often introduced interchangeably as *xeni* (stranger) and *dikia mas* (ours), thus indicating that I was simultaneously near to and far from the raw immediacy of their daily experience (see Simmel 1971: 143–9), I was treated with trust and affection and felt at home with a number of different social groups.[1]

---

1 Having said that, my relations with them were complex and changed over time (see Cowan 1990: 55).

Developing and maintaining trust and rapport with the villagers was a crucial factor throughout my visit. On my part, I consciously tried to fit in with the villagers' views of whom and what I was. I had views about self-presentation with which I was, to some degree, willing to compromise. I was conscious of the fact that assuming certain postures or wearing certain clothes (such as shorts or swimming topless in the summer) may have offended some villagers. I went to great lengths to explain this to friends who visited me in the summer, but I forgot to mention it to my mother, who was a widow, but to the shock of the villagers was not wearing black, thus evoking, in the villagers' minds, a sense of dishonour for the dead.[2] As Crick (1989: 14) has commented,

> ... there is ... a gamble element in regard to the relationships one sets up. One does not know what beliefs will accrue, and one certainly cannot, as with any investment, keep withdrawing from ties just after creating them since one would then never get anything underway. Some act of trust, combined with hope – albeit keeping one's wits about one – has to be made. One may have specific research objectives, but again, the ethnographer-informant link, like any relationship is unpredictable, it unfolds in ways which neither party planned, and requires ... evolving definitions of self and changing boundaries as to what is shared and what remains private.

What was clear to me at the time was that my key informants did consciously or unconsciously affect not only what I was doing, but also to whom or to which data I had access, since the study is based on participant observation (which includes working in the greenhouses, learning to package tomatoes, harvest olives and to make handcrafts, socializing with villagers and participating in village life[3]) backed up by unstructured and biographical interviews, life histories and documentary evidence. In other words, I assumed what Burgess (1989:

---

2   See Mauss (1935). In his essay 'Les techniques du corps', Mauss shows how each society inscribes itself on the body of each of its members, and how resistant the body can be to altering the techniques it knows.

3   Reflecting back to my research experience I recognize that there are some ethical problems in relation to fieldwork: although I did explain the object of the research as clearly as I could to them and I did not give them any guarantees of confidentiality, there were times when people who were not aware of my role were present, for example in public gatherings. In social situations I was still gathering information from conversations that were taking place without announcing that I was going to include this in my field notes. At times I felt guilty. Some expected that this study would bring changes in their lives. Moreover, I could have changed the names of institutions, villages and informants in order to safeguard their anonymity. But I did not; not all of them. This is because I realized that this kind of protection is not feasible since the book contains photographs which make the villagers and other individuals identifiable to themselves and others. 'Inventing pseudonyms is no easy task. Names give meanings to people's actions and activities. Names of institutions have in some sense a symbolic value' (Burgess 1989: 206). As Barnes, cited by Akeroyd (1990) argued, there is no immaculate praxis of

81) calls, 'the participant-as-observer' role. During conversations, informants were sometimes asked to discuss particular issues related to their work and family life, whereas at other times I let the conversation follow a 'natural' course, leaving the informants to express themselves freely and bring up in the conversation whichever themes were in their opinion important, without an input from me. The biographical interview technique was employed because of its advantages compared to a semi-structured or open interview schedule. The non-directiveness of the approach gave my interviewees the opportunity to reconstruct their life, or parts of it, which they wished to share with me. It allowed me to demonstrate that my informants 'are not just responding to static opportunity structures, but are able to change and mould them through innovative behaviour and thereby create opportunities that up till then did not exist' (Kloosterman and Rath 2001: 192). The 'conversations' approach and the biographical interviews resulted in a vast amount of data as well as in data on unexpected areas. In addition, villagers sometimes offered to arrange meetings 'for coffee and a chat' (*gia kafe ke kouvenda*). These quasi-focus groups proved valuable, because they gave them the opportunity to cover themes important to them for me to hear, and also different people felt free to put emphasis on different issues and exchange different opinions.

At times I was feeling uncomfortable and at other times a sense of outrage when hospitality was pressed upon me and a 'no' answer was rarely accepted. In Greece, 'no' really means 'yes'. An assertive refusal of their *filoxenia* (hospitality) would have been regarded as rude, offensive and uncaring, a challenge to the etiquette of guest-host relations; it would have made villagers feel rejected – they sometimes said 'kala, then mas katathehese' (do you disdain us?) – saying 'no' became an anxiety to me when visiting the fourth or fifth house in the same day and offered the fourth or fifth *kerasma* (treat),[4] that is a cup of coffee accompanied by a glass of water and a 'glyko tou kouraliou', which is a sweet prepared by the housewife from a fruit, usually quince, or orange, or cherry, swimming in syrup, and some homemade biscuits, or a piece of chocolate (the favourite brand being an imitation of the Italian Baci). In the summer, different flavours of ice-cream or home-made sorbet break the conformity, or *hypovrihion* (submarine), which is a spoon of sweet paste of vanilla flavour in a glass filled with cold water, accompanied by home made lemonade. Such exuberant generosity can be attributed to the host's pride/self regard; 'the height of *eghoismos*, self-regard, is a lavish display of hospitality, since it speaks volumes about the social importance of the actor' (Herzfeld 1985: 36). As has been noted by other researchers, although the host-guest relationship is

---

fieldwork and the competent fieldworker is s/he who learns to live with and be worried by an uneasy conscience.

4 'The *kerasma* ... is a conventionalized exchange within many contexts of Greek sociability that establishes the relationship between host and guest' (Cowan 1990: 100).

idealized as a reciprocal one (ibid.), villagers' generosity can sometimes be an ordeal for the researcher (see Cowan 1991: 183), especially when 'hospitality' is competitive.[5]

I cannot claim that my experience is identical to the experiences of long term residents. Sonia Greger (1985 :17), in her thesis on Cretan mountain women in Magoulas, a village in the eastern part of the island, parallels an anthropologist's first few weeks of experience in the field with that of a child's in his/her environment. She writes: 'it felt like a "booming, buzzing confusion". Slowly, however, it begins to make some sense and coherence, and one can begin to live with its rhythms and occasional reassuring feelings of predictability'. My experience in the field cannot be compared with that of a child initiated into the community. Being Greek, I already had insights into some basic rules, values and meaning contexts related to Greek culture. Although I was not an insider, in that I came to the area already having my own values and attitudes (which did influence my interaction with the villagers as well as the issues I investigated and my interpretation of the information I collected), I was not an outsider either – I entered the area having a mix of insider and outsider characteristics. This was not a novel or shocking experience for me, because I had been through a similar one when, after having lived for most of my childhood in a Greek community in Ethiopia, my family migrated to Greece and also I was of Greek origin. Therefore, I did not experience the emotional tensions created in fieldworkers by 'the uncertainly about the culture meaning of any one's own words, gestures, movements, or other action ... and the impact of unfamiliar and sometimes shocking sights, sounds, foods, and the like' (Friedl 1986b: 197). Moreover, the fact that I was not from the area did provide me with a detachment which enabled me to see things from a different perspective than I would probably have done if I was 'one of them'. I agree with Greger's claim (op. cit.) that

> there are ... [no] pure data to be collected and presented with objectivity and neutrality which could, at the same time, convey any understanding of what it is to live as a member of the ... community. Each element of experience and information only makes sense when seen in its relation with other elements. In order to understand that part we must understand the context and try progressively to get more 'on the inside of' it!

My background as a sociologist and my interest in development issues, combined with my female gender, influenced my selection of the research topic and the subsequent direction of the research; my age at the time facilitated

---

5   For example, people wanting to know whether I have eaten in other houses in the village, what I had been offered, and expecting me to demonstrate that the food and drink they were offering me was better than what I had been offered by their co-villagers by not only not refusing to eat it but asking for a second helping.

my communication with the young, whereas my gender put barriers in terms of socialization with men[6] and limited the progress of research in certain directions.[7] This study is the outcome of my own experience and of those I have studied.

I also collected statistical, demographic and other data from the local government and state archives, as well as reports from other organizations and institutions, such as the Bureau of Gender Equality in Athens, the Orthodox Academy of Crete, the Women's and Youth associations in Nohia and Platanos, as well as the Union for Women's Rights, the National Statistical Office of Greece in Athens, local cooperatives, cooperatives' associations in Kastelli and Kolymbari to name a few. Semi-structured interviews were conducted with agricultural scientists working in the area and based in Kolymbari for Nohia and in Kastelli for Platanos and some government agencies working in Chania and in Athens. Contemporary local newspapers like the Annals of Kisamos and Selinon were also analysed.

Data collection in the various government offices was at times enjoyable and at times an ordeal. When visiting a government office or a private organization for the first time, I was almost always asked to approach the person who was in charge. The response I got varied from individual to individual; I was welcomed by some, others bluntly announced that they had no time for me, whereas a few welcomed me but withheld access to information and documents. To overcome this, I approached different individuals who had access to the same material and the negotiations started once more. There were no set rules or rigid procedures in the process of extracting information from them. Many times the document I have been refused access to by one individual was next day handed to me with a smile by another. After a while, some did grant me permission to study various files as they probably thought this to be the only way to get rid of me. Others simply refused. As Burgess (1989: 49) put it, 'there are multiple points of entry which require a continuous process of negotiation and renegotiation throughout the research. Research access is not merely granted or withheld at one particular point in time but is ongoing with the research'. At times officials did not keep their appointment with me. I was then assured by their colleagues that the person was 'somewhere there' and that s/he would be back soon, but after waiting for a couple of hours or more I gave up. There was a

---

6   The realization that because I was an unmarried young woman, I would not have been able to do certain things like socialize with the young men and observe their separate world while drinking in the *cafeneion* and/or playing cards and backgammon, came as a shock to me, when a woman informed me that I should not go in the evenings to the olive-press or the *cafeneion*, because 'there would be gossip in the village'.

7   Limitations faced by other researchers in Greece on their access to the social world due to their gender, marital and parental status, can be found in Clark's (1983) article 'Variations on Themes of Male and Female: Reflections on Gender Bias in Fieldwork in Rural Greece'.

joke among the civil servants as to why certain officials suddenly disappeared from their offices: as I was informed, each one of them has two jackets, one to wear and one to place at the back of his/her office chair. After a couple of hours in the office, s/he leaves and if someone asks for this person, colleagues say 's/he is somewhere in the building and will be back soon – his/her jacket is here'. Access to information always involved befriending an individual, who then introduced me to others within the organization. The Kafkaesque situation of Greek bureaucracy and the feelings of anxiety and perplexity I had made me identify with K, the Land Surveyor in Kafka's novel *The Castle*, and my efforts to gain access to information could always be paralleled with K's efforts to reach the Caste.

Discrepancy between statistical data available and reality posed methodological problems. For example, the Book of Births kept in the local government office of each village contained data only on children born locally; most women since the 1960s gave birth in hospitals in Chania or Athens; these babies did not appear in the local Book of Births. The same is true for the Book of Deaths. Another problem is that of the Population Register (*Dimotologion*),[8] which treats nuclear families as basic units where the husband appears as the 'head of the household' irrespective of what is the real situation. With the exception of those women who have a paid job (for example clerks, teachers, civil servants) all women appear as 'housewives', irrespective of the work they do. In addition, sometimes data on marriage of offspring and on migration was incomplete. Another example of problematic data is that of the 'Local Census of Agriculture and Livestock' (*Deltion Georgikis and Ktinotrofikis Paragogis*). The information contained here relies heavily on the personal assumptions of the village secretary as to the area and volume of production; this is obvious because numbers are always rounded; also since producers started receiving subsidies according to the number of olive trees they owned, they started to declare more than they actually had, which resulted in an augmentation in the numbers of the total olive trees in both villages. Agricultural data was either underestimated or overestimated depending on whether producers wanted to avoid taxes or obtain subsidies. This socially constructed data is also used by the National Statistical Offices of Greece, which suggests that the latter's figures are also problematic. In other words, the data found are socially produced and give us at best a very rough picture of what is going on at local level. Cross-checking is a labyrinthine task, since different figures from those found in the above mentioned book were kept for the same products by the local cooperatives and differently again by the local branches of the Ministry of Agriculture. The local officials were perplexed as to why I did not want to make up all the information instead of going through

---

8   This has information on the 'head of the household' who is always assumed to be the man irrespective of whether this is the case. It also has information on the place and date of birth of the spouses and of their offspring, name and surname of father and of mother of both spouses, place of residence, religion, date of death and occupation.

all their books and papers. 'You don't have to do all this laborious work. We will sit down one day and over a cup of coffee we will make everything up', they repeatedly said. And they added: 'Who would know anyway?'

As mentioned above, the existing demographic data grossly underestimates women's participation in economic activities. For example, it is largely omitted in the section/column of demographic data referring to villagers' occupations. They are labelled as (*nikokyres*) 'housewives', that is, their main occupation is stated to be *ikiaka*, which translates as 'domestic work', or 'housework', not *agrotisses*, that is, agriculturalists. This means that the demarcation line between women defined in the local archives as 'economically active' or 'non-active' is arbitrary and, for the purposes of indicating women's role in local economy, meaningless. Thus, available data on women's work have been treated with caution here.

The reason for this is ideological and is associated with the tendency of government officials (particularly those who work in local authorities) to regard women's work as secondary and subordinate to that of men. When asked, the secretary in Platanos, without going into details, said: 'We all know who does what here. Why do you pay attention to such minor details?' This bias concerning women's work reflects the social conventions prevalent among villagers like those living in Nohia and in Platanos. They hold the view that women's work is of secondary importance – a basic source of women's subordination – despite its actual importance for both the local economy and for the survival of the family. This attitude contradicts statements by these same officials that women's contribution in the greenhouses and their unpaid domestic services are paramount for the viability of these enterprises. The case of Nohia's women and their involvement in the production of handcrafts is similar. The contradiction is also reflected in data collected by the village secretaries in both Nohia and Platanos, where women are defined as non-productive and economically inactive 'housewives'. The reality is, however, that throughout the year women work in the greenhouses and in the fields in general, usually for much longer hours than men. Nevertheless, it is men who are listed in local archives as the family breadwinners. This contradiction appears in data on women's involvement in economies of developing countries, where 'a local economy survives thanks to women's involvement in subsistence production while men are unemployed, yet official statistics show low labor force participation for women and high participation for men' (Beneria 1982a: 140).

The shortcomings of data on women's work due to prevailing conceptual and ideological gender-related biases have been pointed out by many writers (see, for example, Beneria 1982a: 119–47; Beneria 1982b; Boserup 1986: 163; Rogers 1986: 57–78; Joekes 1989: 10, to mention a few). As Beneria (1982a: 139) argues, 'conventional labor force concepts ... are geared to measuring labor participation in commodity production – that is, in production for exchange instead of, for example, for the satisfaction of basic human needs'. She attributes this bias to 'the view that economic analysis and economic categories have been defined in relation to the process of growth and accumulation; only workers engaged in activities directly related to that process are conventionally defined as being in the labor force'. She goes on to argue that active labour should include both those who produce products for use value (which include activities geared towards the biological and social reproduction of the family) and those who are engaged in the production of exchange values either in the form of paid or unpaid labour. The women who took up market gardening in Platanos and handcrafts in Nohia are involved in production for exchange and still not counted as being in the labour force. As shown in the chapter on market gardening (Chapter 4), in the case of Platanos, failure to do so has had repercussions on the impact of development strategies and implementation of programmes adopted by the EC/EU *vis-à-vis* its member states for women and their role as economic agents.

The book concentrates on agriculture, handcrafts and women's associations in these villages and analyses the position of women in the social and economic structure of the two village communities, with an emphasis on the economic importance of women's work, bearing in mind Dimen's (1986: 64) suggestion that Greek village women do not work as persons for themselves only, but 'as merged parts of social units' as well. 'The goals of both men and women may be social rather than personal in nature, concerned with the protection and advancement of family rather than self' (ibid.: 27).

In addition to examining the role of women in the cultivation of olive trees for production of olive-oil, which continued to play an important role in the economic activities of local households, the book explores the way two different developments in the occupational structure of these villages – handcrafts in Nohia and market-gardening in Platanos – have impacted on the division of labour by sex and the lives of those women who took them up. Moreover, the way that these changes have influenced other aspects of the socio-cultural space, that is marriage, family relations, sex and fun and women's associations is analysed, as is the role of culture and of beliefs about the role of men and women in placing some limits to the emancipatory potential of economic change. Some norms and practices have proved resistant to change, while others have not. Emphasis is on the intersection of social and economic aspects and on how women and men relate to these. Changes at household level are linked with wider trends such as the impact of the state and the EC/EU policies and their role in these changes. The view held is that in order to understand the position of women, one has to explore the dialectical relationship between culture and the economy, bearing in mind that women's *positionality* varies with class, cultural context and types of work performed.

The book is composed of eight chapters. Chapter 1 addresses the persistence of small farming in Greece in general and in Crete in particular and the role of the EC/EU policies in shaping the structure of local agriculture. It also provides some basic background information on the two villages. Chapter 2 describes the family profiles of a small number of households in Nohia and in

Platanos. This is an attempt to give the reader an idea of the socio-economic position of different families – typical and exceptional – and the varying roles different activities play for different families. Chapters 3, 4 and 5 deal in detail with economic change and women's work in the two villages, concentrating on three activities women are involved in: handcrafts in Nohia, market-gardening in Platanos and production of olives, which is a common activity in both villages. Chapters 6, 7 and 8 deal with the way these changes have influenced three aspects of the socio-cultural realm, that is marriage and family relations, sex and fun, and women's associations. Among the questions I try to answer are: why did the women in Nohia never challenge the traditional and religious ideals about women's nature and role? Why did women in Platanos, at one stage of their history, move beyond the religious ideals and come to address the needs of the local women? Why had the emphasis on female chastity as an indication of social worth for individuals and their families declined in Platanos and to a lesser extent in Nohia? The book suggests that the answer to these questions lies to a considerable extent in the different economic development of the two villages and the different opportunities this had opened up for the women who live there.

Chapter 1
The Geographical and Historico-Politico-Economic Contexts

Crete[1]

The island of Crete stands at the extreme southern portion of Greek territory and is dominated by harsh mountains. It has an area of 8,261 km² and its population is around half a million people. 'It regards itself as an idiosyncratic and proudly independent part of the national entity, distinct from it, physically separated from it, but yet endowed with qualities that have made Crete the birthplace of many national leaders in politics, war, and the arts' (Herzfeld 1985: 6). Today Crete is one of Greece's leading regions in the production of olives, olive oil, grapes, citrus fruits and vegetables, all exported mostly to the mainland. Due to the morphology of the soil, mechanized agriculture is limited to the Messara Plain, which is Crete's major expanse of flatland and extends along the south-central part of the island for about 18 miles. Most of the arable land is worked in small holdings by independent proprietors. The administrative region of Crete is divided into four departments (prefectures or *nomoi*): Chania, Rethymnon, Heracleon and Lasithi.

Agriculture in Greece and in Crete until the late 1980s: The Persistence of Small Farming

The brief historical account presented here mainly concentrates on the period following Crete's unification with Greece (1913)[2] and identifies some

1   Crete was under Ottoman rule from 1669 until 1898. For reasons that are beyond the scope of this book, Crete was only ceded to Greece in 1913.

2   Greece was under Ottoman rule from 1453 AD to the first quarter of the nineteenth century, though it did not become part of the Ottoman Empire until 1669, nearly 200 years after the fall of Constantinople. Land was nationalized, belonging to Allah and his representative on earth, the Sultan. This, along with laws forbidding those who worked on the land to leave, functioned as a barrier to the development of a class of big landowners. Some land remained in private ownership (church land and land donated to individuals for their services) but in Crete this comprised a very small part of the total. Such privately owned land was divided into small parcels. Moreover, land was organized under the *timar* system of landholdings, according to which the *timar* holders (called *sipahis*) had 'no ownership rights over the land ... they simply had a

of the factors which have influenced social and economic changes in the area. It addresses the persistence of small-scale farming, analyses the role of the European Community policies during the first decade of Greece's accession (Greece became a full member-state of the EC in 1981), since their implementation has had (and still has) a major impact on the working lives of rural women and men.

At the turn of the twentieth century many peasants in Greece and in Crete were landless, whereas a few owned large areas of land.[3] This led to peasant unrest over redistribution of land, and the bloodshed which took place in Kileler (Thessaly) in March 1910 (Kordatos 1973:281). According to Kordatos (ibid.:283), the need for recruiting peasants for the armed forces in the First World War, together with the pressure put on the government by peasant unrest, made the government enact laws in favour of the peasantry. Hence, in 1917 reforms[4] meant the redistribution of land to landless families, which, however,

---

non-hereditary right to part of the produce, in exchange for which they were obliged to provide both administrative and military services to the Porte [the government of the Ottoman Empire]' (Mouzelis 1979: 4). Those who worked the land had a hereditary right to use of the land, but paid no rent to the state. They were taxed heavily though, and in this way the state was extracting surplus from them. However, in its concern to prevent any challenge from local potentates, the state sought to restrict the control exercised by *timar* holders over those who cultivated the land and to prevent them from being reduced to mere serfs. According to Kousis (1984: 45), under Ottoman rule Crete was divided into 17 large units (*tziametia*) and 2,255 sub-units (*timaria*). However, in practice this system was administered corruptly and eventually (after the mid-sixteenth century) developed into tax farming organized in such a way that *sipahis* became landlords, and those who cultivated the land their tenants. Indebtedness to tax farmers or their agents pauperized many of those who worked the land and the land was usurped by local notables and converted into privately owned properties (Inalcik 1985; Kasaba 1988). These developments and the corresponding erosion of state control, provided the basis for the emergence in the seventeenth century of the *ciftlik* system. Under this system, the landlord provides the land, whereas the *agrotes* provide the labour. The landlord was obliged to provide shelter to the labourer and his family as well as a small piece of land for self-consumption. After the deduction of taxes and production costs, the produce was divided into three equal portions, one for the landholder and two for the labourer. Many *ciftlik* owners managed to accumulate land and thus the triangular balance between the peasants, the local lords and the state was upset in favour of the lords. Nevertheless, despite the emergence of the new landlord class and too-intensive commercialization of agriculture, agrarian capitalism did not develop. Greek independence came in 1830, with the mediation of the Great Powers (Britain, Russia and France). Crete was not included in the kingdom of Greece. The Ottomans left the island in 1898 and it was ceded to Greece in 1913.

3   For an analysis of the important developments in agriculture which took place prior to this period see Mouzelis 1978.

4   There are many *conjunctural* factors which can be used to explain why the 1917 reforms took place. First, the military coup of 1909, called by Mouzelis (1978: 107) 'a

did not come into full implementation until the influx of 1,500,000 refugees[5] from Asia Minor in 1922.

However, although small land ownership was thus encouraged or, as in Crete, reinforced, in the long run the *agrotes*[6] were squeezed by impersonal financial institutions (banks) as opposed to private land owners of the past (Vergopoulos 1975: 180). During the early part of the twentieth century, more than 83 per cent of producers in Greece were in debt (ibid.:185). It was during the Metaxas dictatorship (1936–1941) that a series of measures was introduced (law 677 of 1937) under which the interest owed by the *agrotes* was cancelled, the interest rate for new loans was reduced by 3 per cent and they were given an extended period to pay back their loans. Portions of loans which amounted to more than 60 per cent of the producer's property were written off.

State intervention continued to operate through the so-called 'safety prices' (*times asfalias*),[7] on agricultural products such as cereals, cotton and olive oil. Gradually the state took responsibility for marketing some agricultural products. Between 1922 and 1936 a series of public institutions was introduced; each channelled a specific product to other markets. In other words, one institution dealt with cotton, another with olive oil. The world crisis in 1929–1932 meant

---

bourgeois coup', marked the end of oligarchic parliamentarianism in Greece and the entrance into politics of the middle classes. 'The clash took the form of disagreement between the liberal Prime Minister Venizelos and King Constantine over the policy Greece should adopt during the First World War' (Mouzelis 1978: 108), which led to a split between Venizelists and anti-Venizelists. The interests of the peasantry were represented mainly by the Venizelist party. So, Greek peasants were drawn into the conflict between the Venizelists and anti-Venizelists and did not succeed in developing a strong agrarian party which would represent their interests. In his campaign for the December 1910 elections, Venizelos promised the peasants that he would do something to solve the agrarian problem. This led to peasant unrest over redistribution of land, and to the bloodshed which took place in Kileler (Thessaly) in March 1910. The pressure exercised by the big land owners, who wanted to preserve their rights over the land, and the landless who asked for redistribution, resulted in laws forbidding the big land owners to drive away the peasants from the land. According to Kordatos (1973: 283), it was the need for recruiting peasants for the armed forces that made the government enact laws in favour of the peasantry, and it was the 1922 influx of 1,500,000 refugees that made the implementation of the 1917 reforms imperative.

5   Around 32,000 refugees (8,270 families) arrived in Crete. More than half of these families (4,769) settled in rural Crete (Settas 1963: 75–82).

6   The term *agrotis* (plural *agrotes* and feminine *agrotissa*) is often used in Greek literature as a generic term, referring both to those who, with the help of their families, work the land and own their means of production (tools and land) and can dispose of their land and the produce of their land as they see fit, and to those who engage in agricultural wage labour. It is also the Greek term for 'farmer' and/or 'peasant' (Elefteroudakis 1960: 302, 681) – although there is also another term, *horiatis* (peasant), which is value laden, having the connotation of being 'backward' or 'culturally inferior.

7   Safety prices were first introduced by Papanastasiou in 1927.

the decrease of exports (currants, olive oil, tobacco). A number of producers turned to the production of such products as cotton, fodder, cereals and legumes for internal consumption. This, in fact, fuelled industrial development.[8]

Finally, peasants were more heavily taxed than the urban population, thus allowing for transfer of resources from agriculture in favour of industrialization. In this way, agriculture served the needs of capitalist development in Greece.

Small family-based production persisted further. One of the strongest theoretical arguments for this position is provided by Vergopoulos (1975), who argues against the Marxist position. The Marxist position entails two related 'theses': first, that with the growth of the capitalist mode of production and the increasing commoditization in agrarian societies, agriculture will follow the same path of development as industry; second, that there will be polarization of the agrarian class-structure with an increasing concentration and centralization of production into large-scale units, which, in turn, will mean the 'depeasantizing' (elimination or proletarianization) and squeezing out of small family producers by the development of capitalist farming. Small family farming continued to exist, because, as Vergopoulos argues, is served the interests of urban industrial capitalism. This argument is based on a theory developed by Samir Amin, according to which the development of agriculture must be understood in terms of an articulation between capitalist and simple commodity production, which ensures the transfer of resources from the latter to the former (Mouzelis 1979: 75,80). The reasons for this state of affairs are threefold: first, the amount of land available for cultivation is limited and cannot be reproduced at will as other commodities can; second, 'whereas in all other branches of production additional investments succeed in bringing down total costs per unit, it is only in primary production that capital investment comes up against the barrier of constant or increasing costs in relation to the invested capital' (Amin and Vergopoulos 1974: 263, translated from French by Mouzelis 1976); thirdly, small producers are constantly forced to modernize and suffer exploitation by private capital through the market mechanism – for example by paying high prices for industrial products used in agriculture while at the same time selling agricultural products at low prices – in order to increase productivity to cover expenses and pay debts. To quote Vergopoulos (1978: 446–7):

> The peasant who is working for himself does not necessarily consider himself to be a capitalist, or an entrepreneur, whose activities depend on the ability to obtain a positive rate of profit. On the contrary, although the head of his agricultural concern, he sees himself, more often than not, as a plain worker, who is entitled to a remuneration which will simply assure him his livelihood. Moreover, in the framework of domestic economy, the problem of ground rent does not arise ...

---

8 For example, the production of cotton corresponded to increased demand for raw materials by the developing textile industries in Greece, whereas the increased production of cereals for the first time satisfied internal demand for this product.

Family farming thus provides contemporary society with agricultural products at their 'cost price' (which includes the strictly necessary remuneration of labour), as well as putting the totality of his own surplus labour, which would normally correspond to profit and ground rent, at the disposal of the urban economy.

On the basis of the 1929, 1950, 1961 and 1971 agricultural censuses of Greece, Vergopoulos (1975: 211–16) revealed that the amount of farming based on family labour actually increased from 79 per cent in 1929, to 86 per cent in 1961, to 88 per cent in 1971. A survey carried out in the early 1950s revealed that 96 per cent of farmers in Crete owned all or part of their land. The remaining 4 per cent were farming: (a) lands assigned to them by the Greek government in the 1922–1923 population exchange with Turkey; (b) lands transferred by parents but not yet formally deeded; and (c) a tract owned by the occupant's relative and farmed rent free. Three-quarters of *agrotes* owned all the land which they cultivated, with an additional 20 per cent owning some and renting the remainder of the land which they cultivated. Ninety per cent of renting was on a share-cropping basis (Allbaugh 1953: 250). According to Burgel (1965), this is also true for Pobia, in southwestern Crete, where no property being cultivated entirely by wage labourers was found; he writes: 'tenant farming is a phenomenon entirely unknown in Pobia' (Burgel 1965: 61 – my translation). As Niotakis (1958: 57–8) argues, small units of production based on family labour prevail all over Greece; he calls this type of land ownership 'dwarfish ownership'. According to him, in the late 1950s, 67.4 per cent of agricultural units of production in Crete occupied an area less than 29 stremmata and these units were divided into parcels, sometimes lying far from one another. Settas (1963: 83) reveals that in the early 1960s, a family's land in Crete could be divided into six to 12 parcels (average 8.9). This tendency towards parcelization rather than concentration of the land is a characteristic of Greek agriculture.

During the rural exoduses of the 1950s, 1960s and 1970s, those who migrated preferred to keep their attachment to their land by letting it through verbal arrangements rather than selling it. The rent remained low. Vergopoulos does not seem to share the opinion held either by writers like Moysides (1986: 106, 120) who believes that rent acts as a medium for concentration of land, or with politicians like Kanelopoulos and Heleou (Vergopoulos 1965), who believed that migration is closely related to industrialization in that the transfer of surplus population from the agricultural sector to the industrial one, would lead to a rise in population in urban centres which would affect urban wages and at the same time lead to a rise in agricultural productivity and hence reduce the social cost of agriculture. Vergopoulos believes that migration of one or more family members is a key source of supplementary income, perhaps the only one available, which in fact allows for the reproduction of the family unit. As Burgel (1965: 22) writes (with reference to the village in eastern Crete he researched), in the 1960s local industries could no longer supplement farm income.

Moreover, according to Vergopoulos, private entrepreneurs avoid investing in agriculture since investments in other industries are more profitable. As a result, more than 40 per cent of the total investment in agriculture in the period 1954–1970, was undertaken by the state (OECD 1973: 22). Credit was (and still is) provided to the *agrotes* by the Agricultural Bank of Greece (ATE). As in the period after 1917, debts arise not due to bad management but because the *agrotes* are encouraged to borrow money in order to carry on. In 1962, almost all farmers had debts with ATE (Vergopoulos 1975: 229–34). One reason for the debts becoming huge was the high interest rate imposed by the bank. The state was obliged, as in the 1930s, to write off the debts. In 1964, for example, the George Papandreou government announced a partial reduction of the debt and in 1967 the Papadopoulos dictatorship wrote off the debt, which amounted to 7 billion drachmas. This state intervention secured the long-term existence of small family-based production in the primary sector.

During the late 1960s and early 1970s, the government's economic policy encouraged industrialization by keeping agricultural prices and prices of raw materials used in industrial production low, while at the same time allowing industrial prices to increase. Hence, *agrotes* had to work more and more to be able to afford industrial products and at the same time ensure the reproduction of the household. This implies a transfer of revenues via the market from the agricultural to the industrial sector; the squeezing of agricultural labour is not a product of the relation between rich and poor *agrotes*, but of producers' relations with the urban sector via the market (Vergopoulos 1975: 224, 263).

One of the factors which had in the past helped some *agrotes* to continue to exist was migration and in particular remittances. Although by the 1980s emigration from the Greek countryside had almost ceased to exist,[9] new

---

9 The mid-1970s and early 1980s recessions affected international migration movements, especially in western Europe. Many migrant receiving countries, such as France and Germany, put a stop to further immigration and encouraged returns. Thus, for Greek migrants, the whole economic climate of migration changed, the post-war emigration boom came to an end and pressure for return mounted. At the same time, urbanization ceased. Today (2008) cities like Athens are no longer attractive to the rural population. For a number of reasons, pull factors which once attracted them to the urban centres are no longer there. Athens, for example, is often covered by a yellow-grey cloud known as *nefos*, which as Gillman (1990:46) writes, 'is composed of some of the most notorious pollutants in the twentieth century, among them sulphur dioxide, carbon monoxide and nitrogen dioxide'. Moreover, long traffic jams, combined with lack of adequate public transport (despite the new metro), as well as a high rate of inflation and growing unemployment rate, make life in large cities intolerable and hence they have ceased to attract young and active members of the labour force. On the other hand, EC subsidies and the development of tourism have provided rural inhabitants with new opportunities to invest locally (Kenna 1983; 1989) and might have succeeded in orienting their efforts and aspirations to the area where they come from, rather than to the city, as had been the case until the mid-1970s.

mechanisms had developed which helped Greek and other southern European farmers – especially medium-size ones – to persist. These were European Community (EC) subsidies and adoption of a new type of cultivation geared towards new markets along with an expanding informal sector.[10] How recent EU agricultural policies regarding cuts in agricultural subsidies affect Greek and Cretan farmers remains to be seen.

Before proceeding into the next section it must be noted that although Vergopoulos' work is widely respected and regarded as one of the most significant attempts to analyse the relationship between capitalist development and agriculture in Greece in a historical and theoretical manner, it has nevertheless received some strong criticism. Moysides (1986: 120) for example, argues that since the 1950s, there has been a shift from small to large agricultural farms, especially in flat (level) areas of Thessaly, Macedonia and Thrace, where arable cultivation for cash prevails. According to him a significant role in this concentration of land is played by what he calls 'indirect type of concentration', that is concentration of land via letting it. Nevertheless, in areas such as Crete, the Ionian islands, and Peloponnesos, there is a decrease in the available land for rent. This is attributed by Moysides (1986: 116–17) to the crisis of arable cultivation which did not permit small producers (who, due to the small size of their holdings, were unable to use machinery at an efficient level) to extract an income adequate for the reproduction of the unit and so the owners of the land migrated. In contrast, those who grew vegetables, and especially early vegetables in greenhouses, were able to survive with small parcels of land. As mentioned earlier, both Vergopoulos and Burgel argue the opposite, that is they believe that a very small, if any, percentage of agricultural land in Greece is rented, and what is, is rented on a largely sharecropping basis.

Finally, contrary to the evolutionist theories which claim that with the growth of the capitalist mode of production (CMP) agriculture will follow the same path as industry, both Mouzelis and Vergopoulos see simple commodity production (SCP) prevailing in rural Greece and both agree that small land ownership based on family labour will not disappear. However, according to Vergopoulos, small private land holding – characterized by high productivity and low income – persists because it is functional to the requirements of the CMP. Mouzelis believes that the present structure of Greek agriculture and the maintenance of small land ownership must be analysed as a product of, first, a negative articulation of the CMP and SCP in Greece – that is, there is no positive complementarity between the two sectors and both productivity and income in the latter is low compared to the former – and second, the role played by classes in this process.[11] Furthermore, in order, according to Mouzelis (1978:

---

10   The informal sector in Greece as estimated accounts for around 40 per cent of national production (Gillman 1990: 50; Katrougalos and Lazaridis 2003).

11   In *Modern Greece: Facets of Underdevelopment* (1978), Mouzelis tries to explain why small producers dominated in Greece by looking at the way in which various

84–6), to find out why small land owners have prevailed in Greek agriculture, one must try 'to combine a "System" with an "action" approach, to portray human beings as both products and producers of their social world ... For insofar as collective actors are portrayed as passive puppets of a mysterious system with its laws and trends, it is impossible to explain why and how social structures either change or persist'.

Having looked at some of the reasons provided as to why small land ownership based on family labour has survived in Greece and for the underdeveloped state of Greek agriculture, I will now turn to various EC agricultural policies which were implemented in the 1980s, that is during the immediate after accession period of Greece to the EC, and try to identify the impact of these policies on Greek and Cretan agriculture and on the lives of the *agrotes*, given the structure described above.

---

interest groups shaped and were being shaped by history. Focusing on the way in which cultivators, reacting during the period between World Wars I and II to the strains created by the risks and uncertainties involved in the transition from subsistence to market economy during the penetration of Western capitalism into the Greek countryside, and the need to pay taxes, 'were brought into the political game through their dependent integration into the major bourgeois parties' (ibid.: 89–91), he brings to our attention the failure of these people to organize themselves politically. He argues that although the 1917 land reforms (which were imposed from above) did break down the big land holdings and (along with the tendency to divide the patrimony equally among children at death, instead of giving it all to the first child) contributed to the establishment of small land holdings, they 'did not contribute very much to the welfare of the peasantry ... [since] the assistance of the state (in terms of provision of credit, technical assistance, education etc.), a fundamental precondition of successful reform, was minimal if not lacking totally' (ibid.: 91–2). This, combined with population growth, resulted in extreme fragmentation of land holdings and low productivity. The industrial sector failed to absorb the surplus labour in agriculture. Those working in the primary sector either migrated or stayed in their village and suffered the high prices of industrial goods which reached the countryside and which meant indebtedness to the local grocer and the state bank. The 'negative' articulation between the industrial and the agricultural sectors contributed to the deterioration of the living conditions of those living in rural areas. Nevertheless, the discontent of those affected did not contribute to the emergence of a strong agrarian movement in Greece; rather, the 'peasants' were drawn into the 'intra-bourgeois conflict' over the issue of the monarchy, and thus their attention was diverted away from their problems. Finally, one could argue that the Greek peasants were not a class for itself, in that, as Lineton (1971: 175) argues, 'families did not seek to improve the position of the peasant generally ... but sought to push their members or climb themselves into a more powerful class ... this always involved some members moving to the city or establishing connections with members of a class based in the city'. Thus, although Greek peasants were brought into active politics, they 'were firmly kept within the boundaries of the bourgeois political parties' (Mouzelis 1978: 102).

The Impact of the EC during the 1980s

Although in the post-war period the contribution of Greek agriculture to the GDP (gross domestic product) and as a source of employment had fallen (Marsh 1979: 69), the importance of agriculture for Greece remained greater than for other southern European countries (see Table 1.1). For instance, during the early 1980s, agriculture continued to perform a major role in the economy of Greece, contributing 14.3 per cent of the GDP and occupying 28.5 per cent of the working population (Jones 1984: 236–7).

Table 1.1   The importance of agriculture in Southern Europe (1960 and 1980)

	Contribution of agriculture to GDP%		Agricultural workforce as a percentage of total workforce	
	1960	1980	1960	1980
Italy	19.0	8.0	32.8	12.8
Spain	20.0	9.0	42.3	17.4
Greece	24.9	14.3	57.0	28.5
Portugal	26.0	14.0	42.8	25.0

Sources: Yearbook of Labour Statistics 1981; OECD 1969.

Background Information

Greece became a full member of the European Community in 1981. The process of joining the Community started under the so-called 'Athens Agreement' which was signed on 9 July 1961 and came into force on 1 November 1962 (Zolotas 1978: 9). A 22-year-long transitional period was granted for giving time to Greek industries and agriculture to prepare for the competition they would face once all duties were abolished or brought down to EC levels (Freris 1986: 201–2) and to harmonize with the structural policy and prices of the Common Agricultural Policy (CAP). This was not merely a commercial agreement providing for the establishment of a customs union between the EC and Greece; it was also a political act aiming at assisting Greece to become, in due course, a full member of the EC. The process of gradual harmonization was interrupted by the Junta (1967–1974), under which relations between the two parties were frozen. As Stathatos (1979: 5) argues, the 'freeze' had been presented by the Community and had been interpreted, understood and accepted by the Greek people as 'an act to help the latter to recover their liberties'. Greece, under Karamanlis, for economic, political and ideological reasons, applied for full membership in

1975. Despite the opposition of the KKE (Communist Party) and of PASOK (Panhellenic Socialist Movement) which at the time made threats to withdraw Greece altogether from the EC if it came to power, the Act of Accession was signed in 1979.

The most important aspect of EC membership for agriculture in Greece was that it became subject to the Community's Common Agricultural Policy,[12] whose aims (agrarian development, balanced markets, adequate living conditions for farmers, self sufficiency within the community of agricultural products, reasonable prices for the consumer) were agreed upon at the Treaty of Rome (1957). The price-trading policy and the structural policy of the CAP are two important mechanisms with which the CAP tries to solve the chronic agricultural problems of the Community. It is outside the scope of this book to give a detailed account of the price-trading policy of the CAP; however, it is necessary to devote some space to the structural policy during the decade that Greece joined the EC, especially the Integrated Mediterranean Programmes (IMPs), because of their importance in Cretan agricultural development in the 1980s.

During that decade the structural policy aimed at the restructuring of the Community's agricultural sector so that the persisting structural diversity in the Community would not become exacerbated by uniform prices and trade policies, since, as Hitiris (1988: 12) argues, 'under conditions of structural diversity such as that still existing in the Community, a uniform prices and trading policy would take little account of regional disparities'.

The basic structural problem was considered to be the small size and fragmentation of farm units (see Table 1.2). In order to overcome this problem, the Common Agricultural Policy aimed at helping farmers to modernize their farms and to improve the marketing and processing of their agricultural products.[13]

---

12   Greece's agriculture prior to its accession to the EC was characterized by regional specialization. After the accession, various regions began to specialize in the production of products with the highest support from the EC, thus increasing its dependence on the CAP; the regional specific effects of this with reference to western Crete will be discussed later on in this chapter.

13   Many pieces of legislation were passed at the time. Although the picture is confusing because the Regulations and Directives are many and complex, I will mention here Regulation (EC) No.797/85 on improving the efficiency of agricultural structures (which was amended by EC Regulation No. 1760/87, but which remained in force until the end of 1994), both because of its wide use and its importance for Cretan agricultural development at the time. The measures of the Regulation which were compulsory, were the following: 'environmental aid', that is aid given to those farmers who were losing income because of the application of environmentally friendly practices; 'aid for conversion', which aimed at encouraging farmers to shift production to non-surplus products; 'extensification of production' which aimed at 'reduction in the output for a period of at least five years, of a particular commodity by at least 20 per cent without other production capacity being increased within the same utilized agricultural area' (Fennell 1987: 180); aid for afforestation of agricultural land; aid for promotion of

Table 1.2   Distribution of farms by size

Farm size in acres	Percentage of farms			
	Spain	Portugal	Greece	Italy
0–5	57.0	77.3	70.9	68.5
5–20	30.5	18.8	26.9	25.6
20–50	8.2	2.2	1.7	4.2
50+	4.3	1.3	0.2	1.7

Source: Jones 1984: 243.

There are differences between the objectives laid down by the structural policy of the 1970s and that of the 1980s. For example, due to the rise in unemployment in the non-agricultural sector during the 1980s, incentives previously given to farmers to leave the land (for example by financing retraining), were abandoned in the 1980s, whereas at the same time, incentives were given to young farmers to stay in the agricultural sector. Moreover, contrary to the situation in the 1970s, in the 1980s 'the modernization of an agricultural farm did not necessarily imply the achievement of an income level at least equal to that in the non-agricultural sector' (Caraveli-Ioannidis 1985: 60).

Finally in view of the enlargement of the EC to include Portugal and Spain, the so-called Integrated Mediterranean Programmes (IMPs) were introduced in 1985 for assisting Greece, southern France and Italy to cope with the consequences of Spain and Portugal becoming members of the EC. Their objectives were to 'provide an overall response to the diverse problems facing the regions' (Fennell 1987: 214–15) and hence, to improve incomes and the employment situation by helping agriculture to modernize and by creating opportunities for jobs or sources of income in the non-farm sector, both for those who remained in agriculture and for those who deserted it. Moreover, a distinction was drawn between, on the one hand, agricultural measures applied to 'low land' areas, where emphasis was on improvement of quality and on the other hand those programmes

vocational skills. Aid for 'farm improvement plans' was also compulsory, whereas other aid available, such as aid for group farming, aid for young farmers in the form of a premium when a person younger than 40 took over the farm, for farm account keeping, for farm management services, etc. was not compulsory. Anyone who possessed farming skills, devoted more than 50 per cent of his/her working time on the farm, derived more than 50 per cent of his/her income from that farm, could receive aid (which could take the form of capital grant), provided that s/he submitted a plan which demonstrated that the investment contemplated would, at its completion, result in 'a lasting and substantial improvement in the economic circumstances of the farm, in particular in relation to labour income ... The value of aid [was] normally no more than 35 per cent of the investment in fixed assets and 20 per cent in the case of other types of investment. In less favoured areas ... the percentages [were] 45 and 30 respectively' (ibid.: 181–2).

applied to 'mountainous' and 'semi-mountainous' areas, where emphasis was on changing to other varieties or types of products. The Member States concerned contributed 40 per cent to the costs of investment projects and the Community participation in projects was not to exceed 70 per cent of the total cost (Caravelli-Ioannidis 1985: 65–7; Fennell 1987: 215). The countries concerned had to draw up individual programmes of action and submit them by a certain date. These programmes had to be agreed by the Community before any expenditure was sanctioned, so as to prevent haphazard development which could lead to little use of the available resources. The same applied to all forms of aid intended for structural reform. Having described in brief the objectives of the IMPs, I am now going to examine the extent to which the accession to the EC affected the already existing trends in the Greek agricultural sector described earlier.

The Implications of the Implementation of the CAP for Agricultural Development in Greece in the 1980s

The implementation of the CAP in Greece during the first decade of the country becoming a full member of the European Community meant the partial loss of control over the agricultural sector by the Greek state, since some of the responsibilities which the government formerly discharged through its national policies were now embodied within the CAP. It also meant the adoption of the trade agreement with third countries, which had previously been agreed by the EC. In addition, agricultural imports (mainly meat, dairy products, coffee, tea, cereals, oils and fats) could be imported from non-EC countries at higher prices than if Greece was not in the EC, because of the so-called 'threshold prices', which were set (as part of the price-trading policy of the CAP) to protect the EC from low-priced imports. The higher cost of these imports was also felt by Greek consumers, since it was reflected in food prices and in the balance of payments (Maravegias 1989:24). Moreover, any surplus of deficit anywhere within the Community tends to lead to trade flows which affect Greece. Furthermore, the financial backing of Greek agriculture through the CAP mechanisms affected both agricultural production (by stimulating its modernization) and the income of the producers. For example, if the Greek market is over-supplied with, let us say, olive oil, the relationship for sustaining the price level to Greek producers and thus safeguarding their incomes will be borne by the Community as a whole[14] (Marsh 1979: 69). It is these socio-economic effects that I am going to describe and analyse here, in an attempt to give a picture of developments

---

14   There were other factors related to the Community's policies which affected the agricultural sector at the time. For example, the trade policies of the EC could affect the Greek agricultural sector via the changes these brought on the trade exchange of agricultural products with third countries. Moreover, the free movement of capital and labour could affect the agricultural sector via, for example, foreign investments in agriculture, food industries and so on.

in Greek agriculture in the period which followed immediately after Greece's accession to the Community and the implementation of CAP. This analysis can also suggest implications as to the effectiveness of CAP when implemented in sectors which are less developed than the Community's average.

Before proceeding, I would like to stress that it would be a mistake to expect a clear cut analysis of CAP's implementation on Greek agriculture and its effects by looking at the 1980s alone, since EC policies began to affect Greek agricultural sectors (and others) well before that. The Greek government's policies were formulated as early as 1976, taking into account forthcoming full membership of the EC (Maravegias 1989: 29–31); some results, such as the increase in production of some products after the adaptation of their prices in line with those of the EC, were already evident before Greece became a full member.[15] As mentioned earlier in this chapter, unlike the situation in many of its EC counterparts, agriculture continued to perform a key role in the Greek economy in the years that followed the country's accession to the EC (1980s). There had been some developments during the 1960s and 1970s which increased primary production at an annual rate of 3.4 per cent – developments including

15   This is also stated in the preliminary guidelines of the *Economic and Social Development Plan 1978–1982* where it is stated that: 'A considerable part of the effort will be aimed at the presentation of the economy, in particular, and the country, in general, for entry into the EC so as to maximize the advantages to be gained by new opportunities and to minimize the difficulties to be caused by short-term problems' (Centre for Planning and Economic Research (KEPE) 1979: 11–12). As far as the agricultural sector is concerned, the same Development Plan refers to efforts made by the Greek government to adapt to the CAP. More specifically, it is stated that 'with the prospects of full membership in the EC during the course of the Plan ... the policy to be followed during the relevant time will aim at the following:

   i)   To prepare the sector so as to secure the greatest possible benefit both from membership in the EC and from the application of the CAP, and to limit to the absolute minimum any possible unfavourable effects which arise as a result of the competition of Community products or of the products of countries affiliated with the EC by special arrangement.
   ii) To achieve both the quantitative, and primarily, the qualitative adaptation of agricultural production to the needs of the domestic market and to the export possibilities of EC and third countries.
   iii) To broaden the possibilities of exports of agricultural products, both to the markets of the EC and to new markets.
   iv) To improve the income of farmers and to retain the agrarian population in certain regions of special importance so as to avoid a worsening of the regional distribution of population and economic activity in the country' (ibid.: 66).

In the same Plan it is also stated that, as part of the policy of supporting agricultural incomes, the prices of Greek agricultural products and economic supports would be gradually adapted to those corresponding in the countries of the EC.

improved technology, fertilizers, suitable plant varieties and livestock breeds and extension of irrigation. These improved productivity capacity and rural living standards (KEPE 1979: 60). Nonetheless, in the late 1970s the sector was still facing problems. As mentioned in the 1978–1982 Development Plan (ibid.: 61–2), the per capita income in the agricultural sector was still much lower than that of other sectors of the economy and there were per capita income inequalities among different rural regions. Why? Several reasons are summarized in the same Plan (ibid.: 30, 32): first, the productive techniques in use, the low levels of technology used in the sector and the limited supply of aid to producers concerning organization and planning of production and the administration of farms; second, weather conditions; third, the small size, extensive fragmentation and dispersal of plots; fourth, the still large percentage of insufficiently or totally non-irrigated area;[16] fifth, the advanced age of a large proportion of the agricultural labour force; sixth, limited cooperative activity at the stage of production and processing of agricultural products; and finally, the gap between research and the application of its findings.

The government tried to take some of the problems on board with the five-year development plans,[17] but none of these were successfully dealt with. According to Plascasovitis (1986: 105) these plans were characterized by abstraction, lack of quantified assessment of means and targets (in that there was no monitoring of progress towards previously set targets), and lack of continuity (in that each plan seemed to ignore the fact that previous plans were drafted).

By the mid-1980s, the picture presented above had changed, albeit only slightly. Most agricultural holdings remained fragmented and small in size (the average size of Greek farms was about 8 acres, whereas that of farms in the EC was around 42 acres (see Table 1.2 for comparison with other southern European countries)).[18] They were also poorly equipped technically and only

---

16   In the late 1970s, of the 30 million stremmata of available agricultural land, only 8.7 million stremmata were irrigated, a small percentage (less than 3 per cent) indeed in comparison with the 16 million that could have been irrigated (KEPE 1979: 62).

17   According to Plascasovitis (1986: 202), the objectives stated in all five-year development plans of the 1970s and 1980s and in the annual programme of the Ministry of Agriculture were similar to those of the CAP. These were:

    i)   to raise and stabilize incomes and the standard of living of farmers;
    ii) to maintain the rural population in certain sensitive regions;
    iii) to improve the international competitiveness of the agricultural sector by solving its structural, organizational and institutional problems;
    iv) to enhance complementarity with the EC so as to maximize the gains from accession;
    v) to expand exports, substitute imports (mainly animal and forestry products) and to avoid the accumulation of unsaleable surpluses.

18   The average size of farms in Greece varies from region to region. For example, farm size in western Macedonia, Thrace and Thessaly is more or less twice that in the Aegean and Ionian islands, Epirus and Crete. Moreover, the total area per farm

a quarter of the total utilized agricultural land was irrigated (Hubbard and Harvey 1986: 118). This suggests the need at the time for structural reform in agriculture involving extensive investment in basic infrastructure, expansion in the use of agricultural machinery to meet acute labour shortages in peak periods as far as possible, as well as modernization of the marketing and distribution system for certain, if not all, agricultural products.

Moreover, prior to Spain's and Portugal's accession, Greek agricultural products were complementary rather than in competition with those of the other EC Member States; Greek consumption could also ease the market situation for meat, dairy products and animal feed as Greece was not self-sufficient and hence had to import large quantities of them at Community prices, which were usually higher than world prices. This problem was accentuated in the 1980s, since it was not in the interest of the Community to support the development of the dairy branch in Greece, but rather preferred Greece to ease the pressure of surpluses of such products in other Member States. The EC claims for self-sufficiency for the whole Community and not for each Member State *per se* presented Member States with problems associated with trade dependency, which these policies encouraged. Greece, for example, became even more dependent on exports of products like fruits, olive oil and vegetables, that is, items whose production was encouraged in line with agreements signed between the EC and GATT. For Greece, this tendency towards specialization meant a rise in imports of products such as beef and dairy products – one more burden on the balance of payments. The incorporation of Spain and Portugal into the EC resulted in surpluses of products like olive oil and fruits and vegetables. Hence, EC accession modified the Greek government's production targets, in that the self-sufficiency principle advocated in the pre-1980s decades was in retreat by the mid-end 1980s.

The fact that Greek agriculture became subject to CAP meant that the latter had a major impact on prices of Greek agricultural output and on its structural formation (as structural reforms were encouraged or imposed on farmers), and thus also had an impact on production and consumption levels. In the mid-1980s Hubbard and Harvey (1986: 129) predicted that agricultural production in Greece would increase as a result of EC membership. Nevertheless, the level of support and incentives granted by CAP to Community farmers proved not to be so attractive from the 1990s onwards given the over-supply of certain products and the problems associated with CAP's budgetary concerns and resulting reforms associated with cuts in agricultural subsidies etc.

In addition, the adjustment came at the expense of small farmers, since it had been the policy of the EC to assist only the 'viable' farms (that is, farms

---

is not continuous; each farm is divided into detached parcels, some of which may be few kilometres away from the rest. The average number of land parcels ranges from 3.9 in Epirus, to 7.0 in eastern Macedonia and Thrace, to 9.6 in Crete (Plascasovitis 1986: 67).

capable of providing for the reproduction of the labour force, plus a small profit); nevertheless, this, and the fact that agricultural income increased since farmers took advantage of the available subsidies, did not make the consolidation of small into large farm units inevitable in the years that followed, as ownership of agricultural land continues to be characterized by the small size of the units.

By the new millennium, the CAP had contributed to the creation of almost 50 per cent of Greece's total agricultural income but there are regional imbalances in the distribution of this support; this, together with Greece's inefficiency in implementing CAP properly, has resulted in the persistence of structural problems in the sector and hence, compared to the rest of Europe (EU-15), Greece continues to have the smallest size of farm holdings and per farmer size of farmland and the second lowest added value produced per farmer (Demoussis 2003: 174–5).

The Case of Crete

Here, I examine the implementation of the CAP in Crete during the years following Greece's accession to the EC and try to assess its impact on Cretan agriculture. Before doing this, I will briefly mention the problems encountered by the agricultural economy of Crete during the 1980s.

Two major factors of change in the structure of the Cretan economy have been the expansion of tourism (mainly in areas alongside the north coast, that is, Heracleon Chersonnesos, Malia, Agios Nikolaos, Rethymnon and Chania), and the introduction and development of market-gardening since the late 1960s (which spread out in the southern flat areas, that is Ierapetra, Tymbaki, Paleochora, Platanos etc. There has also been expansion of areas cultivated with olive trees and an increase in the production of olive oil; this is due to improvements in techniques of cultivation and the modernization of oil-producing factories (*eleourgia*). In addition, there has been an expansion in the cultivation of citrus fruits and the introduction of new varieties of fruits, such as avocados and kiwis. As a result, according to a study by Donatos et al. (1989: 36–7), the per capita income in Crete increased and did not differ much from that of the rest of the country (that is, 153,000 drachmas in the early 1980s compared to 179,000 drachmas, which was at the time the figure for the whole of Greece).[19] As will be apparent below when discussing the IMP for Crete, these figures do not imply that the standard of living in Crete was approaching the average one in Greece, as this should be viewed solely on income grounds. For example, a fundamental component of a rise in the standard of living of people is health services offered in the region where they live. According to Plascasovitis (1986: 46), in 1980 the number of doctors per 1,000 inhabitants in Crete was 13, whereas the average number for Greece was 24 and for Athens 44. This,

---

19   Donatos et al. (1989) used current prices to indicate incomes. They do not indicate whether earnings were real or not.

together with the fact that in almost every aeroplane flying to Athens there is a stretcher with a sick person, shows that Crete is dependent on the health services of Athens. In addition, the condition of the road network and the provision of recreational amenities are far from adequate in rural Crete.

The Cretan agricultural sector in the years after Greece's accession to the EC encountered, and still encounters, many problems similar to those found in the rest of Greece. These are: small and fragmented holdings, which, in turn meant under-occupation of the labour force during certain months of the year and under use of mechanical equipment, which implies a higher cost of production per unit and low labour productivity. Also, the lack of labour at peak periods (for example, during the olive and tomato harvests) presents additional problems. In addition, the low percentage of irrigated land (because of the inadequate infrastructure available for exploiting under surface water) and the lack of infrastructure in marketing and distribution and insufficient and inadequate roads, hold back further development and expansion of cultivations like vegetables and fruits in greenhouses (see Chapter 4). The persistence of traditional cultivations, such as vineyards or some varieties of oranges, adds to the burden of chronic surpluses in various sectors or of limited demand in relation to supply (of such products) in the CAP's budget. In addition, the lack of infrastructure in marketing and distribution makes it difficult for certain sensitive products, such as tomatoes, to reach the market before they are too ripe for consumption; this brings about substantial losses to the producers. Moreover, the insufficient and inadequate roads, especially in the southern and western part of the island, present more problems for both cultivators and shepherds; the latter also suffer from being unable to cross pasture land through cultivated areas without the danger of their flocks destroying production, since there are no adequate roads/paths for them to use without causing trouble to the producers; sometimes the outcome of this is bloodshed and massacre, although such actions are often the outcome of feuds (*vendetes*).

As mentioned earlier on, amongst the most important instruments implemented at the time by the CAP for the regional development of the Community were the Integrated Mediterranean Programmes (IMPs). The IMP for Crete, locally known as *MOP Kritis*, covering the whole island, was in operation from 13 November 1985 until 12 November 1992. The island was and still is regarded as one of the less privileged areas of the Community and the standard of living of its inhabitants was lower at the time than the average living standard in Greece; more than 51 per cent of the active population in Crete in 1981 – the year that Greece became a full member of the Community – were earning their living from the primary sector. The economy of the island faced special problems, characteristic of the fact that Crete is on the periphery of the country and also an island. Therefore, the Commission of the EC regarded Crete as one of the areas more likely to feel the impact of the enlargement of the Community with the accession of Spain and Portugal, because of its particular dependency on Mediterranean products.[20] The IMP was designed in such a way as to ensure and facilitate the incorporation of the Cretan economy, as part of the Greek economy, within the European one and also to avoid a probable over-dependency on the tertiary sector (mainly activities related to tourism).

The aims of the IMP for Crete were the following:

a) reduction in the difference between the per capita income and the standard of living of Cretans and that of the rest of Greeks;
b) expansion of the working possibilities/opportunities;
c) concentration on the future development of tourism in areas such as western and southern Crete, which had not yet been overfilled with tourists; also, encouragement of the development of alternative, environment friendly tourism, or agrotourism. The Greek Tourist Board (EOT) and the Council of Equality supported such schemes elsewhere in Greece (for example, Lesbos, Chios). Tourism has always been a way to supplement family income of rural households, especially in inland areas, where the opportunities for earning an income outside the primary sector without migrating are limited;
d) the development of the secondary sector – mainly small scale industries and production of handcrafts;
e) development of vocational training schemes;
f) improvement of welfare and health services;
g) establishing links between research and production;
h) infrastructural developments (irrigation, transport, electricity production, telecommunications, information technology and the like);
i) protection of the environment.

Crete's IMP contained six sub-programmes: one dealing with the primary sector, another with tourism, a third with industrial and handcraft developments, a fourth with the development of inland areas, another with infrastructural developments and finally, one dealing with the implementation of the IMP itself. Since I am concentrating on the agricultural sector, the first and fourth sub-programmes will be looked at in detail.

The IMP sub-programme on Crete's primary sector was divided into two parts. The first part dealt with the redirection of production, improvement of product quality and decrease in cost of production. The second half of the sub-programme dealt with the development of fisheries. In both parts the need for care for the environment was stressed. Here I shall be dealing with the first part.

The goals of the first part of the sub-programme were:

_____

20   These products include olive oil, citrus and other fruits, vegetables, rice, durum, tobacco, wheat, flowers, wine and meat from sheep. This does not mean that these products can only be found in Mediterranean areas.

a) to gear production towards the demand of the market;
b) to substitute 'traditional' cultivations with more competitive ones;
c) to encourage the cultivation of avocado in an area of 1,630 hectares; although farmers were entitled to receive up to 6,000 ECU per hectare as compensation for this over a period of five years, very few producers were, at least in western Crete, persuaded to replace 'traditional' cultivations with new ones. This measure aimed at re-orienting production towards the cultivation of products for which there was a demand in the market. The same principle lay behind the encouragement given to producers to uproot their vineyards;
d) to introduce modern and more efficient irrigation methods in (a) approximately 6,000 hectares of non-efficiently irrigated land (thus avoiding wasting available water resources, which become scarce during periods of lack of rain) and (b) 7,330 hectares of previously non-irrigated land. The expectation was that the income and standard of living of the farmers who would benefit from such programmes would rise;
e) to build two market centres, one in the prefecture of Chania and one in the prefecture of Heracleon. The plan, which was to be administered by a confederation of local agricultural cooperatives, foresaw the construction of warehouses with freezers, places where the standardization and packaging of products would take place and parking areas for the transport vehicles. The plan was based on the need to reduce transportation costs, as well as the gap between the cost to produce and the cost to the consumer and to overcome the problem encountered by producers in relation to the standardization, packaging and marketing of their products. It also aimed at providing a better service to consumers;
f) the training of people who would then act as advisers on new production methods and the various Regulations and Directives of the Community of which producers can take advantage, for example to help them use the various chemicals available efficiently and correctly and thus protect both the environment and the producers' and consumers' health. These are likely to be welcomed by local producers, since many people in the area expressed their concern about lack of personnel capable of giving useful advice on various problems encountered in production, as well as on various EC Regulations etc., which seemed incomprehensible to them. During interviews I carried out with local producers, many claimed that whenever they asked government officials to provide them with this kind of information, the latter replied that they had no access to it, or the technical equipment to store such data (computers, etc.) and make it immediately available to whoever needed it. This was not just an excuse since, to my knowledge, the department representing the Ministry of Agriculture in Chania (*Georgiki Hyperesia Chanion*) had only one computer in the late 1980s, and this was not used because no one knew

how. Furthermore, many producers, and in particular women, expressed
their suspicion that these measures were not implemented properly by
the various government officials in charge;

g) provision of vocational training programmes (teaching methods
on administration and new technology, mainly computers) for the
personnel of branches of the Agricultural Bank of Greece and local
cooperatives;

h) finance research related to the construction of greenhouses and related
production, as well as production of tropical fruits such as avocados,
kiwis, and other research projects related to marketing.

In order to avoid over-production, especially in the kinds of product where
the Community has surpluses, the CAP's measures intended to modernize
production methods and thus reduce their cost and increase the market
competitiveness of the existing cultivations without, however, causing an
increase in the volume of production *per se.*

The goals of the sub-programmes for the development of inland areas are
similar. Additional programmes encouraged improvement in the quality of
sheep, cows and calves and other animals, as well as animal products (meat,
cheese), the substitution of existing varieties of cherry trees with different
varieties, along with various infrastructural developments.

Almost 30 per cent of the total cost of the IMP of Crete was borne by the
Greek national budget and the rest by the EC.

The implementation of the IMP required the submission of programmes
from the Greek authorities well in advance. In a conference which took place at
the Orthodox Academy of Crete a couple of years after the IMP of Crete started
being implemented, a member of the European Parliament, Papagiannakis,
accused the then government of using the IMP money for lightening the budget
of Greek telecommunications and of the Greek Electricity Board, instead of
using this opportunity for achieving restructuring and for proceeding with
costly investments, such as construction of greenhouses similar to those used in
the Netherlands, where 40 tons of tomatoes could be produced per stremma,[21]
as compared to the corresponding number of 15 in Crete. As Papagiannakis
said, the opportunity offered by the IMP would be missed, since new products
were not adequately encouraged neither were new forms of group cooperative
farming (which would encourage more efficient use of land and machinery),
developed; instead, almost all investments in Crete were concentrated on
infrastructural works.

The IMP in general, was part of a large programme of regional development
in the island, which also included measures not financed under the IMP. Such
measures were the completion of the northern and southern road network

---

21 Stremma (pl. stremmata) is a unit of land area equivalent to 0.25 acres or 0.10
hectares.

of the island, together with other roads connecting the north with the south, necessary for the further industrial, agricultural and tourist development of Crete along with the improvement of the means of transport, communications and of water and electricity facilities. Also, the preparation of a land registry book, necessary for observing the implementation of the various measures of the CAP in Crete, had been planned. In addition, the modernization of food industries and of industries processing agricultural products as well as the modernization of agriculture, were at the time under the aegis of Regulations (EC) 355/77 and (EC) 797/85 respectively.

The (EC) 797/85 Regulation was at the time one of the most important regarding investments in agricultural holdings. Depending on the area and the nature of investment, 30 per cent to 50 per cent of the capital invested was subsidized, up to a maximum of 12 million drachmas per family holding/ business, or 80 million drachmas if the applicant was a cooperative or association. In addition, younger farmers received a premium of 350,000– 750,000 drachmas for starting a business and also received a subsidized credit from the Agricultural Bank of Greece. Many women in Crete resented the fact that, whereas both men and women contributed equally to the family business, one person was recognized as the head of the family business and thus the grant and loan was given to the man. In a society where patriarchal practices were the norm, it was difficult for a man to let the wife appear as the head of the family; nevertheless, it seemed to be even more difficult for government officials to give way to the demands of the few women producers to be recognized as heads of the business for a particular investment, without the written consent of the man, who both men and women recognized as the only 'head' of the family unit (see also Chapter 4).

How Some EC Schemes Aiming at Restructuring Agriculture Were, at the Time, Received by Producers in Western Crete

There was strong pressure on producers to switch from cultivation of some products, such as some varieties of the same product (in the case of oranges, 'Valencia'), or to products new to the area, such as avocados and kiwis. Such suggestions were met with anger and bewilderment by local producers, who, on the one hand, 'did not even like the taste of avocados or kiwi', as some producers told me and, on the other hand, knew from experience that trees have a slow rate of maturation, live for many years, represent several generations of labour and capital invested on their behalf and have a symbolic significance for the family and the community. Freris (1986: 205) argued that similar pressure was also applied to those who were engaged in the production of olives. However, this was not in line with either my observations at the time or informal conversations with government officials at branches of the Ministry of Agriculture in Chania, Kolymbari and Kastelli. Also, if it was within the aims of the EC to make olive oil producers switch to other products, this was set aside by the generous production subsidies paid in the 1980s directly to farmers; subsidies encouraged olive producers to plant more trees and produce more olive oil. Because of the subsidies given, some uprooted their vineyards, leaving only a small parcel of land for growing for household consumption, and replaced them with olive trees, thus moving towards monocultivation. This, of course, was not part of the EC's interests, since in order to export any excess supplies it had to provide export refunds, which compensated the exporters for the difference between world and EC prices. Hence, 'the number of olive trees in Greece was to remain constant' (Maravegias 1989: 61). This shows, on the one hand, the ability of the administrative institutions responsible for carrying out the CAP's programmes in rural Greece to be rivals of traditional institutions and on the other hand, their inability to find solutions to the complex and often contradictory set of relationships between local culture and the growing impact of the European Community's agricultural policies in the 1980s.

To recapitulate, it seems that during the 1980s, the European Community's position regarding the agricultural development of its Member States was a mixture of a belief in the capitalist road to development and foreign investment and a perception that the Community is divided into two areas, a centre and a periphery, comprising the southern Mediterranean regions. It was perceived that the latter had a raw deal during the years that followed their accession to the EC. Acceptance of the notion of a bifurcated Community implied that the EC recognized the opposition of interests between the advanced industrial nations of northern central Europe and the semi-developed areas of the south and the need for assisting their development, in view of aspirations for economic integration and a united Europe. A form of intervention through IMPs was considered to be the way to a prosperous future; IMPs would serve as an agent for the transfer of technology, new organizational techniques required by the agricultural sector in order for the process of development to take off. However, a wide variety of social variables were not dealt with. For example, farmers with a medium-sized area to farm were the ones to enjoy the benefits offered by this system of development policies. Moreover, this approach did not take into account producers' reactions and needs or the reluctance of people to give up their traditional occupations and adapt to new forms of life and their inability to take full advantage of the benefits IMPs were designed to offer because of their poor implementation. This aspect became even more obvious in the years that followed with the CAP reforms and the resulting substantial cuts in subsidies given to farmers, reduction in EU subsidies intended for the development of less favoured areas and the emphasis placed on sustainable development.[22] Having said that, Agenda 2000 conceded a significant role to national and local authorities, which could be said to be advantageous to the

---

22   Despite policy initiatives towards sustainable development, funds continue to be directed predominantly toward policies that follow the agricultural *productionist model* (Kasimis and Stathakis 2003: 8).

southern Member States because of the possibilities it offered for the adjustment of policy to the needs of a specific area and the room for manoeuvring around the rigid regulations applied to the whole of Europe. I am not sure how this would impact on Greece, a country which 'since its admission to the EU, has consistently exhibited its own inability to institutionally intervene with effective national reforms in areas that were not directly in the narrow interests of the CAP' (Kasimis and Stathakis 2003: 14). The Ministry of Agriculture's plan for the development of agriculture in the Third Community Support Framework (Third CSF) with emphasis on 'integrated development of the countryside' – as opposed to the Second CSF's 'sector specific approach' – was a step in the right direction (see Demoussis 2003).

Having addressed the persistence of small farming in Greece and in Crete and the role of EC/EU politics in shaping the structure of local agriculture, I now move on to provide some basic background information on the two villages under study.

The Villages

Nohia[23] (population approximately 260) – see Figure 1.1 – and Platanos[24] (population approximately 1,190) – see Figure 1.2 – are both located in the

---

23   Nohia is located 22 kms west of the town of Chania and around 10 kms from a larger village, Kolymbari. Local legend has it that in ancient times the village was situated a couple of kms to the south, but was deserted when an epidemic killed many of its inhabitants. Those who survived came to live in the present location. Most of its commercial establishments can be found either in the central square or on the road leading from Nohia to a nearby village called Gerakiana and on the main road which connects Kastelli with Chania. Behind these buildings the rest of the houses are clustered along narrow roads and paths that wind through the settlement and are surrounded by fences and walls.

24   Platanos is situated at the north-western end of the Prefecture of Chania, in Crete, about 53 kms west of Chania. It sits on the crest of a hill at an altitude of 240 meters. The sea is visible on a clear day from Platanos, although one cannot see the coast, since this is hidden behind a hill. Below the village lies a hilly area full of olive trees and below that, nearer to the sea, greenhouses and a few tourist establishments. On the north-western side of the village lies the ancient harbour of Falasarna. Little is known of its history; it is estimated that it was destroyed in 184 B.C. There seem to be two distinct centres of activity, the village square and the crossroads where the bus to and from the town of Kastelli stops and where the road leading to the greenhouses and the coast cuts through. Physically the village is a cluster of one- or two-storey houses, some with clay roofs, whereas others have flat roofs on which the family can add another floor and on top of which is a solar water heater. Platanos took its name from the plane trees (*platani* in Greek) located at the centre of the village in the main square. In earlier times the village was located near the sea but the inhabitants were obliged to transfer it to where it is today because of raids by pirates.

Figure 1.1   Nohia: the village

Figure 1.2   Platanos: the village

western part of the island, in the region of Kisamos.[25] Each village has its own president, democratically elected at local elections (*dimotikes ekloges*) every four years from amongst the village council members (all men). Women in Nohia have not challenged the monopolization of the most important public roles by men, whereas women in Platanos mounted such a challenge in early 1980s; however, the incident was treated as a bizarre quest, out of the norm and the women who did so were mocked for this attempt. The village council acts as a liaison between the villagers and other governmental units and aims to further the interests of the village in whatever situations may develop (Friedl 1964: 96). It is responsible for taking decisions about the maintenance of the village infrastructure as well as the allocation of water resources and for keeping the annual statistics on agricultural production, livestock, births, deaths and marriages in the village, preparing tax, pension and voting rolls, preparing information for eligibility for EC/EU subsidies and so on. The main figure in the local government office is the village secretary, who is appointed by the prefecture upon nomination by the village council. The position is a permanent one. The role of the village secretary is to keep in order and update regularly the Population Register, the books on births and deaths, a census for males which helps the authorities trace those who have to do their military service, a book mentioning all decisions taken by the council regarding infrastructural works and the budget, to prepare data on the agricultural produce of the village, and provide the prefecture with all information it may require and the villagers with any necessary documents.

Until 1981 almost all villagers between 18 and 65 years of age were expected to offer their services providing labour for public infrastructural works in the village. This obligation, which enabled the village council to receive money from the government for public works, was common in other parts of Greece as well (see, for example, Friedl 1964: 93). However, in practice, in most years women were exempted from this chore, on the grounds of prevailing village customs ('dioti topikes synthikes ke ethima then to epitrepoun afto'). On the few occasions when women were asked to offer their labour despite local customs, this was valued less than that of men, vehicles and even animals. To give an example, in 1957 in Nohia, men's labour was valued at 30 drachmas per day, that of transport animals at 20 and women's at only 18. Similarly in Platanos the work of men was valued at 40 drachmas per day, whereas that of women and transport animals at 30.

---

25   As is the case in many parts of Greece, (see Kasimis 1983: 15, 188), an adequate demographic analysis of the villages is almost impossible because the data available is scarce and unreliable. The extensive outmigration and/or temporary mobility of men and women in search for work and/or a spouse makes Nohia's demographic basis quite unstable. Although Nohia has not experienced massive depopulation *per se*, many Nohiani (people from Nohia) live elsewhere.

Law and order is maintained in Nohia by a police station situated in Kolymbari and in Platanos by a detachment of the national rural police who live in the village, as well as by the *agrofylakas*, who is usually a villager appointed by the local council and is responsible for detecting and preventing animals from passing through cultivable fields and sees that arrangements regarding watering of crops are kept. Another important figure is the *hydromeneas*, a man responsible for the distribution of water in the area and the general maintenance of the irrigation system. In Platanos there were rumours about him favouring friends from time to time by turning a blind eye when they abused the system, and these problems, deriving from a patron-client relationship, were eventually settled by hiring someone else to do the job.

Both villages have a primary school which is supervised and controlled by the Ministry of Education in Athens. Nevertheless, most middle-aged and elderly women in both villages are illiterate, some unable to even sign their own name and/or count. Schoolteachers enjoy respect, and villagers show this by offering the teacher fresh eggs, olive oil, fruits and vegetables, the locally produced *raki* called *tsikoudia* (see Figure 1.3), and the like.

As in other parts of Greece, both villages have a main church and several others scattered in and around the village, each dedicated to a specific saint of the Greek Orthodox Church. Although the local priest has an important role to play in the minds of the villagers, in that he is expected to act as a liaison between them and God, many nowadays criticize him. For example, during my fieldwork people in Nohia complained that the language used by the Greek Orthodox Church (the Greek of the New Testament and Byzantine times) was incomprehensible to the congregation; this, combined with the fast-speaking priest and the 'ancient Byzantine plain-chant, with its eight "tones"' (Ware 1987: 274) sung by the choir, makes the service largely incomprehensible to them. Furthermore, instead of being respected, the priest seems to be pitied, in that many villagers said that he was so incompetent and lethargic that if he was not made a priest and thus able to receive a salary from the government, he and his family would have died of hunger. So in Nohia the priest had almost no influence on most decisions. The former priest was called 'the devil' because of his temperamental personality and the fact that he used to be a butcher who cheated when weighing the product. At the time of the fieldwork he was teaching pottery in the nearby village of Kolymbari. In both villages the priests were criticized for their lack of education and eloquence. Unlike western congregations, where the worshipper is expected to arrive when service begins and stay until it finishes, in the Orthodox Church people can come and go freely during the service, which is long, 'limitless and unhurried' (ibid.: 279), without causing a disturbance. The congregation does not come to church to meditate and say private prayers but to 'pray the public prayers of the Liturgy and to take part in the action of the rite itself' (Ware 1987: 278). If the church is full, men and sometimes children sit and chat or play outside. This lack of formality and freedom allows people to feel at home as well as to

Figure 1.3   Making *tsikoudia*/raki

treat the occasion as an opportunity to socialize, exchange information and pay compliments to and impress each other. Church attendance varies with age and sex. It is almost 100 per cent during major religious festivals such as Easter, which is the biggest religious feast for Greek Orthodoxy, Christmas and the Assumption, or 'the Falling Asleep of the Mother of God' as the Greeks call it, on 15 August. The major local festivals celebrated by the village church are the patron saint's day, during which a *paniyiri* (feast) takes place; this consists of food and drink and is celebrated by the entire village as well as attracting visitors from other villages or towns. Attendance during the Sunday service is 30 per cent and consists by and large of older people and women. Attendance in Platanos is even less. 'We have no time for Church. On Sundays we sit at home doing the household chores we had no time to do during the week', a woman said. In addition, although in Nohia all the family attends baptisms, funerals and weddings, in Platanos a representative of the family (usually the wife) attends. Most elderly people do fast – a way of disciplining the body and the soul –during Great Lent, which begins seven weeks before Easter, whereas the younger generation fast only during the last week before Easter. Individual people have different times in the year when they worship, such as name days or days when one has made an offering (*tama*) to the local saint to safeguard the health of a member of his/her family. The role of lecturing and moralizing is assumed by the priest's wife.

The Local Economy

Although in both villages a pattern of multi-occupation seems to be the norm (in that most households derive their income from a variety of sources, such as agricultural produce, small commercial activities, wage labour,[26] pensions and remittances), the local economy is based on agricultural production, primarily for commercial markets, but also for subsistence. Members of almost all households are engaged in the cultivation of olive trees and the production of olive oil for a living. In addition to the cultivation of olive trees, as already mentioned, two different forms of cash income, market gardening in Platanos and handcrafts in Nohia, have influenced the division of labour by sex since the early 1970s. These, both of which will be discussed in detail in the chapters that follow, affect the timing of the various agricultural tasks performed during an agricultural year in the areas under study. For example, whereas the olive harvest in is Nohia finished by the end of January, in Platanos – because of the additional work most villagers have in the greenhouses and despite the fact that many hire seasonal labourers to do the job – it continues well into the end of February, sometimes mid-March. The way this affects women's work and lives will be analysed in the chapters that follow.

The first sharp increase in the use of agricultural machinery occurred in the mid-1970s, triggered by shortage of labour due to urbanization and emigration and the search for low costs and high productivity. This process was encouraged by the inflow of remittances and by the then government (Junta), in an attempt to consolidate the support of the rural areas.

In both villages, variations in income are often related to fragmentation of land holdings; social forces like the tradition of dowry and inheritance accentuated the land fragmentation problem. Depending on the number of children in a family, a land-holding is broken up into smaller parcels and in most cases distributed equally between all children, the emphasis being on fairness rather than on taking into account the integration of the holding and the distance between the plots. As at the time of my fieldwork there was no land registry in Greece (and this is still under construction at the time of writing), a complete picture would have required a detailed list of inheritance, dowries, purchases of land and other transactions; the labour required for such task was

---

26 *Pluriactivity*, that is, multiple sources of incomes, both agricultural and non-agricultural, generated by farmers and members of their households, is a well-recognized phenomenon in the European countryside and within Greek agriculture. Some have analysed it as an economic adaptation strategy, adopted by farmers to help them combat harsh market conditions (see Etxezarreta 1985), others as a lifestyle of farmers' children and rural newcomers (Barlett 1986) and yet others focused on rural identities and pluriactivity (see Eikeland 1999). As Kinsella et al. (2000: 483) argue, 'pluriactive farming remains largely outside rural policies and institutions' and therefore there is a need for a specific policy framework for pluriactivity and its impact on rural development.

enormous because the *Hypothikophylakion*, the bureau in Katelli which keeps data on property transactions for the whole region, does so in alphabetical order rather than in separate files for different villages; thus one would have to go through thousands of names for generations in order to form a complete picture, provided the researcher could work there every day, which is not feasible since the office is extremely busy throughout the year.

Distribution of wealth in the two villages differs. In Platanos the villagers can be classified into three categories, according to the number of olive trees they own, whether or not they own one or more greenhouse/s and their employment; only 1.12 per cent of villagers owned more than 1,000 olive trees. The majority (80 per cent) owned fewer than 500 trees. Most of these, however, also had one greenhouse or more, occupying on average an area of four to six stremmata. It would have been a mistake to arrive at conclusions regarding the distribution of wealth relying on these data because, in the first place, many of those with an average or small number of olive trees might also own a large vineyard or even have a small business other than agriculture in the village. For example, there is a small group – fishermen, builders, shopkeepers, civil servants and members of other miscellaneous non-agricultural occupations – who are not landless but have varying amounts of stremmata, usually of olive trees and a small vineyard. In Nohia, a typical family owning around 600 to 800 olive trees divided into an average of 6–8 parcels of land posed a disadvantage for the development of an economically viable agricultural enterprise. An attempt to solve the problem of fragmentation by *anadasmos*, that is, redistribution of land, was met by reluctance on the part of the villagers. Similar to those in Platanos, most households supplemented their income from olive oil in various ways; some had olive orchards or pensions, others had a business and yet others worked as temporary wage workers in or outside the village. Most important in supplementing income were the handcrafts discussed later in this book.

Having given a picture of agricultural development in Crete and of the two villages under study, the next chapter looks in detail at the family work profiles of a small number of households in Nohia and Platanos. This is an attempt to give an idea to the reader of the socioeconomic position of different families – typical and exceptional – and the varying roles different activities play for different families.

Chapter 2
Family Work Profiles

The family work profiles which follow are based not only on information derived from accounts given by individual members of each family from their recollections of events of everyday life and autobiographical information from some (not all) members of each family. They are also based on information derived from a variety of documentary materials and archives held by the local government office (*grafio kinotitas*) in the two villages, as well as from tales told by the other co-villagers (including the president, secretary and priest of each village) and by people who lived in nearby villages. The stories that I was told about each family were not all the same but were varied, with everyone trying to present certain things in a favourable light and at the same time to conceal others. Also, as Hammersely and Atkinson (1990: 130) maintain, 'authors have a sense of audience that will lead them to put particular glosses on their accounts'. In addition, one has to take into account the blurred line between memory and imagination in storytelling. According to Barclay and DeCook (1988: 92) autobiographical recollections 'are not necessarily accurate, nor should they be; they are, however, mostly congruent with one's self-knowledge, life themes, or sense of self'. To quote Rushdie (1980: 253),

> I told you the truth … Memory's truth, because memory has its own special kind.
> It selects, eliminates, alters, exaggerates, minimizes, glorifies, and vilifies also; but in
> the end it creates its own reality; it is a heterogeneous but usually coherent version
> of events; and no sane human being ever trusts someone else's version more than
> his own.

Similarly, my own preoccupations are bound to have influenced the results in one way or another. For example, although taking life histories was left until late in the fieldwork period when I was no longer suspected of being a 'spy' or a tax collector, the selection of a handful of families as typical or extreme cases rather than others and the presentation of material concerning these families highlighting certain issues rather than others, and the exclusion of much that seemed to be trivial and inclusion of much that seemed to be important all presuppose some bias on the researcher's part.

So, the accounts that follow are not to be read at face value, since even the data one can derive from the local archives are not accurate representations of reality. These accounts are presented, though, in order to give the reader an idea of the varying roles different agricultural and other activities (for example, production of handcrafts, running a coffee shop, having one or several greenhouses and so on) play for different families in Nohia and Platanos. In other words, this is an attempt to grasp the socio-economic position of different families via the range of occupational activities pursued by their members at the time of the fieldwork.

Family Work Profiles in Nohia

Case 1: The Voyatzakis and Farandakis Family

As you enter the village of Nohia on foot, it is likely that you will meet a man with a goat; the man's name is Stelios, the goat, although a pet, does not have a name. Most people in rural Crete do not give names to their domestic animals or treat them with affection. Stelios addresses his goat as *I katsika mou* (my goat), but is affectionate with her and so his daughter and other villagers often pull his leg saying *kouzoulathikes more* ('Are you off your head?'). Although Stelios is a widower and has a married daughter in Nohia, Koula, but he lives alone, that is, in his own house. Nevertheless, he has his meals at his daughter's house, and she also does his laundry and at times helps him clean his house.

Koula, who was 50 years old when I met her, is one of the most respected people in the village. Daughter of Stelios Voyatzakis, one of the poorest people in the village, she grew up with her brother Andonis in the care of their stepmother. As Koula recalls, when her mother died in 1941 at the age of 34 from some form of infection, there was nobody to look after the children – Koula was at the time nearly 7 years old and her brother 2 years old. Two years later, at the age of 37, her father married his second wife, a local 'sour spinster' as Koula described her, who used to be the village midwife. 'It was not an act of love', Koula said once, whereas another time she remarked 'tou pire ta myala' (she made him lose his head over her). According to other villagers, the stepmother was strict with the children, who were beaten and made to work hard in the fields.

Koula remembers that in those days she had to help her father collect the olives during the harvest – in those days the olive trees were tall and people had to wait until the fruit fell to the ground before collecting them by hand (see chapter on production of olives). When the harvest was over, women and children wandered around the olive groves and picked the odd olives that remained uncollected; the income from selling them to the local olive press was their pocket money and their compensation for a hard winter's unpaid labour. Moreover, in those days each house produced its own wheat. However, if the household had no boys, or the boys were too young to labour, it was the girls who helped. Koula was one of the very few girls who ploughed, if not the only one in the village.

In the 1950s, poverty and lack of opportunities in Nohia led Andonis, like many others, to leave the village; he took a job in the merchant fleet and later emigrated to Belgium where he married. However, he does come to Nohia every year and spends his holidays at a newly built house – the dream of every Greek who migrated is to use remittances to build a house in his/her village – which is much envied by the rest of the villagers. Koula loves him because he is a caring brother, always bringing expensive presents (for example, in 1987 he sent her a washing machine and the year before a blood pressure gauge, which was regarded as 'deus ex machina' by Koula who needs to have her blood pressure taken regularly); but Koula also complains about the burden of 'hospitality', of having to spend the whole month cooking and looking after them.

In 1955, when Koula was 21, she married a fellow villager, George. They were one of those rare couples who fell in love with each other. George, born in 1926, was one of the six children of the Farandakis family and one of the two that stayed in the village. The rest migrated; one of the sisters married a man from Chania and later migrated to the Nea Ionia area in Athens, while a brother married someone from the island of Paros and migrated to Germany. Another brother was a policeman in Athens and is now retired and offers rooms to rent on the coast in nearby village, Kolymbari and another sister married and lives in Petroupolis, a working class suburb in Athens. George and his sister Katina are the only ones left in Nohia (Katina's story will be discussed in Chapter 6).

As Koula recalls, when George married her, a few years after the end of the Civil War (1949), times were difficult. He was poor and Koula did not have a dowry. Later on, he took up an apprenticeship with a blacksmith, which he regards as his main occupation. They also have olive trees, vineyards and a garden in the area around Nohia. Their property is a typical small landholding, fragmented into small parcels. Both spouses work in the fields (although it is George who looks after the vineyards – he produces his own wine each year – and the garden where vegetables are grown for subsistence); although Koula is not well and suffers with a heart condition, she still helps her husband around the olives so as to avoid hiring someone else to do the job. As women's participation in income-generating activities is regarded as supplementary to that of men, it is always the wife's and not the husband's labour that is weighted against hiring labour.

Koula and George have three children. The oldest son, Takis, completed primary school, but a couple of years later failed secondary school exams and preferred to leave school rather than repeat the year and risk being ridiculed by his friends; he is still in the village, helping his father in the blacksmith's shop and also labouring by contract in construction works in Chania. In the summer months he plays Cretan music in a tourist place and claims also to be working in a nearby campsite although, as he once confessed, this was just an excuse to get away from Nohia and his parents and spend some time with his friends. Although families in Nohia tend to be stricter with their daughters than with their sons, this does not mean that no pressure at all is exercised on the boys. Parents make sacrifices for their children. Contrary to what is the case in other parts of Greece, it is the custom in western Crete for the man to provide the house when he marries – Koula and George built Takis a flat above the blacksmith's shop in readiness for his marriage. Thus the obligation is created for the children to look after their parents when they are elderly. For example, Koula looked after her mother-in-law when she was ill and bedridden and expects her daughter and daughter-in-law to do the same for her. Children, on the other hand, try to live up to parents' expectations and comply with their restrictions when they are young (see Chapter 6 for details).

The second son finished some sort of low level public tertiary education and works for a private firm on the island of Chios, where his wife comes from. However, the parents are not happy and try to use their connections in Crete and Athens so that their son may become a public servant, which is regarded as the pinnacle of achievement and guarantees peace of mind because of the security and pension prospects. At the time of fieldwork, George was trying to mobilize all his personal contacts to achieve this.

The daughter studies politics at the University of Athens; she stays with George's sister and as George put it, 'thus we have peace of mind' (*Ehome to kefali mas isiho*). She visits Nohia in the vacations although, as she said, she feels bored in the village and irritated by the restrictions imposed by her parents on her movements. Her parents' aspiration for her is that she finds a good person and gets married. 'We won't relax until the children get settled', they often said. Children settling down involves two things: marriage and acquisition of property. As far as marriage is concerned, there isn't much they can do. 'Things have changed now', George said, 'Young people choose their own spouses'. As for the property, both Koula and George are concerned mainly with providing the oldest son with enough to live a comfortable life. They have already provided the youngest son with education and a flat in Chios and the daughter with *prikia* (dowry: see Chapter 6). To buy these, Koula spends a large proportion (if not all) of her earnings from selling the cocoon handcrafts she produces (see Chapter 3), while at the same time she lives in a house where there is no proper bathroom and toilet (there is only a small room in the back yard, with a wash-hand basin, a plastic pipe used for a shower and a toilet without running water) and the eldest son sleeps in a bed in the kitchen, while the living-room is used for growing the silkworms.

Koula is one of the pioneer cocoon producers in Nohia. When younger, she used the loom, but she fell ill from sitting at it for hours and hence moved it to a warehouse. From the mid-1970s onwards, she has made handcrafts from cocoons and sold them via intermediaries to customers in other parts of Greece (see Chapter 3). The money she earns all goes towards the successful placement of the children, which consists of 'occupational mobility via educational attainment, and the provision of residential property by parents' (Cavounidis 1985: 79).

Koula and George appear to love each other very much. They take decisions regarding spending and children together. However, their roles in the public life of the village differ. Koula used to be one of the most active members of the women's association. Her new occupation as a producer of handcrafts, however, took all her time. George, on the other hand, was for years the president of the village. Some women villagers commented that Koula was the one who always worked, whereas George spent hours in the *cafeneion* and involved with the presidency. Today, as with all couples their age, George spends his free time in the local *cafeneion* whereas Koula sits at home embroidering, usually alone, with the company of a TV set. 'In the old days, we used to visit other houses in the neighbourhood, sit together and chat. Nowadays, women sit at home alone watching TV, whereas men are in the *cafeneion*. This is how things are', Koula said.

Case 2: The Nicos Chatzidakis Family

Nicos Chatzidakis is one of the poorest in the village. In the old days, when pottery flourished in Nohia, his father used to work as an assistant to a potter. Nicos joined the merchant navy, but later (1980) married through arrangement a woman from Rodopou and, as he preferred to work the land than travel the sea, he came back to live in Nohia. At the time of the fieldwork he had two young children. He earns his main income from labouring at all kinds of construction jobs and also, from time to time, by working for a daily sum during the olive harvest and helping with the spraying of olive trees.

Although his wife tried to take on cocoon handcrafts, she was unsuccessful because she had no contacts who would act as her intermediaries. She complained that the other craftswomen would not introduce her to their intermediaries because they were afraid that she might make a better deal with them and destroy the market for their own work. Sometimes (roughly once every two months), however, when they have a lot of work and find it difficult to meet deadlines, they call her for help and pay her by the piece.

One of Nicos' sisters is married and lives in Nohia (the others married men from other villages and left – according to local customs the woman tends to migrate to the husband's village). At the time of fieldwork, Nicos' father had fallen ill. Although the old man was living with his wife in their own house, the question arose as to who would help the old woman look after him. This became a source of conflict between Nicos' sister (a cocoon producer and owner of a *cafeneion*) and his wife and also became a source of village gossip. Most women in the village seemed to agree that since the old man had a wife and a daughter in the village, the daughter-in-law should not be expected to look after him. 'After all, she has young children to look after, whereas his daughter's boys are old enough to look after themselves', a villager said. This tension and conflict between the two women culminated in the one assaulting the other and Nicos, who during the dispute was trying not to take sides, developing a heart condition. In the end, the old man's daughter agreed to take care of him.

Case 3: The Eftychis Chatzidakis Family

Eftychis Chatzidakis was born in Drakona in 1925; he moved to Nohia in 1958, because he married a Nohiani called Georgia. Two years later, their first son Kostis was born. Kostis is one of the few young men still living in the village. He is an *agrotis* but also has a tractor and works on other people's land for a wage. The second son went to the polytechnic in Athens. The couple decided that since they had spent money on the youngest son's education, they had to give property to the son who remained in the village (25 stremmata of land divided into small parcels). The remainder of the property (that is, 27 stremmata of land covered with olive trees, 7 stremmata of vineyards, 10 stremmata of pastureland and three sheep, two goats and three lambs) is still in the father's name and will, according to the parents, be equally divided between the two boys when the father retires.

Both Eftychis and Georgia work in the fields. Like Koula's husband, Eftychis is the one responsible for looking after the vineyards (mainly for consumption within the household) and the maintenance of the olive trees. Nevertheless, unlike Koula's situation, it is Georgia's job to look after the garden and the domestic animals.

Similar to Koula, Georgia is one of the pioneer women producing cocoon handcrafts in the village and was also involved in the local women's association. Because both of her children are boys, she does not have to worry about *prikia*. However, when her youngest son got engaged to someone in Athens, she bought them a flat and furnished it. Many people in the village pulled her leg afterwards because, as they said, 'tin piasane koroido' (she was fooled by the in-laws) since in Athens the custom is that the girl's parents and not the groom's should provide the couple with a place to live. Georgia said that she was happy because the children would be better off now than if they had to pay rent.

When the young couple was still engaged, the bride-to-be used to come and visit the parents. Georgia was condemned by many villagers for letting the couple sleep in the same room. 'She is not her daughter, that is why she doesn't care', one woman said. She continued: 'Although I know that my daughter and her fiancé sleep together, when they visit I always make sure they sleep in different rooms' (see Chapter 6).

Georgia is the daughter of Kostas, a potter, and Eleni. The couple had four daughters and a son. The son and two of the daughters migrated and married working-class people in Athens. Another daughter married an *agrotis* and went to live in the village Vassilopoulo, whereas Georgia stayed in Nohia.

As with Stelios (Koula's father), since his wife died in the early 1970s, Georgia's father has lived in his own house in the village and his daughter has looked after him and his house.

Case 4: The Basakis Family

The Basakis family is one of the most affluent in the village. The oldest brother, Michalis, born in 1940, is an *agrotis*, a bee-keeper and the co-owner of the sole olive press in the village, which is the family's main source of income. At the time of the fieldwork, Michalis, still a bachelor, lived with his parents. He was, however, building a house for himself and many villagers teased him that this was a sign of preparing to get married. Gossip has it that many years ago he was engaged to a woman in Athens but the engagement was broken off for reasons that nobody seemed to know or remember. Others were convinced that he would eventually become a priest, because he used to spend hours sitting at the local *cafeneion* quoting long passages from the gospels and the bible in general.

Michalis' brother George is married to Dimitra, a young woman from a poor family in the village of Faleliana, and has four young children. 'The couple met at a *panigyri* (local feast), liked each other and the rest was taken care of', a villager said. Although the two brothers do not have many olive trees compared with other villagers, they hire seasonal labourers from the north of Greece to collect their olives, because all the winter they are occupied in their olive press. It is Dimitra's task to look after these men – cook for them, take food to them in the fields, wash their clothes and look after their accommodation. It is part of the deal: they provide the labour and receive in return food, shelter and part of the produce (usually two kilos of olive oil out of every seven). The same applies to those hired to work in the olive press.

Case 5: The Androulakis Family

Athena is the wife of Pericles Androulakis. She moved to Nohia in 1979, when they married. Pericles is one of the relatively poor people in the village. He owns a small area (19 stremmata in total) covered with olive trees, 2 stremmata of vineyard and 1 stremma planted with citrus trees. To supplement his income he works in construction. Athena works every summer in a hotel ten miles away from Nohia, near the coast. Many in the village criticize her, because working in a hotel and being exposed to the 'unethical behaviour of tourists' is considered inappropriate.

Pericles' brother Dimitris is the clerk in the local government office, whose involvement in agricultural work is mainly for self-consumption. He is liked in the village, although some complain that he is never in his office. Most, however, sympathize with him, or even admire him, because he stood by and supported his wife who had a nervous breakdown and took care of his children and the household in general during the years when she was unwell.

Case 6: The Afiniotakis Family

Manolis Afioniotakis was born in Kamara in 1929. He has lived in Nohia since the late 1950s. He has a *cafeneion* at the back of which is a small room used as a store. Although most villagers buy their supplies from the supermarket in Kolymbari, and hence profits from the store are small, it continues to function since it provides villagers with cigarettes, stationery, canned food, soft drinks, sweets etc. Its main service for many years was providing a telephone for the area because, prior to the introduction of mobile phones, there were not enough lines in the village. The couple has two sons. At the time of the fieldwork, the eldest was studying medicine in Salonica, whereas the younger stayed in the village and managed the coffee shop alongside his father, supplementing his income with his agricultural produce.

As you walk into the coffee shop you will meet two women sitting side-by-side; the younger is Maria, Manolis' wife, and the older is her mother. Although it is part of the moral code in the village that women should not visit the *cafeneion*, the owner's wife is expected to be there and assist her husband in the chores involved. Maria suffers from arthritis and is confined to a chair. According to village gossip God punished Maria – the story is that she is an illegitimate child, which is regarded as a sin. The bodily signs are seen as evidence of the disgrace of being illegitimate. Despite this, Maria is accepted in the village like everyone else, is accorded the respect and regard which other women in the village are accorded and the *cafeneion* is one of the two busiest in the village. Is it very popular among the young men in the village, who go there to watch TV, play cards, read the newspaper and exchange information on prices of agricultural goods and politics.

The *cafeneion* is not the sole income-generating activity for them. They also have a relatively sizeable agricultural property and rent small parcels of land which their son then cultivates. Maria's main concern is that he should find a good girl to marry. At the time of the fieldwork he was building a new house in Nohia, a sign of getting ready to marry.

Family Work Profiles in Platanos

Case 1: The Koundourakis, Triandaphyllakis, Photopoulos Family

Dimosthenis Koundourakis was born in 1914 in Platanos. He was one of the five sons of a local *agrotis*. In 1947 he married the daughter (one of four children) of a local *agrotis* and started working as a carpenter having his own shop, which later on (in the 1970s), was converted into a *souvlatzidiko* (kebab shop) and in 1987 his youngest daughter Mary turned it into a modern cafeteria. The old wooden chairs were replaced by plastic white ones, the previously whitewashed walls were half covered with plastic grey tapestry, one of the walls features an image of Asterix and the old sign *Souvlatzidiko* outside the shop has been replaced by large neon letters saying 'Cafeteria'. The shop now serves soft drinks, ouzo, sandwiches, beer and sometimes sweets brought from nearby Kastelli. The changes drove away some of the older customers but have attracted the young and children since it now has facilities for video games, which are very popular in the village.

Born in 1962, Mary graduated from high school but stayed, like many others, in the village to work. She is considered by both young and old as one of the most active people in Platanos. At the time of the fieldwork she organized the village youth association and served as its president for some years. Despite the pressure she encountered from older co-villagers, she rented somewhere where the members of the association (boys and girls) could meet and play, listen to music or organize various activities, such as excursions, a local play, music gigs. During the harvest period Mary, along with other young people, worked for 'pocket money' for a local tradesman packing tomatoes. When I asked her why, she replied that 'the money is good, but it is also fun'. Later on she used this money to buy umbrellas and chaise longues which she rents every summer to sunbathers on one of the two local beaches. Mary married for love and now has two children.

The oldest Koundourakis' daughter, Androniki, was born in 1948, and was 19 when her parents, despite her negative reaction, arranged for her to marry a local man, Andonis Triandaphyllakis, who had just returned from Germany where he had worked as manual labourer in a factory. Initially, he worked with her father as a carpenter and later they decided to set up a greenhouse. Some years later, she opened a grocery shop which, being situated on the crossroads to the sea and to the nearby village, Sfinary, turned out to be a very successful business. Her husband Andonis still manages the greenhouse and part of the produce is sold at their shop. From the profits Androniki bought a piece of land a mile from the sea with some rooms to let. It is easy for her to find customers for the rooms., since the bus which comes from Chania and Kastelli to the village stops just outside the grocery shop. In the summer months she rents the rooms to the tourists and in the winter to the olive pickers and those who come to work in the greenhouses.

Although this is technically against the law, Androniki's son left school after completing his primary education and helps his father in the greenhouse. The daughter, a bright girl, graduated from high school and wanted to attend university, but her parents put pressure on her to stay in Platanos where, as they argued, 'there was plenty for her to do'. This created conflict between daughter and parents; in the end, she stayed in Platanos and got married.

Between Androniki and Mary there is another sister, Photoula. When she was young she went to live with some relatives in Athens, where she worked as a needlewoman (machinist). Although her parents did not approve, she married a man from the Peloponnese whom she met in Athens and they opened a *taverna* in the centre of Athens. Tired of life in the big city, in 1987 they returned to

Platanos where they built a three-storey building on a piece of land given to them by her father – a *taverna* at level, rooms to rent on the first floor and a modern flat with all the amenities for themselves on the second. Photoula works in the *taverna* all day (her daughters help) whereas her husband, besides taking care of the shopping and the accounts, sits all day 'entertaining the customers'.

Case 2: The Dedakis Family

Costis Dedakis (in his early 20s when I met him in 1987) is the son of Yiannis and Efthymia. His father, the son of an *agrotis*, was an *agrotis* himself and also had a *taverna* by the sea serving fish to supplement the household's income. In 1984 Yiannis died, followed a few years later by their daughter. Efthymia closed down the *taverna* only to reopen it a couple of years later, not as a *taverna*, but as a kind of café. Costis decided to try his luck with a greenhouse, which proved to be successful and the next year he opted for a second one. Because there is a lot of work involved (the two greenhouses occupied 3.5 stremmata each), each year they hire labourers, especially during the harvest period when things get hectic. Moreover, although Efthymia helps Costis with the café, it is his job to serve the *meze* to the customers. Still in deep mourning, she sits on a chair and is reluctant to talk to strangers. When I first met her, I was carrying a small tape-recorder which she did not like at all and ever since called it 'the little devil'. Also, because of the tragic events in her life, she had put on a lot of weight and is therefore conscious of the fact that she might either fall over while carrying the dishes or get stuck in a chair, unable to get up.

Efthymia's wish for Costis to get married 'because he needs some help; he cannot always rely on hired labour', did not come true. A couple of years ago when I visited the village she told me: 'Instead of getting married all he does is run after these filthy tourists; he is going to catch some sort of disease one of these days.'

Case 3: The Bihakis Family

Bihakis was a lorry driver before marrying Theano, a woman from Kastelli 18 years his younger. Later on he became *agrotis* and intermediary acting on behalf of a tomato wholesaler in Salonica. In common with all intermediaries (there were around four or five in the area in the 1980s but now there are none), during the harvest period he used to open a kiosk[1] where the packaging of tomatoes took place. Every day he visited all his clients and negotiated prices of the tomatoes, which he then transferred to his kiosk to be packed by labourers (usually young people from the village paid by the crate) and transported to

---

1   Although this is larger that what one might imagine a kiosk to be – that is, a small booth with only enough room for one or two people – the word 'kiosk' is used here because that is what the locals called it: *kioski*, meaning 'kiosk' in Greek.

Salonica (see Chapter 3 for details). They also have a greenhouse managed by Theano. When I last visited the village I heard that Bihakis had died and that Theano was running the greenhouse by herself.

Case 4: The Koufogiannakis Family

The Koufoginannakis family is typical of a family with middle-aged parents (both spouses in their 40s) with a greenhouse in Platanos. Both Alekos and Eftychia are offspring of local *agrotes* and both have siblings who have migrated to other parts of Greece. They earn a living from their olive trees (around 300, which is an average number for Platanos) and from the three greenhouses they own, which range from 1 to just over 2 stremmata each. As in almost all cases, the bulk of the work in the greenhouses is done by the wife, whereas the children (two teenaged daughters at the time) helped both with the greenhouses and with household chores whenever they had time off school. 'We do not expect much help from our daughters. We prefer them to concentrate on their homework and be able to study and perhaps get away from this life here. We do not want them to spend their lives working here', they said. Efthymia has also been involved in the local women's association (see Chapter 8). When I met her she spent all her spare time knitting for her daughters' *prikia*.

Case 5: The Nilolakakis Family

The only person in the village who seems to rely solely on hired labour throughout the year is Stelios Nikolakakis, the president in Platanos. When he married a woman from Sfakopigadi in 1980, the arrangement was that she would not have to work in the fields. Although he has 11 stremmata of greenhouses, she refuses to help and spends all day looking after her children and house. This is condemned by most village women, who have nicknamed her *kifina* (lazy-bones), because she allows her husband to spend money on hiring labour, a part of which could have been saved if she worked with him.

Having described the family profiles of a small number of households in Nohia and Platanos, I will now turn my attention to women's work in the two villages and, in particular, to their involvement in the production of handcrafts, market gardening and production of olives.

Chapter 3
Production of Handcrafts in Nohia

Introduction

This chapter concentrates on female involvement in the production of craft objects[1] in Nohia. The women who make a living from this activity regard themselves as skilled handcraft producers and refer to themselves as *koukoulia* (meaning cocoon) producers.[2] It begins with a brief discussion of some debates on the position of women in Greece and the Mediterranean which have been developed in the ethnographic literature. This is followed by a section on the development of the occupation and a description of the production process, which gives the reader an idea of the skill and labour involved. Then, discussing the marketing of the end product, the relationship between the craft producers and the traders is analysed.

The engagement of women with handcrafts is of particular interest since it is controlled by women both at the level of production and in the market. Before engaging in this production, women were working alongside their husbands – the 'head of the household' – in agriculture as part of the unpaid family labour force, trying to secure an income for the family's livelihood. Despite the constraints imposed by the local value system,[3] which underpins gendered social relations,[4] and by the nature of the work itself, which confines women to the home, here,

---

1 By craft objects I mean objects the production of which involved manual artistry. The producers use neither the term handcrafts (*ergohira*) or *erga tehnis* (*tehni* has two meanings, art and craft). They simply call them *koukoulia* (cocoons).

2 As mentioned earlier in this book (see Chapter 1, fn 26), a pattern of multi-occupation seems to be the norm. Most households derive their income from a variety of sources, such as agricultural produce, small commercial activities, wage labour, pensions, government salaries, remittances. Most men work in agricultural-related activities (they own their own land and/or at the same time, work as labourers for other landholders). In addition to this, most are themselves self-employed craftsmen (for example, one is a carpenter, another a blacksmith, a third a potter).

3 Here I refer to the 'honour and shame' value system, which has been used by some anthropologists – notably British structuralists like Pitt-Rivers (1965) and Peristiany (1965) – to characterize 'traditional' Mediterranean societies. For details see section in this book on sex and pleasure.

4 This is used here as a substitute to the much criticized notion of patriarchy. It was first used by Anthias (1998) as an alternative to Walby's 'gender regimes', that is, sets of social relationships whose object of reference is the construction and reproduction of gendered social practices. Unlike Walby (1997), Anthias (1998) treats gender as an

for the first time, women are given the opportunity to earn cash and contribute more visibly than before to the family's income. Thus they have more say in the decision-making process regarding spending and investing money. At the same time, because the workplace is the home, this does not in itself enable the *koukoulia* producers to question the reluctance of men to take on responsibility for domestic tasks like childcare, cooking and washing. Moreover, although women in Nohia value men as the main breadwinners, contrary to the embroiderers studied by Lever (1984; 1988: 4) in rural Spain where such work is defined as 'non work', not only do men in Nohia praise the women for their work and earnings, but women are also given a new 'meaning', that is a 'new significance', by their men. However, they also stress the advantage of work confined in the domestic premises to the 'smooth running of the household'. In other words, the chapter shows how women, whose work traditionally lay in the home, fields and vegetable gardens, became 'independent' producers working alongside men. This gave them some influence within the domestic group (especially in the decision-making process regarding not only expenditure on children's education, but also new land, dwellings for offspring, agricultural equipment and kitchen gadgets[5]). Men, on the other hand, are reduced in the sphere of *koukoulia* production[6] to occasional participants. However, the spatial non-separation of production from reproduction activities means that *koukoulia* production has remained a 'hidden' occupation, and hence in their social appearance the *koukoulia* producers are housewives. The chapter suggests that the 'semi-domestication' of these women has its roots in gendered social relations and practices to be found in local society, which reinforce the hierarchical relationships between men and women, where men are supposed to control the means of production as well as the marketing of the products as heads of the household unit.

The Context

Within debates on gender relations in Greece and 'traditional' Mediterranean societies more generally, gender has been implicated in the complementarily opposed moral values of 'honour' and 'shame', which are often used to evaluate social worth and to order social relations between individuals (see for example, Peristiany 1965; Pitt-Rivers 1965; Cowan 1990; Chapter 7 in this book). This

---

ingredient that enters into different societal mechanisms rather than being constituted as a discrete system.

5   This is contrary to what some researchers (Oakley 1985) suggested back in the 1970s, namely that when women become involved in decision making, it is limited to issues concerning children.

6   *Koukoulia* in Greek means 'cocoons'. Because these handcrafts are amongst other things made of 'cocoons', which (as explained later on in this chapter) are cut and glued on a cloth, the handcraft producers call their products *koukoulia*.

value system institutionalizes practices that, to quote Giovannini (1987: 61) 'affect and reflect gender-based relations of authority, dominance and coercion'. In Nohia, this is a key dimension to gender ideology and related social practices, and to understanding the dichotomy between private-public space in relation to women's position and needs to be taken into account despite the shift of anthropological attention in the 1980s from structure to systems of meaning and from society to culture.

The division between the two realms can, in crude terms, be seen as being physically demarcated (house versus public space) and behaviourally demarcated (house is associated with women), thus representing two sets of values which are significant for both sexes. However, as Hirschon (1989: 141) points out,

> Since men and women are endowed by nature with different capacities and capabilities, they are not interchangeable entities ... their relationship is defined as one of complementarity, of fundamental interdependence ... the complementarity of the sexes is matched by the separation of their lives into distinct and especially different sets of experience.

Similar to Yerania (an area in Attica studied by Hirschon in the late 1980s), in Nohia these principles demarcate appropriate areas of activity for men and women both within and outside the home. However, the division between public and private spaces is not as clear cut as it may seem. As this case study shows, both genders have during the years acted in both arenas, but to different degrees and for different purposes, which shift over time.[7] My interpretation of gender roles in Nohia will rest on the complementarity of, but also on the differences between, men and women.

Within Greek ethnography, two further arguments exist: one attributes women's lower status to their association with the private realm, and the other suggests that the domestic domain is a source of power for women (Friedl 1986a; Dubisch 1986). Others have suggested that women's involvement with rituals and religious observances outside the home and other 'sociable' social *practices*[8] (such as coffee drinking, dancing, etc.), gives them 'an accepted role in the public world' (Hirschon 1989:142; Cowan 1990). Although in Nohia, after the introduction of the *koukoulia* production, women's involvement in such activities gradually weakened, women's possession of earnings is of

---

7   For example, prior to the introduction of *koukoulia* production, women worked alongside men in the fields. They were also active in religious activities. Hence, public involvement for women also concerned 'the spiritual welfare of family members, both living and dead' (Hirschon 1989: 221). The introduction of *koukoulia* production meant that producers became more concerned with and had more time for worldly temporal economic gains than with more metaphysical ones.

8   According to Cowan (1990: 16) 'practices are the means through and the site in which gender ideas and relations are *realized* – that is, comprehended and made real'.

considerable importance in that it gives them power over the allocation of household expenditure, and places them in command of handling resources. Money, once seen as an integral part of masculine competence (similar to the situation in Yerania – see Hirschon 1989) is now earned by women too. Hence, although their association with traditional values is also important in that women must 'perform' as good wives and mothers,[9] their earning capacity has become highly valued. Values which were resilient and persistent prior to the introduction of the *koukoulia* production are no longer so, as, for reasons given later, this type of production does not threaten a man's reputation and does not challenge 'key values designated to a woman [such as] a chaste image and the attainment of virtue within her family' (Hirschon 1989: 100).

Moreover, as the construction of 'manhood' is shown to be an active, creative and reflexive process, so is the construction of womanhood both enabled and constrained by certain social practices and ideologies. In the case of Nohia, ideas about gender and related practices also bear the imprint of local circumstances and history, including Orthodox religious culture and long-term economic underdevelopment, which has reinforced the 'traditional' division of labour by sex.

The priorities of a married woman centre on the family (see Chapter 6). Once married, a woman takes her position as a 'mistress of the house' (*nikokyra*) and her obligation is to control household boundaries and transform polluting disorder into domestic order (Loizos and Papataxiarchis 1991: 11). In doing so, 'women mould their own nature and eventually redeem themselves from their symbolic handicaps as "daughters of Eve"' (ibid.; Hirschon 1978: 79–86).[10] Similar to the case of Yerania studied by Hirschon (1989: 99), in Nohia too, 'since marriage [is] the aim and female chastity [is] the primary concern for most families, employment outside the home with the dangers of a girl's exposure to the outside world posed problems for the parents'. Hence, 'whatever employment a girl took up ... it was always seen as entirely secondary to her ultimate destiny ... in marriage, childbearing and housekeeping' (ibid.). Womanhood, in other words, means 'nurturing, cooking, cleaning' (Loizos and Papataxiarchis 1991: 8). A woman's economic role lies within the home and is of considerable importance. As mentioned above, men and women alike subscribe to the notion that their roles are separate but complementary. As in Sohos, studied by Cowan (1990: 54), men in Nohia are generally thought to be 'unwilling or unable to' perform domestic duties and take care of dependents (children and elderly). To do so is to risk being ridiculed by male peers. Further,

9   If Herzfeld (1985) is correct in what he says in *The Poetics of Manhood* – namely that men must perform their masculinity – then equally women must perform being good wives and mothers.

10   A process of redemption is also initiated by women as mourners in their capacity to live not for themselves, but for others; they can thus transform sin into forgiveness and redeem the dead (Loizos and Papataxiarchis 1991).

in theory, the status relationship between the two sexes is not one of equality, as the husband has ultimate authority over his wife.[11] This subordination has in practice been challenged due to women's success in the *koukoulia* production, which gave women more control over the household budget.

Attitudes regarding a woman's employment after marriage have remained modelled on this rigid division of labour by gender, despite decades of requiring additional labour on the family farm, which forced contradictions in practice. As in Yerania (Hirschon 1989: 100), earning money is seen as 'an integral aspect of masculine competence'. A husband's social reputation and self-respect depends on his ability to support his family. So the *koukoulia* producers in Nohia have embraced one of the values associated with competitive, masculine activity. Nevertheless, these women are not seen as acting in a manner inappropriate to their designated role – the role of the *mistress* of the house – as the site of production of these handcrafts has been the house and thus has not undermined in any way women's association with the domestic sphere. It therefore allows the participation of women in 'men's world of earning cash' to coexist with powerful assumptions about a woman's proper place and her obligations. What it has challenged, however, is her position as economically dependent on men. The above-mentioned approaches provide a useful starting point for understanding the experiences of *koukoulia* producers in Nohia and for conceptualizing relations of dominance and assessing the extent to which women's activities are controlled by men.

History

As in most of the Mediterranean, embroidering in western Crete is, with few exceptions, the exclusive domain of women. The forms of embroidering produced in the area range from crochet work (see Figures 3.1, 3.2 and 3.3) which, according to Greger (1985: 201), 'is ... popular, as it can be worked in small, very light pieces taken from house to house in a plastic bag for afternoon all-female gossip sessions', to textiles produced by spinners and loom-weavers (*hyfanda*), to knitting and crafts made out of silkworm cocoons and called locally *koukoulia*. Traditionally, all such craft products were made for daughters' dowries and still the best handwork is made for the home.[12] The different designs have been the subject of study (Cocking 1987) and will not therefore be touched upon here.

---

11   Some women make use of irony, silence and submission as strategies of subverting male dominance (Herzfeld 1991: 81, 96).

12   Specimens of these handcrafts can be found in the Benaki and in the Folk museums in Athens, in Heracleon's historical museum in Crete and in the Victoria and Albert Museum in London.

Figure 3.1   Woman crocheting while talking to her father

In Nohia old traditional methods of embroidering and other handwork are
dying out. By the mid-1980s only two women, both in their late 50s, were still
spending a large proportion of their time weaving on their loom, kept in a room
at the back of the house. The other looms in the village are carefully packed
away and stored in cellars. As a young woman said: 'we are modernized and
we are very busy – we no longer need to display these items in our living rooms
to be considered as good housewives. Times have changed. Time is money now
… One can always buy nice machine-washable embroideries from the market.'
Since most of these articles were produced for self-use rather than for sale, the
main loss is aesthetic rather than financial.[13]

In view of the fact that *koukoulia* making has been, for many households in
Nohia and other villages in the area, a major household occupation since the
mid-1970s, it is surprising that so little official information is available about
its production and marketing and the people involved in it. During the 1940s
there was considerable production of *koukoulia* in the province of Kissamos[14]
in general and in Nohia in particular. During World War II and the Civil War
which followed, the production of *koukoulia* almost disappeared. This was
attributed by a 90-year-old woman to the difficulty in getting hold of raw

---

13   This is not to say that articles produced for self-use do not have an economic
value.

14   The province of Kissamos is located at the western part of Crete, in the
prefecture of Chania and around 10 km west of the city of Chania.

Figure 3.2   The finished product

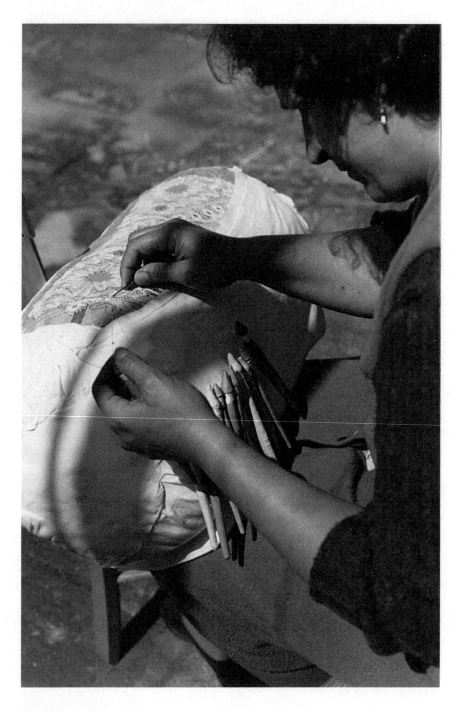

Figure 3.3 Kopanelli

materials because of shortage of money and disruptions in road networks. In the mid-1960s production was resumed, but most products were sold to a factory in the town of Chania, either for cash or in exchange for threads used for producing silk cloth and garments. Production was once more disrupted when the factory closed down in the early 1970s, only to start up again in the early 1980s. The revival was encouraged by a programme launched by the Department of Agriculture aiming at the revival of traditional crafts in Greece and also at the provision of practical training for people to help them to participate effectively in the development of their community.[15] A few women from the local branch of the Department of Agriculture came to the village to teach local women the *koukoulia* craft. Initially, the finished goods were sent as gift parcels to friends and relatives in urban areas as a return for some favour. For example, a woman who at the time had a son studying in a technical college in Athens and living with her sister's family, sent a *koukouli* to them to show her gratitude. In the early to mid-1980s two exhibitions of cocoon handcrafts and other craft work took place in two nearby villages – many women were impressed and thus the craft was extended to other villages in the area. Training was provided by the Department of Agriculture and financed by the Prefecture Committee for Popular Education (NELE). To begin with women in Nohia concentrated on learning how to undertake the handwork itself and not on cocoon production. Cocoons were provided by the Department of Agriculture (see Figure 3.4).[16] The skill is relatively simple and hardly any capital is needed. Gradually it changed from a non-profit-making activity aimed at decorating houses into a form of simple commodity production with an exchange value.

At the time of the fieldwork, approximately 20 per cent of the female population in Nohia was engaged in the production of *koukoulia* – not all full time, because of their involvement in agriculture. They did not work for self-use, as had been the case in the past, but produced for the market. The net income of women who worked on *koukoulia* full time and regarded it as their main occupation was estimated in the late 1980s to be around 200,000 drachmas (€600) per month, averaged out over the months they could sell. If one compares this to the 110,000 drachmas (€330) earned at the time by a construction worker during the same period, the amount earned by these women was relatively significant. The rest of the chapter examines the importance of this for the division of labour within the household, the decision-making process

---

15   Similar programmes were also launched by the Prefectural Committee for Popular Education (NELE) (for example, they provided weaving courses for women).

16   The eggs for the production of silkworms were imported from Japan. These were delivered to producers in spring. Producers were subsidized for each box of eggs they claimed to 'open' (a local expression for hatching). Women often ordered more boxes than they planned to 'open' in order to receive the subsidy, which in the late 1980s was around €45 per box.

Figure 3.4   Cocoons

regarding the expenditure of the household income and the way the position of these women changed within the family and the wider community.

Production of *Koukoulia* Handcrafts and Division of Labour

The means of production owned by the *koukoulia* producer are visible when one enters their houses or verandas in the summer. Apart from a room with big tables, very simply, they consist of needles, scissors, thimble, cloth, chemical dyes, glue, carbon paper, beads and threads. The design is printed on the cloth, which is usually black (it can also be red or blue or green, depending on the customer's preference); this is bought from a cooperative in Chania, although on rare occasions velvet imported from Eastern Europe is used.

Six different stages of work can be distinguished: cutting cloth, sewing and hemming, cutting the cocoons into different shapes, dyeing the cloth and the cocoons, gluing many cocoon pieces together and forming different shapes (for example, a flower or a leaf) and joining these pieces to other pieces or patterns to make a whole piece. As Greger (1985: 202) writes, 'the logical structure of women's handwork designs hardly goes along with the idea that women are transmitters and absorbers of feeling only, and not rational'.

The cloth has to be planned (a task which involves mathematical skills) and cut into different shapes (usually squares and rectangles) and sizes, depending on the orders they have, and in such a way that maximum use is achieved. Then, the cloth is printed. Different prints are used according to the design; these are printed on several pieces of cloth, which are then sewn and 'cocooned'. After the outer coating is removed, the cocoons are cut into several pieces of different size and shape, glued together either on the cloth or on small pieces of cardboard and then, depending on the shape, glued onto the cloth or sewn. Sometimes beads are used as well. Chemical dyes imported from the Netherlands and Germany give the cocoons different colour/shades, although sometimes more natural methods are employed, such as boiling cocoons with onion leaves. With the exception of the chemical dyes, most of the raw materials are produced in Greece. Because cocoons are glued on, the embroidering involved is only a small part of the whole process and that is the reason why one cannot call these craftswomen 'embroiderers' and their products 'embroideries'. The percentage of time spent on each stage/task varies according to type of design and size of product. But, roughly, one could say that the most time consuming task is sewing. This is perhaps why much of the sewing has gradually been substituted by gluing.

Almost all the above mentioned tasks – apart from the embroidering – are performed by the *koukoulia* producers themselves regardless of whether the finished articles will be for their own use or for sale. The embroidering and the hemming are either done by the producer or by an assistant, who is paid on a piecework basis, at the time of the fieldwork receiving between one euro and 4.5 euros per piece depending on the size of the product. The assistant, using the skills she has learnt 'through having been brought up to be a woman' (Lever 1988: 11), sews the different designs which have earlier been copied on the cloth, usually using a golden thread, counting every stitch in the cloth so that the needle goes in and is pulled out at regular intervals, say every three threads. Some producers prefer to do this stage themselves and thus save on labour costs. Others split up the tasks so that the assistant, who is assigned specific tasks (mainly sewing and hemming), for a specific rate per piece, does one stage. In either case, the producer herself controls the whole production process and can assess the quality of her product in the interest of the 'business'. Almost all producers use the extra help of an assistant from time to time; some are mothers and others daughters, who are not always paid for their work in cash, but accept that their help will be reciprocated sometime in the future (babysitting for the daughter, looking after an elderly dependent relative). All in all, two sewers in the village work regularly as wage workers.

The bargaining power of sewers is weak, because of lack of alternatives in a small agricultural village like Nohia, where wage labour is hard to find apart from the primary sector, and the women cannot switch employers if one pays more than another, because this might upset the delicate balance in interpersonal relations that people living is a small community must try to preserve.

This new division of labour does not mean that each woman does not know how to make a whole piece of *koukouli*, as was the case with the lace makers

Figure 3.5 *Agros*

Figure 3.6 'Young girl'

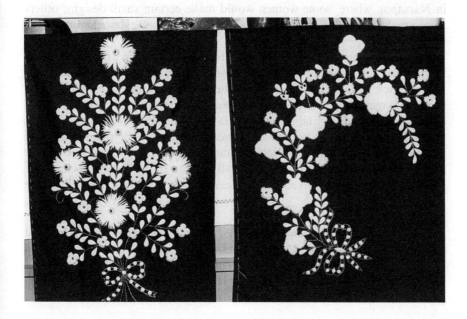

Figure 3.7 Smaller items

Figure 3.8   Traditional design in a modern household

in Narsapur, where 'some women would make certain small designs, others would make other designs and again others would make some joining parts' (Mies 1982: 35).

The skill content varies from stage to stage and from article to article. Sewing and hemming are the easiest stages, and designing the most difficult. The pinnacle of achievement is *agros* (the field) (see Figure 3.5). Most of its surface is covered by patterns and the designs are considered by local women to be intricate and very laborious. It is larger than other articles and it does take relatively longer to complete (approximately a day or two longer) and on these grounds the price is higher[17] than that of other patterns (see Figure 3.7). Of course, the more skilled the craftswoman is, the faster she can work and the more she earns. To some extent earnings and skill correlate. To quote Lever (1988: 9)

> These 'tacit skills', for example, an ability to work without counting each thread when embroidering designs which depend on following the threads of the original cloth ... knowing how to disguise mistakes and knowing the best posture to avoid a backache, allowed the embroiderers to earn a living ... and benefit from these tacit skills through receiving high quality work.

---

17   The price of the a*gros* design is ten times higher of that of smaller patterns.

Figure 3.9   Traditional design

The prices of the end product vary according to size and the work involved, the cheapest sold for about €3 each, the big ones for around €45. The entrepreneur could earn about €450 to €525 net per month.

As mentioned earlier, different designs are used, each given a different name (see Figures 3.5, 3.6 and 3.7) and some more popular than others (and affected by different fashions). They differ from more traditional designs (see Figure 3.9) in that they are more colourful (see Figures 3.5 and 3.6) – the traditional ones used to be black and white – and some of them involve drawing skills (see Figure 3.6). These new designs have changed to accommodate patterns that have nothing to do with either Cretan village culture, nor the symbolic meaning of the old traditional designs. Some village women insisted that in the old days, the products were of high quality, whereas now the work involved less skill. For example, in the old days they used to sew the beads and cocoons on the cloth, instead of gluing them; they did not use carbon paper for printing the designs on the cloth; therefore, more skill was required. One would often hear words of admiration both for the woman who made it – usually an ancestress of one of the spouses – and for the design, which was 'delicately made', simple, black and white, usually with a wedding photograph of the producer and her husband

Figure 3.10   The 'little huts'

stuck in the middle symbolizing their union, the couple's happiness and the affection they felt for one another. Others disagreed, claiming that old designs were much simpler and easier to make. The designs are numerous, some vary in the amount of skill they demand, others do not. Most are 'poor taste', a fact admitted by the handcraft producers themselves. Characteristically, a woman said: 'It looks disgusting but since there is a demand for it ....' Although these articles were disliked, the ones which women produced for their daughters were rather valued and seen as 'pieces of art'. *Agros* or *kalivakia* (the little huts) (see Figures 3.5 and 3.10) were thought to be the best among the modern ones in terms of skill and labour involved, as well as in terms of design and colours used. These were made with 'care and affection' as a woman told me, 'using the old method of sewing rather than gluing'. Producers are often reluctant to show much overt interest in the designs of others because this may be seen as 'casting an evil eye' via admiration or jealousy, and thus be branded as harbouring antisocial attitudes. The guessing game about the next new design occupies an enormous amount of their energy and time. Nevertheless, aesthetic plagiarism entails social risks; the play of imitation and invention of new designs is a social matter, carefully negotiated and judged by criteria of appropriateness in the particular context they operate in, trying to make profit with a product of limited market in the production of which they invest their personal creative pride.

The craftswomen work on the *koukoulia* between eight and 14 hours a day, and this involves boring routines. The work varies seasonally and according to the woman's responsibilities at home (for example, those with young children tend to have less 'spare time' for producing crafts). During the season of the olive harvest (usually from mid-November to early February) the women devote less time to *koukoulia*, unless their spouses decide to hire labour (*mazochtres*) for harvesting the olives, than they do during spring, when they work for up to 14 hours per day. It was worth hiring labour, the women said, because the amount of money paid for the hired labour was far less than the amount earned from the craft.[18] In early summer, on the other hand, most of their time is devoted to cocoon production (the collection of mulberry leaves, feeding the caterpillars, cleaning the room the silkworms are kept in) rather than to production of handcrafts *per se*.

Generally, in Crete, embroidering and making *koukoulia* handcrafts is considered to be a 'woman's job'. The family helps. Women help both in producing cocoons and in gathering mulberry leaves and feeding the caterpillars, as well as keeping clean the place where these are kept. Men prefer to gather leaves and cut branches for the caterpillars; both men and women justify this in terms of the physical strength required. However, the main reason seemed to be the fact that often this involves travelling about 15 to 20 kilometres with a car which, because women in Nohia cannot drive, requires the presence of a man eager to finish the job as quickly as possible so as to return to his own occupation, or to visit the local coffee shop. Otherwise, it is exclusively women who collect leaves from the few mulberry trees in the village. Furthermore, men help with the packing of the products in large cardboard boxes and their transportation to the nearest post office (or other transport agency). One thing men do not do is sew. A young boy in the village enjoyed helping his mother hem and was reprimanded strongly by other males for this, both by his peers and adults, for doing what 'girls normally do'.

The number of articles they manage to produce per day varies according to the size and amount of labour required. They prefer, however, to sew a number of them and then devote some days to drawing and sticking the pieces of cocoon and beads on them. The main reasons for doing this are: first, because they usually work on the kitchen table (they do not have their own working space) and, therefore, have to take everything off this table before a meal and put it all back afterwards, which is quite laborious and creates a lot of resentment on the part of the women. As a craftswoman said to me,

> this continuous moving of the stuff on and off the table gets on my nerves especially at times when a deadline has to be met; but men are men – they want the table clear when they come home for a meal.

18 The decision to hire help was a consensus decision taken by the women together with their husbands.

This was also noticed by Greger (1985: 201) in the village she researched in Eastern Crete. She writes: 'Men ... profess not to like watching a wife do handiwork, and it is usually put away when the man comes home.'

The second reason for the women's preference is that, because they carry their work under their arms when sewing, they can visit other women who produce handcrafts, or friends, whereas when gluing pieces on the cloth they have to stay in the house, alone (the men are either in the fields or sitting at the local coffee shop drinking coffee or raki and playing cards or talking with other fellow men).

Some women claimed that before engaging in this 'business' they had time to socialize; however, now they did not have the time, since 'time [for them] is money'. Most of the time, each one of them is confined to her house, working on her handcrafts. Hence, unlike the village Hatzi studied by Kennedy (1986: 121, 127), where women's friendships were 'rich, freely chosen emotional bonds that, in intensity, is comparable to – and often surpass – women's kinship ties ... a powerful coping mechanism and a unique expression of special energies that are not adapted to the dominant culture', in Nohia, *koukoulia* producers no longer have time for such relationships. 'Such relationships are rare', a woman said. 'There is no time, and there is much to lose ... people gossip.' It could be said, therefore, that women's involvement with handcrafts signifies their commitment to the values of the household and serves as a mechanism preventing idleness and gossip. In addition, unlike on Lesbos, studied by Papataxiarchis (1991), where domestic kinship (*sigenia*) is of great significance for women, as 'it sets women together in matrilocal alliances' (ibid.: 157), virilocal marriage mitigates against the formation of any separate women's world in Nohia, based on kinship ties.

Moreover, although women know the kind of profits dealers make and hence they are aware of the fact that they are being exploited by market relations, there does not seem to be much economic cooperation between them. 'Other producers are materialistic and jealous; if they learn that my dealer offers better prices for the same products, they may try to contact the dealer .... I wouldn't like that', a woman said. And she continued: 'I am afraid of being eyed' (*fovame to matiasma*). Such behaviour was thus reinforced by the belief in 'a harmful power of both envy and admiration which was expressed in the evil eye' (Hirschon 1989: 181). Another woman added: 'women often like to gossip ... I do not like the rest of the village to know how much I earn.' In other words, these women act in the spirit of *sympheron*, that is, 'the pursuit of material success, translated as "self ... interest" ... [which] is an essentially competitive drive, grounded in gaining advantages, often at the expense of others, and its effect may often be to limit possibilities for co-operative effort' (Hirschon 1989: 103–4). Hence *koukoulia* producers in Nohia embraced competitive, masculine activities; they seem to have acquired what Hirschon calls 'a guideline for masculine achievement' (ibid.), despite the fact that their labour was taking place in household premises and therefore was not detached from their role as 'mistress of the house'.

Handcrafts and the Market

The connection with the market is mainly through intermediaries – here called dealers. Dealers are usually women, who are neither producers nor consumers, but buy the products from the producer, often frame them, and sell them with a 50 per cent to 100 per cent profit. The profit margin varies with size – the smaller the item the larger the profit. The products are sold either to another merchant, who sometimes owns a shop, and who, in turn, sells them to tourists (both Greek and foreigners) or to consumers in other parts of Greece, mainly lower-middle-class or working-class women. The latter either cannot decorate their walls with their own embroideries, (because for one reason or another they have not got the time to make them), or cannot afford to buy a painting.

The dealers are from different geographical areas in Greece. Some even come from abroad; for example, one woman in Nohia sends articles to a relative in Australia who acts as her intermediary, and another one in the US. They are somehow connected to the craft producer either through kinship, or through friendship or *koumbaria*.[19] Unlike Tupperware dealers, they are not consumers/ customers themselves, but like them they do go to house parties to sell and give the hostess a small present as a reward for collecting together so many potential customers.

The whole circulation of the product depends on established networks. If the producer finds the 'right dealer/s' – an 'active and clever' dealer, as they describe him/her – she can make a lot of money because of the big volume of handcrafts sold. As most handcraft producers in Nohia say, 'it is easy to become a producer of cocoon handcrafts; the only problem is to have business connections'.

'How did you come in contact/get to know your dealers?' I asked a producer.

'Usually, when a dealer hears that you are a good, reliable producer that makes handcrafts for the market, she/he approaches you', she replied.

The intermediary does not get a commission. Unlike the putting-out system used by agents in Narsapur, where lacemakers are visited by agents who supply them with thread and collect the finished product (either a whole piece of lace or a partial piece which is finished later by another lacemaker) (Mies 1982: 34),

---

19 *Koumbaria* is the Greek term for the relationship between the godfather/ godmother and the child's parents and also for the relationship between the best man/ bridesmaid and the married couple.

in Nohia the intermediary orders the goods (specifies the designs her customers have ordered and the ones that are more likely to sell), usually by telephone or by letter; both the producer and the dealer keep photographs or samples of the designs customers prefer; these are individually numbered or named, to avoid misunderstandings. The dealer also fixes the time when she wants the goods (in a month, 15 days or even less). When she presses for time, she offers better terms. On receipt of the orders the woman makes the required number of articles. Payment varies depending on the relationship between producer and dealer. If a trust has developed between the two parties, the dealer pays the agreed price after she/he receives the items; if not, she/he pays prior to delivery of the finished articles at the post office. On the part of the intermediaries, payment per piece encourages care and fast delivery. Generally, craft producers prefer to charge the same price (for equivalent items) to all their dealers in order to avoid conflict if one dealer discovers that another is getting the product more cheaply.

The profits made by the intermediaries consist of the difference between the prices they pay to the producers and the prices they get from the consumers. Although their work input is less, they earn more than the producers do since they can manipulate both selling prices and the price they pay the producer. Often dealers deceive producers by claiming that demand is slack and, based on this, manipulate their 'cost' price. Although some women at times feel cheated by the dealers, producers have no way of checking whether the demand for their product has fallen or not.

The dealer has certain advantages too in that no investment in capital, buildings or raw materials is required. These costs are all borne by the producer. If the demand is slack, the dealer simply orders a smaller number of products. On the other hand, an intermediary has no means of forcing a producer to sell to her and to others within a given period, apart from instances when the dealer gives the producer a loan in advance. Hence, although the dealer controls her/his own labour power of selling, s/he does not fully control her own profits. Dealers pay about 10 per cent to 15 per cent more if they want the work to be done at a certain time, when there is great demand (for example, around Christmas). It is then that the producers can bargain and get better deals.

Usually, producers prefer to sell to dealers rather than directly to shops, because shops demand invoices – as, for example, Claudatos in Chania – which almost all women hesitate to provide so as to avoid paying taxes on profits. This is in some contradiction to the fact that they are formally subsidized for their product (production of silkworms and cocoons). The paradox here is that on the one hand they work illegally, but on the other they are legally subsidized, that is, this illegality is tolerated by the authorities. Nevertheless, some of them said that if sales dropped significantly, (as we shall see below, they did so slightly in the late 1980s due to saturation of the market and economic recession), then they would start giving invoices and thus maximize sales by selling, if possible, directly to shops.

Prospects for a Cooperative

In July 1985 a women's cooperative (*synetaerismos*) was founded in Kolymbari[20] (a village near Nohia) for all the villages situated in the nearby regions. Most of its members (only 20) are loom-weavers. It was supported by the then EOMMEX (Hellenic Organization for Small and Medium Sized Industries and Handcrafts), which at the time offered regional development programmes also geared towards the promotion of craft cooperatives alongside an emphasis on the wealth of a long and rich traditional Greek culture which must not be left to perish. The cooperative sold its commodified folklore – mainly *hyfanda* (loom-woven products) – to merchants in Athens and other cities in Greece. It also runs a shop famous for its dear prices, in a village near Nohia. 'It is a coop; it shouldn't have such high prices', was echoed many times by villagers, who reckoned that if prices were lower, there would perhaps have been a bigger turnover. Products of the cooperative were also exhibited in craft exhibitions.

The *koukoulia* producers in the area, as opposed to the few loom-weavers who joined the cooperative, did not set up a cooperative, despite being encouraged to do so by EOMMEX. According to some local women, representatives of EOMMEX came once to the Orthodox Academy of Crete (situated in Kolymbari), made a few promises, but never revisited. However, EOMMEX did organize two handcraft exhibitions in Nohia, in 1987 and 1988, where many embroiderers, *koukoulia* producers, loom-weavers and potters had the chance to exhibit and even sell their products.

Some *koukoulia* producers argued that they were reluctant to join a cooperative, because they lacked information about what their responsibilities, obligations and benefits would be. 'They told us, give €150 to subscribe and then you'll see ...', a woman producing *koukoulia* said. Others did not find the idea of getting a loan for joining the cooperative attractive. This is partly because 'owing money' has a derogatory connotation of failure amongst some people in rural areas of Greece. If they owe money, this at least has to be for a justified purpose, and a 'woman's cooperative' does not seem to be one in a patriarchal society such as Nohia. 'If we get a loan, we might as well invest it in our agricultural property', a producer said.

Another reason is that their job is clandestine; they do not pay taxes on profits, whereas by joining a cooperative they would probably have to. They could not, presumably, see the benefits of joining a cooperative, namely the potential for greater profits because of lower production costs, the fact that dealers could be bypassed by setting up a marketing office, which could negotiate for cheaper raw materials and explore possibilities of promoting exports. Also, the producers of *koukoulia* in Nohia did not find the idea of joining the loom-weavers' cooperative in Kolymbari attractive, because, as they said,

20 Kolymbari is a coastal village situated on the north western part of Crete, around 20 km west of the city of Chania.

loom-weavers need more money for capital goods such as machinery, while *koukoulia* producers do not.

Despite the fact that any proposal that they should enter into a local form of collectivism fell foul of the self-perception that *koukoulia* producers entertain as individualists who do not easily tame their interests to a common goal or cost efficiency, most of them admitted that there could have been some advantages in joining a cooperative or forming their own cooperative, or even some kind of association. These were summarized as follows by a producer who was also the wife of one of the most prominent members of the Cooperatives' Association in Kolymbari. First, instead of having the anxiety every spring as to whether they would be able to get hold of enough mulberry trees to feed the caterpillars, they could join together, buy a piece of land and plant some trees there. 'If we did this when the *koukoulia* production started in the village, we would by now have been able to feed our caterpillars with these leaves. Instead, we have to travel to other villages every day and ask people to do us a favour and give or sell us leaves.' The production of cocoons is entirely dependent on these leaves and, furthermore, one must make sure that the leaves have not been sprayed with pesticides. Second, women could have a systematic production, such as common ovens, warehouses, space for rearing the caterpillars, purchase of raw materials in large quantities and, therefore, cheaper transport facilities for delivering the goods (currently they individually use the family car), a shop and they could work together instead of each being isolated in her own home at her kitchen table. Whereas this getting together would have helped them break their isolation and boredom, it would have depended on the fear of gossip that exists in the villages and the fear that the family will be less respected if other fellow villagers got to know its problems. 'Ta en iko mi en dimo' is a well known saying in Greece meaning 'whatever happens within the house, should not be made public'. As each family is promoting its own interests and relationships are marked by competition, this, as Hirschon (1989: 178) argues, creates 'a level of latent antagonism'. If, therefore, information becomes public, accusations about members of the household may be made 'through commentary (*skholia*) or gossip (*koutsombolia*) without her (the hostess) having the opportunity to reply, whether verbally or non-verbally, to 'what people say' (Cowan 1990: 203). To risk being misunderstood or becoming the subject matter of village gossip is to risk being ridiculed in the eyes of the community, losing one's honour. As du Boulay (1974: 107) argues, honour 'involves the evaluation of the community', that is, public opinion is very important for the individual and for the family. As 'the predisposition of others to pass unfavourable judgements [is] believed to have no limits ... some grounds could always be found to denigrate or criticise the activities of others' (Hirschon 1989: 178). In response to this anxiety, relative isolation was employed as a defensive technique. They seem to think that a cooperative is 'an institution that requires a level of honesty they are incapable of achieving or too fixated on short-term gains to want to achieve' (Herzfeld 2004: 163).

Generally, the attempt to promote the involvement of rural women in cooperatives was part of the PASOK government's attempt in the 1980s to involve women in production and promote their position in a decentralized system of agro-industrial organization of the country. The idea was that whereas the rural woman working in the family business was not paid for her labour, her involvement in a cooperative would give her the opportunity to get paid according to her labour input. This idea did not appeal to the *koukoulia* producers in Nohia, who, despite some benefits from forming or joining a cooperative, opted for working individually rather than cooperatively. This is because, as they said, 'in this way we organize our time better – we work as much as we want to'. The isolation of the *koukoulia* producers from each other (each woman works in her home – apart from instances when they go to each other's houses, sit together and either cut cocoons or sew – and often keeps secret new designs she produces and for whom) and the fact that different women have different dealers and they work they get varies (some get more than others), means that any kind of union is difficult to organize. In spite of the existing structures of mutual help and closeness in the community, production is individualized. Thus, there is a lot of competition, jealousy and distrust among the women, which is the source of deep-seated anxiety amongst them and arguably poses a threat to the 'taken-for-granted' local way of living including cultural norms of cooperativeness and responsibility.[21] Each woman thinks of her handcrafts as the best and believes that, if she joins the others, the quality will fall; because, as they maintained, 'each of us will try to do the job as fast as we can with as little effort as possible'. Relations often appear to be competitive and agonistic. New designs are kept secret for as long as possible. These are often discovered through relatives in other villages or the women who work in the Department of Agriculture in Chania, who give these designs in exchange for other favours, such as samples to exhibit in Chania. There is no formal agreement between producers on the prices of the end products. Although, by looking around, they try to keep their prices at the same level as others do, as soon as one notices a drop in her sales, she tries (with hesitation) to reduce her prices for fear of losing her outlets. A woman in Nohia did this but, as a result, another woman's dealer started buying from her. A lot of criticism followed this action. 'She shouldn't have done this. We have known each other for so many years', the woman who lost her dealer said to me. Others refused to comment on their similar experiences. So, one can be a 'business woman' in the village, but only up to a point. There are some ethical boundaries within the community that one should not cross. Betrayal of trust is one of them. It entails an enormous social risk in a closely knit society like that of Nohia. The potential for *parexigisi* (misunderstanding or upsetting someone) and the potential of an open confrontation erupting between producers is of

---

21   General discussions of trust can be found in Luhmann (1968) and Misztal (1996).

central importance here. Moreover, this individual competitiveness among the producers, where each is striving to protect her own interests at all costs, perpetuated by the organization of this system of production itself, is also curtailed by the community value system; a system which nevertheless has not managed to eliminate the competition between these women and enable them to come together to define their interests against the various intermediaries and market forces and to win each other's trust.

Finally, women avoid (as much as they can) teaching the handcraft to other women, because of fear of saturation of the market. At the time of the fieldwork there was demand for the product; however, when they later encountered market saturation due to recession and rising prices of inputs due to inflation, one would have thought that they would have been forced to consider either joining together or warming to the possibility of production diversification. In fact, none of these occurred. Instead, unable to compete in a world of globalization – which has amplified to unprecedented levels the weaknesses of those whose products appeal only to a specifically small local market, itself weakened by an increasingly homogeneous universalized cultural and aesthetic values – they decided to abandon it. As a woman said when I visited the village a couple of years ago, 'We made enough money, we can't complain; it's over now. No one wants to buy them. Tastes change'.

Implications for Women's Position at Village and Household Levels

The work of handcraft producers in Nohia was accepted with pride by the male population of the village. As men told me at the peak of the cocoon production (1980s), 'This is a very good work for our women, because it enables them to look after the house and work at the same time. They earn good money. Maybe all women in the village should learn the task. Some are so clever they manage to export to USA and Australia. We are proud of them'. Although men reacted negatively in the beginning, as a producer said, 'When they realized that we were making a profit and were able to contribute to the family income, they started encouraging us to work more'.

Some women in fact started earning more than their husbands. In my question about who decides where the money should be spent, women answered that they put the money in the family budget, which is spent on the reproduction of the family, and that decisions are taken jointly. As Koula's husband said:

> Koula and I almost always take decisions regarding household expenditure together; she has more say, however, on matters related to children's education and future dwellings. Without Koula's earnings from *koukoulia*, we wouldn't have been able to build such a nice house for our son Takis, and our daughter Charoula, who studies in Athens, would have had to manage on a smaller allowance.

He added:

> I must admit that in the past, before Koula took up *koukoulia* production, although we both worked in the fields, I was the one who kept the money ... This is how things used to be and this is how things still are for most families if the woman hasn't an independent income.

It is difficult to know whether in practice decisions are in fact taken jointly; almost all *koukoulia* producers and their husbands insist that they do so and attributed this to the fact that the women make a significant economic contribution to the household. A large amount of their earnings is spent on the family rather than on personal luxuries, thus lifting the burden from men; this is important in Nohia in terms of the limited opportunities available. None of the producers who were interviewed seemed to resent this, but saw it as a 'natural' thing to do as members of a family. In practice, however, instead of investing their earnings in other productive sectors of the economy, some women now have the flexibility of spending – within 'reasonable' limits – a small amount of money on themselves (for clothes) and, since most of them support a son/daughter who studies in the University in Athens or elsewhere in Greece, contribute to the daughter's dowry,[22] buy a house for the son (in Crete, as opposed to other parts of Greece, the man has to provide the house) or some 'luxury goods' such as a TV, a video, a washing machine, etc., which are signs of prosperity, for the household. In other words, the production of these handcrafts had a definite bearing on household consumption patterns and hence on the standard of living of these families. However, as mentioned above, very few use their profits for buying consumer goods for themselves and the ones that do are criticized by others. 'She spends all her money on clothes ...', said a producer disparagingly about another woman.

Although in theory the husbands of these producers are expected to support their wives financially, in practice they expect their wives to supplement the family income. Changes in female work participation have meant that most handcraft producers, who previously worked alongside their husband in the fields (and were therefore directly productive, though not independently paid), have given up working on the family land and become women who stay at home as 'housewives', fulfilling and enhancing society's traditional roles as wives and mothers and yet at the same time earning cash independently from their men. As Eftychis, the husband of a producer said:

> The way we used to divide the fieldwork has changed; whereas in the past we were both working in the fields, now Georgia [his wife] stays at home. I now do most of the work alone; sometimes, my son Kostis gives me a hand.

---

22 Although the institution of dowry was abolished in the early 1980s, this still remains one of the most prominent customs in the village.

In other words, there are some very small changes in the division of labour outside the home. With regard to domestic work, though, the spheres of production and of reproduction are closely interconnected. Domestic labour is easily integrated with the *koukoulia* handcrafts, because both take place in the same location, the home; the producer wakes up around 6 or 7 a.m., fulfils her duties as a housewife, in that she prepares breakfast, makes up the beds and cooks lunch, and then, around 10 a.m., she clears the kitchen table and starts working on her craft. She takes a break around noon when the men come home for lunch and starts working again until 7 p.m., when she starts preparing the evening meal. An exception is the summer months, when everyone in the village takes a siesta for a couple of hours in the afternoon. After the evening meal, she works for two to three hours, while waiting for the men to come back from the local café, and goes to bed at about midnight or even later if her dealer is expecting a delivery of goods at short notice. Women with children have to devote some time to helping them with their homework, since the education system in Greece expects parents to help their children study and men rarely do this – it is considered to be part of the mother's responsibilities. Occasionally, time is taken off for cleaning the house, ironing clothes – all have washing machines at home – and preparing more elaborate meals for guests.

Apart from the domestic labour that the producers are expected to contribute, they also look after the *koukoulia* business alongside the other members of the family. Usually, there is a delivery date set by the customer. In addition, the craftswoman tries to meet that date so as to avoid losing the customer's/dealer's trust. It is a kind of self-exploitation and it would perhaps be interesting to link this to cycles of the family (that is, family with small children, children about to get married, married children and so on) and see at what stage of the family life cycle the woman is most overworked and most exploited by market relations. As a result, women have little time for leisure and this is one of the reasons why the women's associations in the village are inactive (see Chapter 8). Having said that, most women tend to emphasize their love for the work they perform, the *meraki* (passions of the artist) with which they work and the sense of enjoyment (*kefi*) they feel. Nevertheless, this type of work also entails calculation, in view of the profits made; they tend to become habituated to the demanding discipline of long hours at the worktable. The profits made in their opinion merit the sacrifices they have to make.

Concluding Remarks

The producers of *koukoulia* in Nohia work at home, which means that their personal life and their working life are not separated and they are paid by the piece by the dealer, who largely determines the designs of the articles. Even so, they do not consider themselves to be homeworkers, but rather describe themselves as 'self-employed'. In addition, they own their means of production, which means that they do not rely on their intermediaries for supplying them with raw materials and are thus much more in control. Nevertheless, production of *koukoulia* handcrafts is spatially confined to the home of the producer and although the conditions of employment may in many ways make one think that they resemble those of homeworking – in that the women define themselves as 'self-employed' and 'self-made' and lack employment rights and security – if one looks closely, one realizes that this is not true. Unlike homeworkers, *koukoulia* producers are not employed but work on their own account and they have some control over the prices they receive (although these are, as mentioned earlier, set by the dealer), in that these are not set by an employer. They often say: 'we have our own work, we are independent.' They are (and see themselves as) independent producers vis-à-vis their men and the market.

Moreover, the non-separation of the spaces of production and reproduction, which is based on the ideology of the housewife, means that although the villagers (both men and women) as well as many government officials (for example, the local secretary and the president), speak about these producers and their handcrafts with admiration, and do regard it as something more than a mere 'leisure activity', it still remains a 'hidden' occupation. Some, for example the local priest, still see the producers as 'housewives who use their leisure time in a profitable way' – and this despite the fact it can occupy many hours a day for much of the year. Such stereotypes are deeply ingrained and do strongly influence people's perceptions of what is happening in the village. The construction and reproduction of gender-specific values which reinforce the separation between the masculine world of public performance and the feminine world of private service, contribute to the invisibility of these women's productive work. This invisibility becomes apparent in the paradoxical situation demonstrated by the fact that although, when I came to the village for the first time and asked to visit some of these producers, everybody knew who they were and where they lived. The coffee shop owners could also give details of the stage of production at the time. However, when I visited the local government office later, I discovered that these women were registered as housewives, or at best *agrotisses* (agriculturalists), and that although the agricultural and livestock census (official statistics) includes the category 'cocoons', this was left empty in all censuses kept in that office, thus leaving the production of cocoons and of these handcrafts in the village unrecorded, indicating that no such production took place. It is also interesting to note here that the local secretary, in his role as a member of the community and husband of an ex-craftswoman – his wife was a producer until she fell ill – recognizes the existence of this occupation and sees it as 'work', but as an official bureaucrat who has to inform the local archives, he sees it as a 'hobby', a 'leisure-time activity'. This contradiction has its roots in the fact that the occupational status of the household is defined according to the occupation of the male 'head', thus making these women 'invisible' by not defining them as workers 'even in the face of abundant evidence of their productive work' (Mies 1982: 54). The reason for this neglect is male bias prevailing in the concepts and definitions used in official statistics, especially in countries with strong patriarchal institutions, as well as the inherent characteristics of this kind of production, located as it is in the home, reinforces the domestication of women and makes them fully 'housewives'. Another material motive in the women's interests as well as men's for this neglect, is tax avoidance.

So, these women are 'semi-domesticated', which means that in their social appearance they are housewives, but in reality they earn a respectable income and are integrated into a market-oriented production system. This has its roots in the patriarchal system which reinforces the hierarchical relationship between men and women where men are supposed to control the means of production and women's reproductive functions. In this context, the symbolic feminization that a woman earning more implies for men and the impact the failure of supporting one's family has on a man's reputation and honour in the eyes of the community is offset by the solidarity needed for the family to survive in an overwhelmingly competitive economic environment. Although they do not refuse to attribute skill and value to their women's work, in that their skills are recognized as such, they tend to relegate the labour contributed by women to the undifferentiated and subordinate category of women's work or housework.

Chapter 4
Market Gardening and Women's Work in Platanos

Introduction

This chapter describes the introduction of greenhouses (*thermokipia*) in Platanos (see Figure 4.1) and analyses the effects of this kind of transformation of agrarian structures and of technological change on the division of labour by sex. It highlights the contradictions that can appear when on the one hand, due to the changes introduced by the 'greenhouse revolution' in the area, the degree of women's economic activities related to the production of greenhouse vegetables and fruits has increased, while on the other, existing patriarchal forms expressed through tradition act to encourage women's subordination. It aims to study the greenhouse as a distinctive space of constructing womanhood and to explore the possible problems that might have emerged within that spatial context.

Figure 4.1   Greenhouses in Platanos

After describing in detail the process of agrarian change, I shall look at the new technology being adopted by some farmers and the differential impact this has had on men and women and how this has narrowed down the tasks done by men and increased some of the burdens of women. Moreover, the way EC regulations and directives were implemented during the 1980s by local bureaucracy shows that, although it is assumed that subsidies (in the form of inputs – technological and other) affect the whole family equally, they are in fact being unequally distributed among family members – since they are geared towards the 'head of the family' – by state officials who thus have furthered (and perhaps, in the case of women officials, are themselves the victims of) the perpetuation of the ideological undervaluation of women's work in the area. The position of women in Platanos may have improved in that, although they say that they do want recognition for the work they do, they do not express feelings of subordination with respect to their work the greenhouse or for the family, but no claims can be made about any overall improvement in gender equality. So the presumption that modernization improves gender equality is problematic, because it ignores the regional, cultural and historical nature of rural societies and the people living within them.

Historical Background

The cultivation of early vegetables and fruit (*proima kipeftika*) is a dynamic and intensive form of agriculture, which first appeared in Greece in the mid-1950s and rapidly expanded since.[1] There is scant information as to why this form of agriculture developed in Greece at all. According to Donatos et al. (1989: 22), and to some government officials working in the local branches of the Ministry of Agriculture and of the Agricultural Bank of Greece whom I interviewed in Chania and Kastelli, the determining factors which contributed to the development and relative expansion of greenhouses in western Crete were: a rise in the demand for early vegetables due to a rise in the consumers' standard of living, the favourable climatic conditions and financial support rendered to producers by various institutions, such as the Agricultural Bank of Greece (in the form of loans, etc.), the Ministry of Agriculture and the EC (in the form of subsidies, technical advice and the like); the favourable soil conditions prevailing in the areas concerned; the expansion and use of modern irrigation systems; the relatively high agricultural income rendered by the cultivation areas; and,

---

1   Until the mid-1950s the production of fruit and vegetables in Greece was limited to open-air cultivation. Local market demands for seasonal vegetables were met with difficulty. However, from the late 1950s onwards the production expanded. For example, from 1966 until 1981, there was a tenfold increase in land allocated for greenhouse agriculture and a further 35 per cent during the 1981–1987 period (Girgilakis 1985: 6).

finally, improvement in the means of transportation (use of ferry boats, etc.). By the early to mid-1980s a large percentage of greenhouses was situated on the island of Crete (45 per cent of land allocated for greenhouse agriculture in Greece in 1981–1982 and 48.5 per cent in 1987 was in Crete); tomatoes and cucumbers were grown on more than 70 per cent of land in Greece and in Crete allocated to this cultivation, while flowers, melons, watermelons, aubergines, etc., were produced on the remaining 30 per cent or less. As will become apparent below, greenhouse agriculture has since been very important for the economy of Crete in general and of Platanos in particular.

Greenhouses first appeared in western Crete in poor areas; Koundoura was pastureland and people in Platanos barely survived by cultivating olive trees, cereals and onions and gathering salt from the sea-shore and herbs from the mountains (Katakis 1987). As a Plataniotis (that is, a person from Platanos, a villager) I interviewed put it:

> At one time, before the introduction of greenhouses in the area, people used to sow barley, wheat, etc., the whole year through and thresh during the summer; some were fishermen and others sailors; some cultivated onions and others were cattle breeders. There was neither electricity nor water in the village.[2] People emigrated to Germany or worked in cargo ships. When we started to use greenhouses in the area, an economic development occurred and as a result, first, many migrants returned to the village and, second, a change in the occupational structure of the village took place.

By the mid-1980s, half of the area occupied by greenhouses in the prefecture of Chania[3] was situated in the province of Kisamos (Girgilakis 1985: 5), and two-thirds of this half was in Platanos. The once uncultivated areas, which were at that time regarded as barren, were made productive after being irrigated. This, and replacing a part of what local people call 'traditional cultivation' (that is, olives and wheat) with the dynamic production of fruits and vegetables cultivated in greenhouses, means that an income of around €1,600 to €1,700 could be obtained from a piece of land occupying an area of 1 stremma, compared to the much smaller return from the production of 100–120 kg of, let us say, barley per stremma in the old days.

---

2   Village economy started developing after drilling for water took place (1970s). Today, there are still problems with the availability of water, especially during the summer months.

3   The main centres of greenhouse cultivation of vegetables in the prefecture of Chania are Platanos, Gramvousa, Koundoura and the coastal zone between Chania and Kolymbari. At the time of fieldwork, the mean size of each greenhouse was 2.9 stremmata (one stremma = a quarter of an acre) (Katakis 1987: 8). The usual products cultivated in greenhouses in the region are tomatoes and, to a lesser extent, cucumbers, melons and bananas.

There was poverty in the village in the old days. Five or six rich families owned a significant number of olive trees and land. Many of those who took up the 'greenhouse business', for the first time, had to rent land which was regarded as barren by its owner. By the mid-1980s almost everyone had his or her own land and a much higher income than before. But, as I shall show below, whether or not this implies a higher standard of living for the women concerned is debatable, since it implies more hours of work in the fields and not necessarily fewer hours of domestic work and childcare, or more hours available for leisure.

Figure 4.2   Low-roofed Ierapetra-type greenhouse

Another factor which, as I shall show later on, has an effect on the amount of labour input required by women is the quality of products being produced, since it is women who undertake the laborious tasks of nursing the plants and cutting off diseased leaves and fruit. The products are poor in quality because most of the tomato hybrids planted produce large fruits, uneven in colour and shape.[4] Yet another factor which affects women's work is the type of greenhouse (that is,

---

4   At the time of fieldwork, most of these were imported from abroad – the hybrids GC-204, DOMBO and B79-622 were imported from The Netherlands, JOLY from the USA – and they did not grow particularly well on Greek soil and in the prevailing

Figure 4.3   Modern greenhouse

the way it is built). For example, the low-roofed Ierapetra-type greenhouses (see Figures 4.2 and 4.3), which are covered with plastic, have no roof windows, no heating or adequate ventilation systems, create a damp and humid environment and cause the plants to be more prone to disease.[5] Moreover, the fact that they are low means that workers can hardly stand upright inside the greenhouse, or breathe when the weather is hot due to the poor ventilation; this makes the work really difficult, and, as I shall show later on in the chapter, particularly affects women, since they are the ones who spend most of their time in the greenhouse tending the plants. Another important factor which affects the labour input requirements by men and women in a greenhouse is the technology used which, in turn, correlates with the type of greenhouse the producer has. For example, the low roofed Ierapetra-type uses trenches for irrigation, rather than the more modern 'drop-by-drop' method; this encourages more weeds and hence more work for women, since it is the women's job to remove the weeds. It also entails manual fertilization, a task which – although the fertilizer (chemical substance) itself is prepared by men – is carried out by women (see Figure 4.4).

---

climatic conditions (Katakis 1987: 7); some (for example, GC-204) were more resistant to disease than others.

5   Until the late 1970s (when the Agricultural Bank of Greece stopped giving credit for construction and producers realized their disadvantage) low-roofed greenhouses were preferred by some producers to the high-roofed ones covered with fibre-glass, because of their relatively lower construction cost.

Figure 4.4   Women applying hormones to plants

So although the work load of both men and women increases, it is not evenly distributed between the sexes.

As shown below, because greenhouse agriculture on the island is labour intensive, the organization of labour is important and control over family members, which is legitimized by the prevailing ideology of the 'male head of the household' and breadwinner, can be paramount.

Labour Relations

Market gardening on Crete usually consists of small family-based units (the average number of household members is five). The producer controls the land, bases his or her production capacity on the use of manual labour provided mainly by family or household members and is dependent on the market for the sale of products. As one producer maintained, 'Everybody seeks to get the job done using the labour of family members. Children help too'. As will become evident in what follows, age and sex, combined with traditional beliefs and values, determine who does what, who is dependent on whom as well as the rewards one receives for one's labour in the family enterprise.

The Importance of Child Labour for Alleviating Women's 'Double Workload'

Child labour is common in the area. Most parents expect their children to 'help out', as they say, in periods when the work is hectic, namely when the olives and vegetables are harvested. During my fieldwork I saw children of different ages (between nine and 14 years old) as well as adolescents working alongside their parents.[6] They performed various tasks ranging from carrying tomatoes and/or leaves out of the greenhouse (a job which requires some physical strength since the containers are heavy), to performing the very laborious task of clearing out greenhouses overgrown with weeds, a task otherwise mainly undertaken by women. Most of the work carried out by children is unskilled and is learnt through practice.

The work done by children varies according to gender and age; this takes place within the shifting parameters of need and reflects assumptions, values and expectations held by the local community and family regarding gender roles. Girls are expected to perform domestic activities such as cooking, cleaning the house and so on, that is tasks which remained primarily a female province, while other family members, that is, the mother, adult siblings who have not

---

6   Instead of working as unpaid family workers, some teenagers, contrary to their parents' wishes, prefer to engage in various income-generating activities, ranging from working in the greenhouses of other, non-kin producers, to packing tomatoes for tradespeople. They are almost always boys, whereas girls tend to carry out domestic work and thereby help their mothers.

emigrated and younger brothers, are expected to help the head of the family (usually the male[7]) in the agricultural family business. Both male and female children contribute substantially to the welfare of the household through the work they perform in the family business and in the household. Hence, they may be classified as 'unpaid family workers'. Yet the vital contribution which children make to the greenhouse business and to household sustenance receives remarkably little attention and remains a somewhat neglected element in the development process.[8]

As is the case in many developing countries, although the use of child labour in greenhouses as well as in the house is known to the local authorities, it nevertheless remains unchallenged by them. The secretary in the local government office attributed this to local traditional values, according to which an attempt to prosecute people would be regarded as betrayal (*prodosia*) and an affront to the Cretan spirit to defy any compliance with authority and law. The reluctance of officials to impose bureaucratic or legal sanctions is also demonstrated by Herzfeld in his analysis of a village inhabited by shepherds in central Crete. Referring to incidents of animal theft, he argues that on the one hand the Glendiots boast that 'the law does not reach here' (Herzfeld 1985: 53), and that, on the other hand, instead of trying to impose legal sanctions, the police show 'respect for the unwritten local rules for dispute management. They recognise fully that any strategy that contravened these rules would eventually backfire' (ibid.: 26). Thus, children are denied the stereotypical 'childhood' which most young people experience in urban centres and certainly the 'pathways to maturity' followed differ significantly.

The time and amount of work that non-waged family workers are expected to contribute daily by the family head are largely related to the size and composition of the family. As this changes through the years, it brings about new patterns of behaviour with regard to the non-waged family workers' daily contribution to the family's enterprise. The same applies in relation to individuals' domestic work, the difference being that in periods when the demands for labour in the domestic domain increase (because, for example, a baby has been born or a member of the family falls ill and needs attention, or elderly members of the family need to be looked after), the female family members' contribution to the family (agricultural) enterprise decreases in favour of domestic activities and labour is hired to compensate. In other words, although by and large the family business is operated by non-waged family workers, it does not rely solely on family labour, but rather labour is 'hired in' and 'hired out' depending on changes in the family's demographic cycle.

---

7   There are cases where a woman is the head of the family business in Platanos. For example, when the husband is dead or has special needs, when his main occupation does not permit him to work full-time in agriculture, or when a woman is single.

8   Development agencies need to identify the effects of development projects on children and to view children as 'social actors' in the development process.

To give some examples, Kostis, a former truck driver in his mid-50s at the time of fieldwork, married a woman 18 years his junior from the nearby town of Kastelli in 1969; they have two children. When greenhouse cultivation became popular in the area, Kostis gave up his employment as a truck driver and became an agent, buying and packing tomatoes on behalf of a wholesaler in Salonica. With his wife, Theano, he also has two greenhouses, which are attended by Theano, with the occasional help of hired labour. When their son was born, Theano regularly hired seasonal labour to help her in the greenhouse while she spent more time with the baby. Sometimes she took the baby with her and left him in a neighbour's hut while she worked. 'I had to stop working and feed him and change nappies every so often', she said. 'My daughter at the time was too young to cope with a baby.' When the son was a little older, his sister, then a teenager, used to look after him, especially after he came out of school and before his mother returned home (after a hard day's work in the greenhouse) to assume her domestic responsibilities; the daughter looked after the house, while her mother looked after the greenhouse. In 1987–1988, the boy, then aged 7, was considered old enough to help his parents. However, he was a bright child; this put additional strain on his mother, since the parents felt obliged to encourage him with his school work and the Greek educational system expects parents to help their children at home with their homework. This task would have been carried out by the daughter if she had not in the meantime become engaged and hence tended to spend the afternoons with her fiancé.

Another example is that of Eleftheria, a woman in her late 40s, married and the mother of five children, who, with her husband, has three greenhouses in Platanos. They are one of the few large producers in the village (the total area their greenhouses occupied at the time of the fieldwork was around seven stremmata and they were thinking of expanding to nine). The three daughters study in Athens and Chania, whereas the boys are still at school. They help in the afternoons and at weekends as well as during the holidays. During the summer, when the daughters come home, they help out with the household chores, whereas during the winter these fall on the shoulders of Eleftheria. During the harvest period, Eleftheria almost always hires day-labourers to help her and her husband in the greenhouses.

However, this is not the case with the Benios family, whose son, after completing his military service, has returned to Platanos and works with his parents in the family's greenhouses. 'We used to hire labourers during the peak season when the kids were young, but now my son works with us, and so we manage without the additional cost of day-workers', the mother (Maritsa) told me. 'If my son was not working with us, we would definitely have to employ someone to help us; we are getting old; our bodies cannot cope with the physical demands of working in the greenhouses', her husband Georgos said.

Finally, the situation with Maria is also different. She was born in 1950 in a village called Lousakies; and in her early 20s she married a fisherman from Platanos and moved to the village. She worked for some years as a seamstress, until the mid-1980s, when she decided to go into market gardening by herself. Her husband Kostis helps her occasionally, more so during the harvest period when Maria cannot cope on her own; he helps so as to avoid hiring seasonal labourers as far as possible. Their three sons, none of whom helps with what they regard as 'women's work', spend most of their free time wandering around the village, watching TV or playing football with peers. So, when Maria gets home in the evening she has to spend time doing housework. Her workload is heavier than that of women who have daughters of the age of her boys.

As can be seen from the above cases, the organization of family and non-family labour displays flexibility – a feature which is of utmost importance for the viability of the family enterprise and the reproduction of the domestic group – as the composition of the domestic group changes over time. The presence of young children in the household implies a greater need for childcare, which, since this remains exclusively a female province, in turn increases the domestic work performed by the mother with the help of older daughters, if they are available. Although there is a pre-school nursery in Platanos, the complexity of many of families' childcare arrangements often implies a considerable degree of negotiation and adjustment on a daily basis within the household. Similar to other rural areas in Europe (see Halliday and Little 2001), in Platanos such adjustment takes place within the parameters of local provision and reflects the values and expectations held by the community, the family and the individual regarding gender roles, the needs of the children and of other members of the household. Similarly, when the children grow older and their obligations at school increase, their contribution to the household activities and to the family's greenhouses tends to decrease. Hence, parents have to choose between increasing their labour input and receiving help from other members of the family (who are either engaged in other work or are pensioners as, for example, elderly parents would be), or hiring day-workers to help them with the work previously performed by the children. In the cases of Kostis and Maria, the domestic unit is divided into two production units (Kostis in the marketing sphere and his wife in the production sphere); Maria attends her greenhouse business and her husband goes fishing and performs various other agricultural tasks (such as looking after their vineyards and livestock – a few sheep and goats) and they reunite for production as well as consumption at different periods of the agricultural year. In the other cases mentioned above, the domestic group is both a unit of production (in that the spouses work together in the production, harvesting and preparation of tomatoes for the market) and of consumption. The reason Maria's husband helps his wife in the sphere of production rather than reproduction must be attributed both to the patriarchal ideology which, in Platanos, dominates social relations of production, as well as to the susceptibility of this kind of production to economic uncertainty, due to conditions prevailing in the sphere of production (such as weather) and in the sphere of marketing (no guaranteed prices, exploitation of traders and their agents). The Benios family is a typical example of how dependent work arrangements, among other things (such as the number and size of the greenhouses and the technology used) can be on the demands created by the three-generational cycle of human life and the growth or dispersal of conjugal residential units. In other words, one must not make the mistake of characterizing those who hire labour as rural capitalists; the issue is more complicated than that, since, as Swindell argues in his book on farm labour in Africa,

> ... at certain times ... farmers may hire-in labour to offset temporary labour shortages, which result from adverse dependency ratios in the domestic production unit caused by the developmental cycle and age-sex imbalances. (Swindell 1985: 62)

This is not to say, however, that family domestic needs alone determine the hiring of labour. There are other factors, such as the number and size of greenhouses a family owns. A family like Elefteria's, for example, who in the late 1980s owned greenhouses occupying an area of around 7 stremmata, although not wealthy in that they owed, as they said, thousands of euros to the Agricultural Bank of Greece for loans they had received to erect the greenhouses, had to hire in labour because of the intensive work required in the spring months. Although other members of their families helped on a part-time basis, this was not enough to meet their needs; when the tomatoes are ripe, they have to be picked immediately otherwise they quickly over-ripen because of the heat. This requires a massive input of labour hours over a short period of time, which can be met by hiring more people – usually day-workers – to do the job, unless the family has a pool of labour to draw on when the need arises.

Generally, the introduction of market gardening in the village has not led to a differentiation among the villagers and the emergence of those who hire labour and those who see their labour power as a commodity to the former. They are rather small-commodity producers who 'are linked to, and part of, capitalist commodity circulation without being *necessarily* capitalist entrepreneurs' (ibid.: 63). Nor is there a marked differentiation among greenhouse producers themselves, based on differing farming inputs or size and number of greenhouses owned. An example here is the economic situation of Kostis and Theano. As mentioned above, Kostis is an agent who also owns, with his wife, two greenhouses, which are tended by her with the occasional help of hired labour. His status in the village is an ambiguous one, since he is seen both as a producer (one of us) and an exploiter of producers (one of them). This does not necessarily mean that he and his wife are richer than the other producers; during the 1987–1988 agricultural year, the whole crop in the greenhouse was destroyed by a fungus and thus they lost money rather than making any profit.

Before investigating the structure of labour in the greenhouses, I shall look more closely at women's participation in economic activities related to the production of vegetables in the greenhouses of western Crete and try to understand the way these are integrated with various domestic activities.

Women's Work

Due to the shortcomings of available data, for the purpose of analysing women's work I shall concentrate on their own accounts of their working life.

Women's domestic life   Here is how one greenhouse producer, Maria, described her daily domestic life:

> I work in the greenhouses fifteen hours a day. When I go home in the evening, I have no time even to take my working shoes off; the saucepan (*to tsikali*) is waiting for me. 'Maria, come on', says Georgos, my husband. 'Come on, come on, come on, get the food ready'. I don't even have time to sit down and drink a cup of coffee. I get the food ready. Every minute is stressful. And when I finish working, at ten o'clock in the evening, I am exhausted ... [My husband] does give me a hand! I can't say that he doesn't. There are even worse [husbands] who never help. But I have three sons too, who make their own demands ... they are men, aren't they? They take turns and ask questions like, 'Have you done this for me?' We have our dinner, I wash the dishes and he goes to the local coffee shop to hear the news [local news or gossip] and I sit with my kids watching TV and tidying up the kitchen. What fun!

Another producer, Evgenia, described her daily life as follows:

> I have a schedule in my life. In the morning, I get up quite late. I never get up earlier than between 7.10 and 7.50. Other women get up much earlier. Well, I get up, I try, let's say, to make the beds; the dishes, etc. have to be washed up from the previous evening and I leave. At noon, when the children come back from school, they do whatever [chore] has been left to be done from the previous evening ... they are girls and I have made it a matter of principle that they should help with the housework. When I get back in the evening, if they haven't cooked, I'll cook, I'll dust a little bit; I don't dust and mop [every day] ... we do these chores once a week ... and it looks fine ... Well, the most essential parts of the home are being kept clean!

From the above interviews, one can draw the following conclusions: first, activities carried out to maintain and care for the family members (such as bringing up the children and helping them with their homework, cooking, keeping the house clean, washing and ironing clothes) are performed by women. Apart from households where there is no woman, because of death or divorce, or the woman is incapable of performing domestic tasks due to illness, women have sole responsibility for domestic chores, even among newly married couples where men are supposed to assist women in such work. In addition to their work in the greenhouses, women in Platanos spend between four and six hours a day on social reproduction, depending on the household appliances they have at their disposal (which save them considerable time and energy), as well as on the type of work they have to do in the fields. Referring to women in developing countries, Momsen (1991: 38) argues that, 'at planting and harvesting times, when more time must be spent in the fields, domestic work must be cut down'. The same could have applied to women in Platanos during the tomato harvest, if women did not have to look after the hired labour (cook their meals and sometimes even wash their clothes and clean their rooms). This task adds a burden to the already heavy workload women have to perform every day at home and in the fields. Generally, the time they have available for leisure is less than that of the men and depending on gender relations and power within the household, some complain about it, whereas others take it for granted.

Second, as mentioned earlier, the time and energy women spend on the household tasks depends on the age of the children and on whether or not there are other females in the family who can alleviate the pressure arising from social expectations of what a *nikokyra* – literally a 'mistress of the house' – should (or should not) do. However, because it is predominantly a virilocal or patrilocal society, a great many women are not Plataniotises (that is, from Platanos) and hence do not have the advantage that women have in other parts of Greece, such as in Kalymnos, where 'mothers, sisters and daughters exchange services and become invaluable to one another in overcoming ... difficulties' (Petronoti 1980:96), or Samos and Karpathos, where the 'wives' position was favoured by the assistance they received from their mothers and sisters with whom they developed relations of mutual advantage ... the participation in female networks helped ... women to cope with daily exigencies' (ibid.: 111). That is why, in most cases in Platanos, the burdens of housework and care of young children fall on the shoulders of older female children rather than on a grandmother.

Also, women do not seem to attach the same importance to keeping their houses immaculately clean as do women in Platanos who are not involved in the greenhouse agriculture, or women in other parts of Crete and the southern Mediterranean[9] in general and Greece in particular (see, for example, Hirschon 1989). Most women I spoke to who were involved in greenhouse agriculture, concurred with Evgenia in that keeping the house clean was not of paramount importance in their lives. Androniki, a former greenhouse owner who now *inter alia* runs a grocery store in Platanos and is regarded as one of the most successful businesswomen in the village, commented on this and argued that women who worked in greenhouses in Platanos simply had no time to be too fussy about such 'unimportant details' (with emphasis). This means that the self-esteem and prestige conferred on a woman from being a 'mistress of the house', has, in Platanos, been transferred to the 'greenhouse'. Women who work in the greenhouses pride themselves on keeping them as clean and tidy as they can (see Figure 4.5) and describe those run exclusively by men as being untidy, dirty and disorganized. A few, such as the *papadia* (the local priest's wife) and the wife of the secretary in the local government office (neither of

---

9   See Lever's account of Lagartera (Lever 1984), and Dimen's account of Kriovrisi (Dimen 1986: 57).

Figure 4.5   Woman cutting off diseased leaves and fruits and 'cleaning her greenhouse'

whom have ever been involved in greenhouse agriculture), also commented on how the women working in the greenhouses neglected their house and children, putting money first and their 'duties' second. In other words, the untidiness of these women is not totally beyond criticism.

Furthermore, few of the women seem to take pleasure in doing their hard domestic work without complaining, as women, for example, in Kriovrisi (Dimen 1986: 57) apparently do. In Platanos, as in Kriovrisi, 'the household organizes biological reproduction because it serves as the cultural locus of kinship, marriage, procreation, childbearing, and early socialization. It also sees to the daily bodily maintenance of the labour force', on which the livelihood of the household depends. So, women do bear the domestic burden by themselves, but, at the same time, some of them seem to be conscious of this and able to complain without hesitation about men's grip on the public domain and their reluctance to share in the tasks which are carried out by women in the domestic domain. Almost all the women in Platanos who seem to resent having to carry the burden of the domestic workload without the help of men, happen to be active in the public domain. Not only do they work in the greenhouses, but they are also active members of the local women's organization (see chapter on women's associations). Other factors (such as being exposed to different ideas from daily exposure to media and contact with tourists, agriculturalists, government officials, merchants, and so on) may also be contributing factors to these women's awareness of their position as housewives and workers in Platanos' households.

Women's work in the greenhouses   What I will argue here is that, first, the sexual division of labour in greenhouse agriculture alters with the introduction of new technology as the demand for labour in some stages of the production process rises while it falls in others; second, that contrary to Boserup's (1988: 356) data on Asia where 'a ready supply of landless labourers available for hire and the "technical nature of farming operations under plough cultivation" discouraged women's involvement in agricultural tasks and encouraged segregation of the sexes, including the seclusion of women in some areas', in the area of western Kisamos where Platanos is situated, the technical nature of farming operations adopted in greenhouses has not discouraged women's involvement in agricultural tasks at all. Technical modernization in the production of vegetables in greenhouses and the process of economic development which accompanies it have not resulted in the marginalization of women. What probably encourages the segregation of the sexes is not technology itself, but, as I shall show below, the way this is implemented by the various development agents. Greek bureaucracy especially – both male and female – is obliged under the existing legislation to treat men and women equally, but they are brought up under a value system which encourages this segregation and makes it seem 'natural' to them and, hence, the implementation of various projects, rather than being gender neutral, is overridden by cultural taboos (Lazaridis 1995b).

Women are becoming increasingly involved in greenhouse production in the area – in fact, most of the men involved admitted to me that it is because of women's labour that these enterprises flourish. However, this is attributed to gender-specific qualities like 'dexterity in handling the plants, as well as patience and delicate fingers'. In the mid-1980s for the first time a few women (fewer than ten) themselves became owners of their own business instead of their husbands being the owners. It is worth noting that in most of these cases the husband's main occupation was not an agricultural one. Although women's dexterity in handling the plants is regarded by most producers in Platanos as paramount for the success of the business, the reality is more complicated than this, since, as I discovered during fieldwork, greenhouses run for one reason or another by men alone were not necessarily unsuccessful. To give an example, Yannis, an unmarried man in his early 20s, who at the time lived with his father, a widower, decided in the mid-1980s to go into market gardening. By the late 1980s he owned two greenhouses. Although there were times when both men complained about not having a woman in the house to give them a hand with both the housework and the work in the fields, he nevertheless managed well. By the time I met him he had already cleared his debts and was thinking of expanding the business. It was in terms of the expansion that he felt he needed additional unpaid help and he thought that marriage would solve the problem for him. The father confessed that 'a woman in the household makes all the difference'. In Yannis' case, even exclusively female activities were being performed by him and his father and Yannis had acquired the supplementary skills which would enable him not only to help his future wife but also to perform all the tasks assigned to the sphere of social reproduction. Contrary to his father, he also at times expressed sympathy for his sister Chrysoula, who worked all day in the greenhouse that she and her husband owned and in the evening, while he went to the local café, worked at home cleaning the house and taking care of their two children. But when Yannis married, both he and his father were expecting a reversal of the situation. This suggests not only that attitudes of men vary with age, but also that these can change according to convenience (Rogers 1986: 19). Generally, men very rarely help with household tasks; it is an insult to their manhood to do so. Let us now look at what women and men actually do in the greenhouse production process.

The crucial operations performed by women in the greenhouses are weeding, planting, removing old leaves and diseased tomatoes, feeding the plants, harvesting and sometimes watering. The physical demands of the work and, hence, the amount of energy and time a woman spends working throughout the agricultural year, are influenced by the type of greenhouse and the level of mechanization (which in Platanos is considered to be relatively low since all other tasks apart from irrigation, preparation of the land, fertilization and spraying are performed manually even in the most modern and capital-intensive greenhouses in the region). The amount of energy and time a woman spends are also influenced by the different types of cultivation techniques applied, that is 'simple' cultivation where only one crop is planted during the agricultural year, or 'double' cultivation, where two crops are planted, one from August to January and another from February to July. Those who plant only one crop can at least relax for one or two months during the summer.

Whether the official owner of the greenhouse is the woman or the man, since the manual labour is mainly provided by the producer's household members, both work long hours every day in the family business. The time they devote to working changes throughout the year. During the tomato and olive harvests they reach a point of self-exploitation, working from sunrise to sunset and even longer, especially since so-called *typopeisis* (that is, the packaging of tomatoes into small packets containing two to eight tomatoes each, depending on the size of the product) has been introduced. During these hectic periods seasonal labour is also brought in. As far as domestic tasks are concerned, it is during this period that children's and/or parents' labour is most drawn on and exploited. In other words, this pressure for more hands has not led to an adjustment of the sexual division of labour within the private space.

Throughout the year, most of the work is manual, intensive and very tiring, since it entails either standing or bending all day long. Most women complain of backache and this gets worse during the tomato harvest, which usually begins in mid-April. As one woman I interviewed said, 'I've been harvesting tomatoes ... tomatoes and tomatoes ... damn them! My back ... Last year it didn't hurt, but now it does ... My back, damn it'. However, backache is not the only complaint suffered by those who work in greenhouses; respiratory problems and skin irritations were also mentioned as well as chronic constipation and, for women, bladder problems due to lack of toilets in the area where the greenhouses were situated.

As in most developing countries, in Greece as a whole and in Platanos in particular, with only a few exceptions, what men and women do has certain common patterns. Men undertake the heavy physical work of land preparation as well as tasks which require knowledge of chemicals, such as applications of pesticides. Women carry out repetitive tasks like weeding, stripping off the leaves of the plants, removing rotten fruit and leaves and cutting off the edges of the plants to strengthen them, planting and so on, as well as tasks culturally associated with their feminine nature, such as taking care of plants affected by diseases and feeding. The above, however, is not a strict division delineated by cultural taboos as is the division of labour regarding the social reproduction of the family, because, as I noticed during participant observation, most of the tasks are in practice becoming gender neutral, when the circumstances demand it; for example, in cases where the family has more than one greenhouse, at times the man works in one and the woman in the another, performing similar tasks – and in greenhouses owned and worked exclusively by men. Flexibility allows for the absence of family members for certain hours a day, when the need arises, for example, to take a child to the doctor at the health centre in the nearby town of Kastelli. Furthermore, whereas men tend to operate the machines or use the various chemicals, this has not resulted in the marginalization of women. On the contrary, many women in Platanos know how to operate the machinery used and some (not all) seem to be even more (if not, equally well) informed than the men about the various sprays, etc., that are currently to be found in the market (in Greece and elsewhere) and how these can be used more effectively so as to produce a product that is both of high quality and high yield. To my amazement, women did not seem to feel and did not express any resentment about the fact that they do not use the machinery even though they seemed to know how. Nor did they associate access to machinery with power. Rather they expressed relief at not having to perform an additional task. At times, one can see women putting sprays in the machines or advising their husbands on which chemical seems to be more effective. However, although most women do give hormone feeds to the plants alongside men, they hardly ever spray. Both men and women rationalize the application of pesticides by men only in terms of their potential danger to health and to future pregnancies. The naturalization of women's biology is used to explain why men should handle pesticides. It seems that men use pesticides (see Figure 4.6) to reproduce and reinforce patriarchal ideologies which exclude women from their application. So, similar to tractors in French farming (see Saugeres 2002: 143), pesticides in western Crete have become 'a symbol of masculine power and domination over women and nature'. Most pesticide containers have the poisons warning symbol on their labels (see Figure 4.7). When asked, most producers, irrespective of their gender, said that 'chemicals are too dangerous for women', or 'men are tougher than women' and in order to convince me, brought a container/box to show me the symbol. This is an example of how gender differences regarding access to certain chemicals and related tasks are legitimized in terms of the biological differences of the sexes, which in turn determines their respective roles in biological reproduction (see also Momsen 1991: 50). The application of pesticides creates a *masculine space* which excludes women from at least a part of the greenhouse production; they have become 'the symbol of masculine identity and power through which ... [men] define themselves in opposition to women and nature' (Saugeres 2002: 155–6).

With regard to decision-making processes, women who own their greenhouses take decisions regarding their 'business' by themselves and discuss matters concerning their work with other male and/or female owners of greenhouses on an equal basis. Women who happen to work with their husbands in the family business where the greenhouses are owned by the man, also take part in the decision-making process, some on a more equal basis than others. Some men prefer to take all the decisions themselves related to technical matters, such as the purchase of a tractor or the choice of chemical sprays, etc. It seems that young couples or couples of a more radical political orientation tend to share more equally in the decision-making process than older couples do; the latter seem to expect men to be involved in the construction of the greenhouse (possibly due to the physically demanding labour associated with it) and the marketing

Figure 4.6   Man applying pesticides

of the products rather than women, and, therefore, to take the appropriate decisions associated with these tasks. Further investigation would be necessary in order to highlight possible changes in the decision-making process in view of the penetration of feminist ideology in the Greek countryside during the last decade.

Finally, what about the social working conditions? Dimen (1986: 61), speaking of domestic work, argues that 'by working alone, and by feeling both proud of doing so and lonely while doing it, women symbolize as social figures, communicate as social participants and re-create as social actors, the social and economic isolation of the household itself'.

Women in Platanos go to their greenhouses every day and most of the time also work alone (usually the husband works in another greenhouse or at the other end of the same greenhouse), feel lonely and have a battery-operated radio to keep them company. Nevertheless, one cannot claim that the lonely woman who works in the greenhouses in Platanos mirrors and 'communicates the self-protective isolation of the household in the public sphere' as, according to Dimen's account, women in Kriovrisi do (ibid.). As in Kriovrisi, each household in Platanos does depend on its own labour for its own livelihood, even though they all may hire or exchange labour occasionally. The difference in Platanos, however, is that during the tomato harvest, women's isolation in the workplace comes to an end, due to the influx of agents, buyers, those who transport the products to the markets and seasonal labour; furthermore, during the same

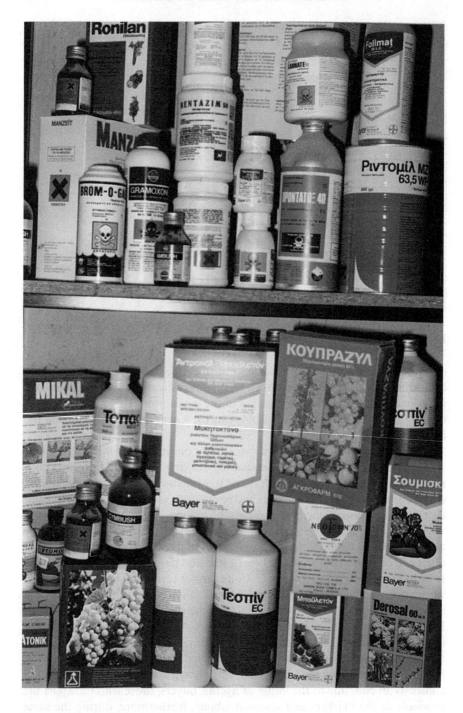

Figure 4.7   A collection of pesticides

period, producers tend to visit each other in their greenhouses and discuss prices paid by buyers, packaging of products and so on.

Generally, women's work is well respected by the men of the village. Some claimed that women work more than men in the greenhouses and others that without women's contribution the greenhouse business would not have flourished in the region. 'Countrywomen are heroes', one man said. 'We work more than men', a woman added. Women are expected to help their husbands in these family businesses; women who, for one reason or another (for example, if an informal agreement before marriage has been made between the two parties), refuse to work in their husband's greenhouse are referred to as *kifines* (lazy bones) – a word which demonstrates shame due to lack of work. The *kifines* tend to be wives who come from villages where greenhouse cultivation does not exist and/or who regard such work as hard and dirty and as being at the bottom of the agricultural work hierarchy and who justify their domestication in terms of the idea of 'maternal deprivation', 'from which children would allegedly suffer if their mother, or another woman working full-time as mother substitute, did not provide them with "constant attention night and day, seven days a week and 365 days in the year"' (Rogers 1986: 23–4).

Whether or not a woman's refusal to help in the greenhouse is the result of a premarital agreement between the two parties does not seem to be a justifiable reason to the villagers. Hence, no matter what their reason for not helping their husband, they are not respected by the rest of the village; they are regarded as hard-hearted individuals who prefer to see their poor husband's earnings being used for hiring in labour and they are resented for this. As Androniki, a woman in her early 40s who owns a grocery store and rents rooms to tourists and whose husband still has a greenhouse where she used to work, said about a woman who refused to work and help her husband,

> She feels no compassion for him; the poor man has greenhouses occupying an area of eleven stremmata, is indebted to the bank and also has to hire labourers in order to help him in the fields, all year through. What a waste of money ... Her behaviour is inexcusable. Her husband is a nice man. What can he do about it? He promised her that if she agreed to marry him she wouldn't have to get her hands dirty ... She can twist him round her little finger.

Therefore, women in Platanos are expected to produce both use values within the home (goods and services such as washing and cooking meals) and goods for exchange within the family-based agricultural business (mainly products such as tomatoes, cucumbers and melons). This view is in contrast to that in Yerania, where Hirschon (1989: 98) found women's work outside the domestic space legitimized only in exceptional circumstances (for example, young girls working outside the home for the purpose of providing for their dowry). With women under this kind of pressure, women's work outside the domestic domain indicates either the start of a gradual erosion of the division of labour by sex in non-agricultural household tasks, or the fulfilment of these tasks by migrant labour, as is currently the case in big urban centres (see Lazaridis 2008; Lazaridis and Koumandraki 2007a, 2007b; Lazaridis 2007a 2007b; Lazaridis 2003; Lazaridis 2001; Lazaridis and Wickens 1999; Lazaridis and Psimmenos 1999; Lazaridis 1999; Lazaridis and Romaniszyn 1998).

Forms of Labour Cooperation

As has already been mentioned, manual labour in greenhouses in western Crete is mainly provided by the producer's family members – generally spouse and children – with the occasional help of parents, aunts and uncles, cousins and so on, who, unlike the immediate family members, are paid for their work, or expect a favour in return. Sometimes friends help each other too. These mutually beneficial, reciprocal arrangements (with no money exchange) between producers (or producers' families) are based on conditional loyalties and are called *thaneika* (borrowed). Under these arrangements, a producer and his or her family receive help from other family members or a friend with the obligation to return this help in due course; this is grounded in *trust* and informal norms that promote cooperation between individuals or groups. Participation in such activities is voluntary. They resemble Putnam's (1993) 'bonding capital' in that they reinforce and sustain a sense of *trust* and *loyalty*.[10]

Although, as I have mentioned above, labour is hired in Platanos, *thaneika* is a type of labour cooperation which can be seen as the antithesis of proletarianization and it indicates that differentiation of the agriculturalists – whereby there is a small agrarian bourgeoisie (capitalist farmers) and large numbers of agricultural labourers – does not seem to be the case; rather, 'middle farmers' who are not separated from their means of production and mainly use their own family labour and are little involved in selling their labour power or buying in the labour power of others, seem to be surviving. Polarization between agriculturalists is weakened because of the persistence of small land holdings due to the existing inheritance traditions and due to the morphology of Crete's soil which encourages parcelization, that is, a lack of large plains which would

10   According to the World Bank's 'World Development Report 2000/1', social capital is 'the capital of the poor'. It refers to 'norms of reciprocity and networks/ associations which can promote co-operative actions and which can be used as social resources for mutual benefit' (Das 2004: 30; see also Putnam 1993; Woolcock 2000). *Reciprocity*, according to Putnam (1993: 172) is of two types: *specific reciprocity*, which refers to simultaneous exchanges of items of equivalent value (for example, the women interviewed exchanged *inter alia* information for jobs). The other type is *generalised reciprocity*, that is, a continuing relationship of exchange that is at any given time unrequited or imbalanced (for example, capital, etc.). Each act within the generalized reciprocity type is characterized by a combination of short-term altruism and long-term self-interest. 'I help you now in the expectation that you will help me out in the future.'

have permitted the concentration of land in a few hands (see Chapter 1). If what Swindell (1985) argues is true, namely that 'the persistence or decay of communal labour may serve as an indicator of ... capitalist farming', then one may say that the latter has not become a characteristic of Platanos' rural economy.

Thaneika are very common in Platanos during the tomato harvest and also during the period when new greenhouses are being constructed, depending on the type of greenhouse. In other words, like other forms of labour cooperation (see ibid.: 129–51), *thaneika* is particularly important 'at times when farming practices demand short bursts of heavy work ... which lie beyond the capacity of domestic groups, at least if they are to be accomplished in good time' (ibid.: 129). Many producers prefer to buy the raw materials and put up the frame of their greenhouses themselves (with the help of friends and/or relatives) rather than paying the manufacturer to put it up (because this is much more expensive). Sometimes, however, installation is included in the price of the greenhouse. Nevertheless, the producers themselves, no matter how experienced they are, cannot erect a greenhouse which has a metallic frame and/or is covered with glass or fibre-glass. The manufacturer usually takes care of that. As years pass and more producers are replacing their old greenhouses with more modern ones, this type of reciprocal labour exchange is declining, at least in respect of this particular type of work, which is almost always performed by men.

The basic definition of the *thaneika* relationship is that, first, the tie that develops between the two parties is relatively equal in terms of status and wealth[11] (although the latter is not essential); they can be friends or relatives who either live in the same village/area or where one member of the party has emigrated. Second, it depends on reciprocity in the exchange of services; and third, it relies heavily on face-to-face contact between the two parties, the relationship being friendly, warm, informal, unwritten and one which depends on personal accountability. This is true whether the parties are individuals, kinship groups, extended kinship groups, informal or formal voluntary groups or institutions.

It differs from relationships of power such as clientelism in that the latter, as Powell (1970: 412) maintains, develops between two parties unequal in status, wealth and influence. Furthermore, *thaneika* tends to be a short-lived relationship which can be renewed whenever necessary whereas patron-client relationships are more likely to be continuous and long lived. Finally, whereas clientelistic ties are vertical chains cutting through horizontal class interests and ethnic groupings, *thaneika*, by its nature, cannot, at least, prevent the emergence of class and interest demands or hinder class mobilization. As has been mentioned above, it is a short-lived relationship and its function is, mainly, to provide the parties involved with labour at times when need and demand for manual labour

---

11   If a tie which develops between two parties is unequal in both status and wealth, then a patron-client relationship rather than a *thaneika* relationship may develop.

is high. In other words, this is an institution which functions, to the extent that this is possible, as a mechanism (on behalf of the parties involved) to avoid hiring labour and therefore paying out wages. This is, however, affected by the family lifecycle: when the children are young, given the fact that in rural Crete, due to the prevalent male ideology, the bulk of tasks associated with nurturing infants and young children falls exclusively on women, it is more likely that women will not participate or will participate only as part-time labourers in the *theneika* arrangement and thus be replaced by hired labour.

The work done under the *theneika* arrangement is usually measured by its duration and the tasks performed by both men and women are all labour intensive and vary from harvesting to removing old leaves (but not application of chemicals). As mentioned above, there is no payment except for lunch, which is provided by the family on whose land the work is carried out. It appears, however, that this way of organizing labour flows may not be as efficient as the villagers think, since they do not take into account their own *merokamata* (remuneration for one day's work) and the fact that by using it they leave their own business unattended, a whole day sometimes, during the time when they repay the services to the other party of the relationship. Although this may not be so bad per se, it nevertheless means that the next day the owners will have to spend more time in their greenhouses, trying to regain the ground they lost the day before.

It differs from other forms of cooperative labour, such as 'festive labour',[12] for example, in that the latter – which is known in East Africa as 'beer parties' – as Swindell (1985: 131–2) argues,

> is organised on an *ad hoc* basis for specific tasks and the reward for work in drinks and food can be quite lavish, depending on the status of the host. Kinship and clientage may be the basis of their formation, but reciprocity is poorly-developed and may only apply to the host's kin giving their labour, rather than himself. Festive work parties are large and the rewards for work are immediate rather than delayed, as in the case of labour exchange groups.

Thaneika helps to keep the use of hired labour less than it would have been if this form of labour cooperation was not used. It has advantages over hired labour since it is cheaper and more flexible, in that an arrangement to harvest can be cancelled without charge if the weather is bad, for example, and helps out in periods where a shortage of labour is foreseen. It is used more in Platanos than in Nohia, where the labour demands of the most economically important crops (that is, olives and tomatoes) overlap at certain times of the year (especially between November and February). It may, however, decline in the future, with

---

12   'Festive workgroups' were formed in both Nohia and Platanos every autumn for pressing the grapes; this tradition has, however, declined because women refuse to undertake the arduous task of cooking for such large groups of people.

the introduction of new technology; this could entail a reduction in the number of participants and, at the same time, an increase in demand for skilled workers who can operate these machines effectively. I also anticipate a change in the sex distribution of the group in favour of men, since these machines are most often operated by men. An exception to this is, of course, when the appropriation of agricultural technology by men becomes challenged by women and is used as a space for contestation of male power.

The alternative to the *thaneika* institution is the hiring of labour, though in practice both are treated as complementary to each other, especially during the tomato harvest. Regarding tomato production in Platanos, most paid labour composed of non-family members is casual labour, that is 'labour lacking a moderate degree of security of income and employment' (Bernstein 1988: 651). In some cases, however, casual labour may apply to family members as well – when they are paid for their work in the family business. This mainly applies to male adolescents who, for one reason or another, have decided to drop out of school and work in the greenhouses as casual labour. In this case, they ask parents and/or relatives to pay the same wage that they would pay to a non-family worker; they are preferred to 'tourists', because they are more reliable and also because, as they have occasionally helped their parents in the past, they have acquired the necessary skills for the job. Moreover, the parents feel that the money remains within the family and can make an arrangement with the son whereby they keep some of the money for him – for his future – and he receives the rest (usually less than half of what he earned) as 'pocket money'.

In the late 1980s casual workers received at least €10–12 per day for their work and were offered lunch and transport if they came from a nearby village. Local labourers were still in demand because they are 'very efficient' (*avgatizoun*). Apart from the adolescents mentioned above, these tended to be relatively young women (between 25 and 45) who came from relatively poorer villages near Platanos and who were in need of extra work to supplement their household income from olive growing. Most had worked in Platanos before, usually for the same greenhouse owners. Since they knew the work and were reliable, they were preferred and were better paid that the 'tourists'. 'We speak the same language, and this is important. Whereas with the tourists we have to use gestures, like monkeys', Plataniotes explained.

Since the early 1990s, this dwindling indigenous non-family labour force has been gradually replaced by an increasing number of 'third country' migrants, offering more hours of work for lower wages. They are a labour force 'suitable for all tasks'; some live permanently in the village and are employed on a constant basis by one employer, whereas others work for different employers and yet others return periodically to Platanos to work at tomato harvest time. Employment relations between the greenhouse owner and the migrant worker are characterized by informality and vagueness (lack of proper contract), payment in money and/or in kind, adaptability on the part of the worker, a general distrust leading to a gradual building of trust over time which has culminated in some instances in formation of kinship ties (baptism) (see Kasimis et al. 2003).

Packaging and Marketing

There are two ways in which the trade of early vegetables produced in the greenhouses of Platanos takes place: the so called 'productive way' and the 'commercial way'. The 'productive way' (*paragogikos tropos*) was described by a greenhouse owner and producer, Maria, as follows:

> Marketing conditions here resemble those of the Middle-ages ... I harvest my tomatoes, put them in crates, do the packaging – I bear the cost of the packaging – I load them on a lorry and send them to Athens. I pay for the transport costs ... The merchant in Athens ... he receives the tomatoes and sells them on my behalf. I know neither the price he sells them, not what he does. Also, they aren't weighed and even if they are, there is always a discrepancy between the weight quoted by the merchant and the weight quoted by the producer ... he gives the excuse that some of the produce has been damaged on the way to the market ... After he sells the product, he deposits the money in a bank in his name and ten to 20 days or even a month later, he send us a settlement which states that such and such tomatoes of such and such delivery, had so many costs, so much produce had been damaged on the way to the market etc. and sends us an amount of money ....

The 'commercial way' (*emborikos tropos*) of marketing used in the areas was described by the same producer as follows:

> There are some merchants who come here and open a kiosk, and they buy tomatoes. They say, for example, 'today we pay so much per kilo'. Price fluctuations depend on the market. When the demand is high, they pay more, because if not, they won't be able to buy them ... you sell your products here instead of sending them to Athens.

In other words, the product is sold to a wholesaler via an intermediary/middle-man (see Figure 4.8) at a price agreed with the producer after careful negotiation. In the 1980s there were four intermediaries covering the area of Platanos, all of whom were men. When I re-visited the area in 2003, intermediaries were no longer being used.

Tomatoes are usually packed in crates before leaving the place of production. Who does the packing depends on the way the marketing of the product is being done. Under the 'productive way' of trade the sorting and packing of the tomatoes is done by the producers, who bear the packing labour costs themselves. Some of it is done by hired labour but the bulk is carried out by family members. When the 'commercial way' of trading was in vogue in the area,

Figure 4.8   Intermediary

Figure 4.9   Tomatoes packed into crates

the packing was done in the intermediary's kiosk[13] and the cost of the packing was carried by the wholesaler. Either way, the crates used (see Figure 4.9) are provided by the wholesaler and bear the name and the location of his business. Packing is a relatively well-paid job, done by either men or women (usually local adolescents who want to earn pocket-money, or young single women, or nowadays migrants) who are employed daily as piece-workers. The faster they work, the more money they earn. Their earnings depend on fluctuations in labour demand throughout the agricultural year. When the harvest season is over, they go back to what they used to do before.

In the late 1980s they introduced for the first time a new packing system called 'standardization'. Under this system, good quality tomatoes were placed onto small trays and covered with cellophane and could be sold at higher prices (see Figure 4.10). This brought changes in the way work was arranged. The burden fell on the family, who had to adjust their lives to the new conditions and intensify their labour input in order to continue being competitive in what were for them deteriorating market conditions. Nowadays, some employ migrants to do the job whereas others insist on keeping it strictly *en famille* and thus over-exploiting themselves and other family members such as parents, in-laws and small children. The 'standardization' process has not led to the marginalization of women but rather to the accumulation of more market-oriented skills, which in turn has resulted in them working longer hours in the greenhouse business without this in any way altering demands made on their time by domestic commitments. Stress levels are high and the way in which the social organization of the standardization process has structured the way in which men and women experience stress needs to be researched, along with ways in which men and women have adapted to, handled and/or resisted, work-related stress.

The cooperatives' association in the nearby town of Kastelli offered as a solution the construction of a large 'packaging factory' in the area. However, this was received with scepticism by the producers, mainly because of its location, 15 kilometres away from the site of production; the argument put forward was that tomatoes are a sensitive product and have to be transported to the place of consumption as soon as possible and hence the transport of tomatoes to the packaging factory and then to the urban centres would be time consuming and would have an adverse effect on the quality of the product which would impact on the price.

The producers also discussed the idea of having a tomato producers' cooperative which would deal exclusively with the marketing of the product and would empower the producers, particularly in the negotiation of commercial contracts and help them improve their response towards market fluctuations in supply and demand. However, this attempt was unsuccessful. The reason given by most producers was: 'we can't organize', 'we are like wild sheep' (*apolola provata*). *Bridging* social capital is a powerful means by which producers can

---

13   See fn 1 in Chapter 2.

Figure 4.10   Producer packing/standardizing tomatoes, using a *roaster*

address their problems and create spaces of control, but Plataniotes have little bridging social capital. It seems that the sentiment of '*we-ness*' amongst them is weak. This lack of social capital was reinforced by strong clientelistic ties used at the time as a mechanism of social control in particular party interests. There was no scheme set up to assist producers to concentrate on post-harvest processing and set up a tomato juice plant. Instead, they were encouraged to expand their production rather than divert their attention to other possibilities.

Limits Set by Bureaucratic Structures on the Possibilities of Women in the Greenhouse Business and Concluding Remarks

As I have shown above, the success of the 'greenhouse revolution' in Platanos has been attributed by policy makers to local 'ownership' and by local women and men alike, to the women's contribution. Although the visibility of women and their crucial contribution in both sectors cannot be denied, their contribution in the spheres of production and reproduction is often undervalued by development planners and/or those who are responsible for the implementation of projects who, working within existing power and social structures, do not address women's needs. Bureaucratic structures set limits on the possibilities of women in agriculture, because of the belief in the 'myth of the male breadwinner' and 'male head of the household unit' and women's and children's dependency on men, which, as Rogers (1986: 65) argues, 'obscure the fact that women in fact bear heavy responsibility for supporting genuinely dependent people'. As already shown, in Platanos it is the so-called 'head' who is dependent on the family labour (usually wife and children) and not vice versa, since, if support from family members is denied to him, the viability of the business will be threatened by the higher costs of outside labour; the family members, however, can find work elsewhere, since there is a shortage of labour in the area. So, as Rogers (ibid.) argues,

> In many cases where women are officially classified as 'dependants' of a household head, it is clear that in fact they play a crucial part in the maintenance of individuals in that grouping, and that, in some cases, the man classified as the 'head' might more accurately be described as a dependant from the point of view of productive activity.

Local government officials and bureaucrats are themselves victims of institutions, traditional values and ideology which inculcate such beliefs and, to quote Rogers (ibid.: 50), 'would not tolerate any attempt to involve women in development' or would only tolerate women's involvement under conditions which would not give them full power and control over resources. Such exclusion may be reinforced by men coming to effectively 'own' the community development intervention in the eyes of bureaucrats and planners. The tendency of planners to overlook women is supported by evidence from the case of Platanos. So, although women's work in the greenhouses has changed in response to various development policies which expect women to make up a major part of the labour force and encourage the introduction of new technology, and so on, if one looks carefully at administrative practices, one realizes that these policies favour men as far as control of resources and distribution of inputs are concerned. Many of the women in Platanos complained about government officials – irrespective of their rank or sex – favouring men in providing credit and including them in development schemes whereas, in the mid-late 1980s, if a married woman wanted to appear as head of the household and under the EC Regulation 797/85 be awarded a development project (*shedio veltiosis*) for the household enterprise (and of course receive credit, etc.), she needed a paper from her husband confirming his willingness to recognize his wife as head of the family. The reason one agricultural scientist, who at the time worked in a branch of the Ministry of Agriculture in Chania, gave for this discrimination against women producers was that they have instructions – she did not want to specify from whom – to deal with only one member of a household and thus only one head per household unit was to be recognized.

The failure to understand how agricultural change has altered the division of labour between men and women in Platanos, together with the importance of the role of women and the need to give them financial independence and power of their own, has generated tensions within households and the community. Men are reluctant publicly to give up their role as breadwinner and provider in case they are ridiculed in the eyes of their co-villagers and accused of being 'wimps' who cannot control their wife or feed their family. These factors have meant that, of the approximately 200 families who at the time lived in the village and had greenhouses, fewer than ten women appeared on paper as head of the family enterprise and had a development project issued under their name. As Elefteria informed me,

> I am one of the first women to have a development project under my name. Until two or three years ago [mid-1980s], bureaucrats did not accept this. They kept saying that the head of the family enterprise is the man. The woman has no right of claiming to be so.

Other women who happened to be present when the conversation took place agreed with Elefteria's comments and expressed their dissatisfaction too. One woman said: 'We hear them saying that things changed back in 1981 ... [in favour of women]. But this is not true. Things changed only recently, one or two years ago [late 1980s]'. Elefteria's story is one of the few exceptions; it is a story of complex attempts at coexistence between the cultural scripts and the modern individual, who is free from fixities of tradition with respect to gendered division of labour. The majority of women remain victims of the *traditional script* where a man dominates even when the head is a woman. Similar to the case of farmers in Finland studied by Silvasti (2003: 162), in Platanos 'institutionalised values and practices may ultimately close the space found by the individual for new interpretations of cultural scripts'.

When I tried to ask government officials their view on this, they changed the subject. They refused to admit that these development projects were directed towards male greenhouse owners. They seemed to find it difficult to challenge their *traditional script* that establishes men as the natural and rightful heads of the family. The case of women in Platanos has confirmed, once more, Momsen's (1991: 51) argument that, 'even when included in development projects, women may be unable to obtain new technological inputs because local political and legislative attitudes make women less credit worthy than men'. The sole difference is that it is not so much the political and legislative attitudes that discriminate against Greek women (after all, legislation was passed by the PASOK government abolishing institutions which previously institutionalized gender inequality). Rather, it is various traditional values, beliefs and customs embedded in Greek and Cretan culture, which legitimize the attitudes that perpetuate gender inequality and ignore the multiple and complex roles women actually perform. In the eyes of government officials women lacked something essential, an important quality that is needed to legitimate their position, 'a male body'. They faced problems in assuming their social position as the master of the greenhouse, as their identity as greenhouse owners was regularly questioned. Similar to the women farmers in Finland studied by Silvasti (2003: 161), the stories of women in Platanos lead one to examine the meaning of the gendered body from the framework of the social construction of agricultural occupations. Referring to Bryant's work (1999a, 1999b), Silvasti (ibid.) writes: 'Body politics is the central way of using power in the field of agriculture. At the same time, that special way of using power is also shaping the context wherein young girls and women construct their self-identity as women and as farmers or farm wives'. In the case of Platanos, we have a battle between traditional cultural scripts,[14] according to which it is the man who is the head, even when the head is a woman, and the modern woman who is 'free from the fixities of tradition', with respect to gendered division of labour. The failure of bureaucrats to recognize women as head of the greenhouse is a manifestation of *traditionality* and of the rigidity of wider institutionalized values and practices.

When I asked the local bureaucrats about whether or not a woman who is the mainstay of the greenhouse business *deserves* to be recognized as such, it quickly became apparent that contrary to the Weberian bureaucratic ideal, *merit*

---

14 'Social interactionism defines "social scripting" as a process where people are subconsciously and consciously conditioned to follow rules and adapt values and behavioural patterns determined by society, its subculture or some ethnic or socioeconomic group .... Scripts are a kind of mental map .... that are developed and used to organise behaviour along socially appropriate lines' (Silvasti 2003:156).

is not a gender-neutral means of making objective decisions about the worth of individuals, but, as Pini (2002: 66) puts it, 'is value laden and embedded within the gendered organizational contexts in which it is invoked'. In the case of Platanos, *merit* appeared to be a gendered construct, whereby greater value was given to men's role over women's, resulting in women's requests for recognition of their role being not granted despite their greater involvement, interest and knowledge in the greenhouse business and in men being positioned as having more *merit* in the public world than their female counterparts. Excluding women from a position of 'leadership' and denying them visibility is a failure on the part of local bureacrats to understand that resistance to change leaves them open to criticisms of overt gender discrimination.

Although the European Community, through various directives, was at the time promoting equality of opportunity and treatment in economic, social and cultural life, a shift in attitudes towards that direction required at the time, and still requires, that

> More systematic and carefully targeted large-scale campaigns [should be carried out]. They should be aimed at decision-makers, individuals and the various groups concerned, those active in politics and in the social, occupational and educational field, while increasing media involvement. Equal treatment should figure as a permanent topic in information and awareness campaigns. (Commission of the European Communities 1986: 16)

Unless there is a change in traditional attitudes about gender roles and some positive discrimination on women's behalf over and above general measures intended to benefit both sexes equally, because traditional stereotypes held by local bureaucrats assign the role of breadwinner and the head of household to men and that of household worker to women and budgetary constraints favour men in allocation of new technologies via various development projects, there is a danger that segregation to the disadvantage of women might even increase; this might also be fuelled by fear that women's increasing economic and social independence might prove damaging to children and the institution of the family.

So, key to my findings is the recognition that, although greenhouse production ostensibly provides women with financial independence and the potential to negotiate more equitable gender relations within the household, the strong gendered ideology underpinning agriculture mediates this development, restricting its impact on household gender relations. The main project developments that appear inclusive and transformative turn out to be supportive of a status quo that is highly inequitable to women. The severity of constraint to agency and public engagement for women and the extent of 'male' capture of 'new spaces' for decision-making is apparent. Similar to the case of Northern Ireland studied by Shortall (2002: 172), in rural Greece 'the approach to rural development may have changed but a particular gendered ideology persists.

This is no doubt linked to the masculine institutional apparatus that manages rural development programmes'. The data from Platanos revealed the limited engagement of many women with formal public institutions and the importance of varying degrees of 'informal' extra-familial collective action (often conceived as the basis for social capital) like for example the organization of the annual tomato feast (see Chapter 8 on women's associations for details), in enabling women to shape collective spaces and to use these as a claim to positions of leadership. Local norms around the right of men to lead are shifting and women are able to exert more active agency than they did prior to their involvement in the greenhouse business, depending of course on personal motivations and individual responses to the opportunities offered and constraints encountered which play a role in shaping patterns of participation.

Chapter 5
The Production of Olives and
Olive Oil in Nohia and Platanos

In the previous two chapters I looked at the way in which two different developments in the occupational structure of Nohia and Platanos, handcrafts and greenhouses, affected the work and impacted on the lives of the women (and their households) who took up these activities. Here, I will try to look at an activity common to almost all households in the two villages; that of the cultivation of olive trees for production, mainly of olive oil. This cultivation formed the basis of household income before greenhouses and handcrafts were introduced and has continued to play an important role in the economies of the households ever since. I will also try to highlight the differences in the work demands for those women who combine the cultivation of olives with either market gardening or production of handcrafts, with those who do not.

Background Information

Greece is the third olive oil producer in the world after Spain and Italy. Most Greek olive tree cultivators live in Peloponnese (around 24 per cent), Crete (around 22 per cent), Thessaly (around 20 per cent) and the islands (around 19 per cent).

The cultivation of olive trees is one of the most traditional and widespread agricultural activities in Crete, alongside vineyards, oranges and vegetables grown in greenhouses. Although in some villages or agricultural communities in Crete these other cultivations are regarded by the producers as more important income-generating activities than olive trees, the economic prosperity of the majority of agricultural communities in the region is connected with the cultivation of olive trees for oil production, including on terrain with steep slopes inaccessible to the plough. The area covered by olive trees has been increasing since the mid-1960s, especially during the 1980s with Greece's accession to the European Community (1981). For example, in the prefecture of Chania, between 1971 and 1981 the production of olive oil increased by 33.15 per cent and in the period 1981–1986 by 58.4 per cent. A similar pattern seems to prevail in Nohia and to a lesser extent in Platanos, due to the fact that in Platanos greenhouses supplemented the household's income from olives. The few alternative solutions, for example replacing olive trees with avocado or kiwi, were not met with enthusiasm by the producers who felt unable to uproot their olive trees which they inherited from their ancestors and would eventually pass on to their children. Olives and olive oil have always been part of their staple diet, whereas avocados or kiwi were new to them and, as a producer told me, 'we can't even eat them, they have such a bad taste'.

The variety of olives grown in Nohia and Platanos is lianes, a small fruit used only for oil. The trees are no more than 4 metres high and in a good year can give up to 10 kilos of oil. At first glance, the distribution of households with regard to ownership of olive trees looked similar in the two villages; at the time of the fieldwork, between 80 and 90 per cent of people in Nohia, and slightly fewer in Platanos, owned up to 500 olive trees. However, a closer inspection of the data shows that a larger percentage of households in Nohia owned fewer trees (up to 250); in addition, a slightly smaller percentage of households in Nohia (around 17 per cent) than in Platanos (around 20 per cent) had more than 500 olive trees. This difference is important because in Nohia the income from the olives was more important to the basic survival of most households. Having said that, because (unlike Platanos) under Directive 85/148/EC Nohia was at the time of the fieldwork classified as a semi-mountainous village, under European Community regulations geared towards helping people to remain in areas which were in danger of becoming depopulated, the producers in Nohia were entitled to some extra financial assistance, however modest.[1] Six women from Nohia were encouraged by their husbands to apply for this subsidy; in all six cases, it was the woman who provided the land for which the subsidy was to be received, whereas the husband had another full-time occupation. Some *agrotes* expressed worries about their lack of understanding of the various regulations and directives imposed from above and the long-term implications of receiving these grants on the financial viability of their farm and on local autonomy and national sovereignty.

Olive Harvesting

The harvesting period is a period of intensive work for almost all households in Nohia and Platanos since they all produce olive oil for sale and for domestic consumption. Moreover, throughout my stay in the area, people from both villages repeatedly stressed that they sent olive oil as a gift to relatives in urban centres or to friends they felt obliged to or to whom they could turn for favours in the future. Every gift was used or seen as a means of creating an obligation on the part of the receiver, which would potentially be fulfilled sometime in the future. Harvesting starts sometime in early November when the olives are

---

1   At the time of the fieldwork, they received around €1.5 per stremma of olive trees and/or vineyards producing sultanas and edible grapes, and around €20 for every seven animals, provided the producers owned or rented at least 10.5 stremmata of pastureland for every seven animals.

ripe and swollen and finishes by the end of February. Some people who hold many jobs start to harvest later on (that is in early December); this depends on the time they can get off from their other obligations and on whether the olives have ripened or not.

There are several ways to gather the olives. One way is to leave the olives on the tree and wait for them to fall either directly onto the soil (a method used until the late 1960s and used mainly by women) or onto nets/cloths called *dychtia/ kapes*, laid under the trees by the producers who then collect the olives, either manually or with a machine similar to a vacuum cleaner, which sucks the olives in. This method is not very popular because it is labour intensive and results in a lower oil quality due to the prolongation of the harvesting period. The picking of olives from the *dychtia/kapes* was mainly women's work and hence the word *mazochtres*, meaning gatherers, which is a word of feminine gender with a 'low status' connotation. There are still women in the villages who well remember this harvesting method. As Koula said:

> Before *kapes* were introduced, we, the women used to collect the olives from the ground one by one, put them in our pockets and then place them into the sacks; it was back breaking. At the end of the season, we used to go to the fields and search for the odd ones which were left lying on the ground; we picked them and sold them; this was our pocket money.

Another woman, Andonia, added:

> In those days, even pregnant women went to the harvest. I was in the field picking olives when I started having labour pains. I kept on picking them up. When at noon it started raining and we returned home, I told my husband to call the midwife; in the beginning he didn't believe me .... I had the baby that afternoon, and three days later I was back in the fields, with the baby in a basket near me, gathering olives. I had to carry her with me, because I was breastfeeding her. In those days this was common practice.

The word *mazochtres* is used nowadays to refer to 'hired labour' (see below).

Another method is to remove the olives directly from the tree. This can be done either by hand-picking them, or by beating the branches using either a wooden stick (*ravdi*) (see Figure 5.1) or a giant plastic fork (*pyrouna*). The 'beating method' can also be done with the use of machines (see Figure 5.2), but if not used properly, they can damage the tree. Another way is to use big machines that shake the tree; these can be used only on level land and in areas where there is a large corridor between the trees for the tractor to pass. They cannot be used in Crete due to the morphology of the soil, the small space between the trees and the fact that olive trees have been and still are planted in a haphazard way.

Figure 5.1   Woman harvesting olives using a *ravdi*

Figure 5.2   Man harvesting olives using a machine

When the harvesting season starts, both men and women 'go to the olives' (*pane stis elies*), as the locals say. They spend all day there, from dawn to dusk. The actual 'beating' of the trees is done both by men and women. Most of the work done exclusively by women concerns the laying out of the cloths under the trees and their mending (see Figure 5.3) and washing at the end of the season. It is mostly men who bag up the olives into sacks, weighing 60 to 70 kilos each, to be transported to the olive press (see Figure 5.4). Men also prune, prepare the soil, apply chemical fertilizers and pesticides. Similar to Lineton's (1971) Mina, in Nohia and Platanos, households without a male head were at a disadvantage in protecting the property from the depredations of others' livestock and in working the olive presses. The introduction of harvesting machines made the division of labour between men and women more acute, in that, as a producer said, ' my wife tried to use it but she did not last more than ten minutes; it is so heavy ...'. Physical strength and agricultural technology are used to reinforce patriarchal ideologies which marginalize women in the olive oil production. Although as mentioned above the machines, if not carefully operated, could damage the trees, as a producer said, 'anyone who wants to save on labour costs buys a machine'. In Platanos the majority of those who bought machines were greenhouse owners, that is, people who wanted to save on harvesting time as well as labour costs. The decision about whether or not to invest in a machine was made by men. For example, I attended a Panhellenic exhibition for olive harvesting machines and, although the exhibition was very well attended, there were no women there. When I asked women in Nohia why, they replied: 'but my

Figure 5.3   Woman laying out the *kapes* under the tree

husband is the one who makes this kind of decision; he is the man, he knows;
I know nothing about machines. These are not things a woman should worry
about'. A woman said: 'I tried to persuade my husband to buy a machine but he
wouldn't listen to me. We have around, I don't remember exactly how many, eeeer
... 780 olive trees and as both of our children live in Athens, we cannot manage
by ourselves and hence we hire *mazochtres*; a machine in the long run would
save us money towards labour costs. He holds firm on his belief, saying that the
machine will damage the trees. But, in reality, he knows that this would mean
more work for him, and that's why he doesn't want it; I can't use the machine,
it's too heavy.' A man who bought the machine said: 'Now my wife will do the
easy work; all the heavy work will fall on me. She won't even have to cook for
the workers, since we won't need to hire any. The machine has replaced them.'
In other words, not only did men's work in olive harvesting increase in relation
to that of women but, at the same time, it was the labour of women that seemed
likely to become marginalized, especially since the introduction of harvesting
machines, and the division of labour became even more distinct than before.
These machines have become an important symbol of masculine power and
physical strength and stand as a boundary between men's and women's work,
thus creating an exclusive male space in the olive harvest process; women, treated
as inferiorized others, now concentrate on laying down the *kapes* and bagging
the olives into sacks for transportation, a task which was previously performed
by women and men, and still is when a harvesting machine is not in use.

Figure 5.4   Men perform the tasks that require greater strength

The whole process of transportation of olives to the processing factory and the marketing of the oil which is produced, including the decision making involved, was, and still is, handled by men (see Figures 5.5, 5.6 and 5.7). Women are simply excluded from this process. Men talk about these procedures and/or the decision taken as if all the olives of the household belong to them and ignore or tend to forget the fact that some of the household's olive trees belong to their wife and were brought to the household as part of her dowry or inheritance. Much agricultural produce is seen in this way, that is as men's, despite women's vital contribution to it. An exception is involvement in greenhouses where, as shown in the previous chapter, because women's work is recognized and accepted by men and women alike as being very important, and in many cases even more important than that of men, agricultural produce is not seen as men's and thus women are involved in the decision making process related to the production and marketing of early vegetables. Moreover, women actively involved in the production of early vegetables in greenhouses seem to have more say in the processing and marketing of olives as well; for example, in Platanos women can be seen in the olive presses, chatting about the acidity of their household's olive oil and in the cooperatives' association in the nearby town Kastelli, discussing the EC/EU subsidies they will receive and/or whether the olives would be included in the development project designed to improve their greenhouses and other agricultural endeavours. In Nohia, on the other hand, most women producers who, under EC/EU schemes for developing

Figure 5.5   The olive press

Figure 5.6   The olive press

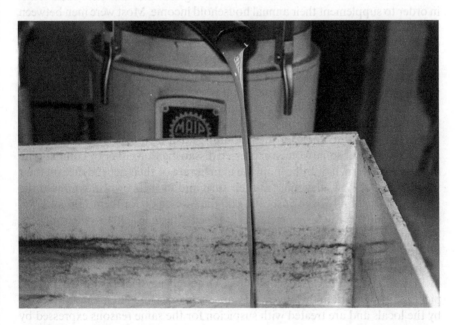

Figure 5.7   The olive press

semi-mountainous regions, are entitled to receive financial help for every olive tree they own, have given their husbands, fathers and sons power of attorney to act on their behalf; hence, the male 'head of the family' turns up in the local government office to complete the required documents and discuss how many olive trees he should declare for receiving this form of subsidy, in addition to the subsidy the household was entitled to at the time for the production of olive oil. The latter also went into the 'man's pocket' so to speak, since he is the one who collects it from the cooperative, which is responsible for distributing the money to the producers. An example is the Farandakis family: although some of the olive trees belong to Koula, it is her husband George who deals with the bureaucracy; when asked why, Koula replied: 'I know nothing of these things' (*Ego then xero ap' afta*).

Hiring Labour

Olive production in Crete is labour intensive. Households that cannot keep up with the work hire labour. As mentioned earlier in this chapter, these workers are called *mazochtres*, that is, 'pickers'. Most are day-wage labourers. The use of day-wage labour during the harvesting period is extensive. Until the early 1990s, labour mainly consisted of Greek seasonal migrants who came to Crete from either northern or central Greece, at a period when they are kept idle there due to adverse weather conditions that affect agricultural activities back home, in order to supplement their annual household income. Most were men between 25 and 50 years of age, usually from relatively poor families. Very few women came, usually with their husbands. They received a day-wage for their work or were paid in kind, that is, in oil, depending on the deal they had made with the employer. The majority preferred oil to cash, as they stood a fair chance of earning more if paid in kind, due to oil price fluctuations. They were offered food and shelter as well, which meant more work for the employer's wife since, on top of the work she contributed to looking after the family and the household property, she had to cook for the labourers, wash their sheets and clean their rooms. As a result some women expressed dissatisfaction either by complaining directly to their men or by keeping the man 'aware of their dependence on their womenfolk, of how they must in their turn and in their own way uphold the honour of the family by reciprocating all the women do for them' (Friedl 1986: 52). Gradually, many olive producers stopped offering shelter to their pickers. The latter rented rooms in the village in Platanos and in the surrounding villages of Nohia since there were no rooms for rent in the village itself.

In addition, there were and still are tourists who, as in the tomato harvest in Platanos, come to work as pickers. Although most of them are 'orange pickers', some work in the olives; they are cheaper to hire but are not preferred by the locals and are treated with suspicion for the same reasons expressed by greenhouse owners in Platanos, namely for drinking, being unreliable, taking dope and wearing shabby clothes.

Locally-hired pickers were mainly people who either had very few olive trees of their own or had no olives at all. Local workers were hard to find since most preferred to share-crop on a half-share basis for migrants, who maintained a holding in the area but had neither any relatives to look after their property nor were they able to come themselves and gather the olives. Similar to Mani (Lineton 1971: 134) some took care of migrants' property for fixed annual payment of olive oil. This is similar to the situation in Corfu, where, under the so called *paktoma* arrangement, absentee landlords or people who, for one reason or another, did not have time to look after their olive trees, arranged with someone else to look after their property, harvest the olives and so on, in return for part of the produce (Couroukli 1985: 87). It was difficult to tell whether they worked for others to make as much money as they could or because of obligations.

From the early 1990s onwards, Greece experienced the inflow of hundreds of thousands of Albanians, Bulgarians, Ukrainians, Poles, Romanians, Africans, Asians and other nationalities, a large proportion of whom settled in rural areas, employed mostly in the construction industry, tourism-related activities, in-house services and agriculture. These migrants provided a solution to the long-standing shortages of labour in rural Greece in general and in Crete in particular, that have come about with agricultural restructuring, depopulation, the rejection by the younger generation of agricultural labour and the increased opportunities of those who stayed in rural areas to find off-farm employment (see Kasimis et al. 2003). Migrant labourers changed the character of hired labour in olive harvesting. They offer more hours of work for lower wages (up to 50 per cent or 60 per cent less than the average wage paid to Greek workers) and have replaced internal migrants who had previously met seasonal labour needs. Increasing migrants' wages following their regularization will put pressure on agricultural income and is likely to make it more difficult for small farmers to cope with increasing production costs and hence will encourage increasing polarization within the Greek farm structure brought on by the competitive global economic environment, thus leading to more inequalities.

To cut down labour expenses many migrants and locals try to either pick their olives alone or make an 'arrangement' with some neighbours or relatives and take turns to help each other in the field. This is similar to the *thaneika* arrangement described in the chapter on market gardening (Chapter 4) and is widely used especially in villages where people have to attend to their greenhouses as well as to their olives. Since, as mentioned in the introductory chapters, land is divided into small parcels scattered in different parts of the village area, people usually arrange to gather all the olives from the parcel belonging to family X and then go to a parcel belonging to family Y and so on. Those who migrated and still have olive trees in the village try to cut expenses by coming themselves during the harvest period to pick their olives. Most stay in relatives' houses. Although they were welcomed, because they brought news and life to the village, many women complained about the additional work this meant for them. As Katina said:

> I look forward to the time when the relatives are going to leave; they stay in my house – obligations you see – after all it wouldn't look good if we let them stay elsewhere, people here gossip. They are an additional burden to me. I have to cook for them, clear their room, wash their clothes. I wish my sister-in-laws came as well. Things would have been different if they did. But they can't; their children are young and have to attend school in Athens.

Marketing

Women's work in Nohia ends in the field. The decision as to which olive press should be chosen for the processing of the household's olives, the transportation of the olives to the olive press, their processing and the sale of the end product are, with a few exceptions, exclusively the men's responsibility. In Platanos, by and large only women who work in the greenhouses get involved in the marketing of the olives and olive oil, are knowledgeable about the business and sometimes visit the olive press, a space that is exclusively male in Nohia. When asked why, men replied: 'This was always men's responsibility and there was no reason for things to change now.' Women on the other hand argued that they could well do without it; 'one worry less for us', *(mia skotoura ligoteri)*, they said. Some of these women have never set foot in the press, whereas others have occasionally come to have a look at the processing.

After harvesting, olives are taken to the olive press (*eleotrivio* or *eleourgio*[2] – see Figures 5.5, 5.6 and 5.7). Nohia has one privately owned olive press, whereas Platanos has two, both cooperatives. On rare occasions villagers take their olives to be processed by another olive press outside the village. George,

---

2   Two different words are used locally for olive press. *Eleotrivio*, which refers to the old type of press, which consists firstly of large stones in a large vat driven around either manually or by a petrol engine and secondly of a press, which is tightened on one of the revolving shafts that drives the mill (Lineton 1971: 127). The *eleourgio*, on the other hand, refers to the new electrical machines, based on centrifugal force, where one person loads the olives into the machine. The olives are automatically washed and separated from leaves and other materials, enter into the machines, are reduced to a pulp and then oil is extracted from the pulp with the help of centrifugal machinery which separates the oil from the water. Whereas in the *eleotrivio* six or seven people are needed because many tasks are manual, the *eleourgio* needs just three people, one to work the machinery and look after the books and accounts, one to unload the sacks of olives and feed the machines with olives and a third to test the oil's acidity, collect it into large plastic containers, weigh them and give them to the customer. The workers can be either migrants from other parts of Greece – as was the case in Nohia – or local people – as was the case in Platanos. The atmosphere in the press is very friendly, since customers (men) gather, watch and drink raki.

for example, takes the household's olives to be processed not in the olive press in Nohia, but at another village, because his son works there during the harvest period. Eftychis takes half of his olives to a nearby village because his father was born there and the man who owns the olive press there is a relative; he takes the other half to be processed at the local press in Nohia, because he feels that he should support his fellow villagers *(tous synhorianous tou)*. Depending on the deal, the producer either transports the household's olives to the olive press himself or the factory sends someone with a tractor to collect them. Almost everybody in Nohia and Platanos sells the oil to their Cooperatives' Association; nevertheless, it is traditional for each family to keep a relatively large amount of olive oil (around 300 kilos) for self-consumption. In villages like Kamissiana (near Nohia), where there is one privately owned and one cooperative olive press, most people are likely to support the cooperative for political reasons. 'It is here that all the progressive people bring their olives', the president of the local cooperative told me. 'Unless they have an obligation to the owner of the private one, or the man is a relative of theirs', he added. In this case, a *proodeftikos* (someone with progressive, that is, centre to left, political ideas) would bring half of his produce to the private press and half to the cooperative one, whereas a 'conservative' would take them all to the privately owned press because the deal offered was better. As a *proodeftikos* said to me, 'we must support the cooperatives, no matter what the cost'. Another producer added: 'I am with PASOK; the person who owns the private olive press is with the New Democracy, so, I will never support his business endeavours by processing my olives in his press.' The same feelings were expressed at a gathering where even PASOK followers expressed their dismay at the cooperative's relatively high prices. In addition, some accused the privately-owned presses of cheating on the weighing of the produce.

Another reason for supporting the cooperative is that people think that by doing that they will get a favour in return. Also, since interpersonal relations are important, some prefer the cooperative either because one of the members of the Board of Directors is their friend or relative or because they owe him a favour. 'I can't use the local olive press' said a small producer from Nohia, 'because my wife's brother works in the cooperative in Kamissiana. I have to show my support ... he has been very supportive to us in the past, that is when my wife and I needed financial help for building our house'. Another producer said: 'I have to support them; my second cousin is married to the president's sister-in-law and they have always been very supportive whenever we needed them.' So business transactions are not based so much on potential profits or losses as on personal contacts and reciprocal obligations and political affiliations. These principles also apply when deciding where to take the oil for sale. Although 80 per cent of producers take their olive oil to the nearest cooperatives' association in Kolymbari (near Nohia) and Kastelli (near Platanos), a few producers go to the private traders called *lathembori*. These traders give lower prices but are 'chosen' by producers who in the past obtained a loan from the Agricultural

Bank of Greece but did not pay back the debt. To the dissatisfaction of many producers, the Agricultural Bank keeps in touch with the association and therefore the latter knows immediately whether a producer owes the Bank money or not and might refuse to buy his olive oil unless he clears his debts. Personal contacts are also a factor in the sale of some olive oil to private traders. When I asked the secretary of the local government office in Platanos why he sells his produce to the *lathemboros*, he replied: 'He is a personal friend of mine, a good friend; this year my son is going to attend a vocational school in Athens. His son, who lives in Athens, is going to look after him. Athens is a big city. We are afraid that he might be led astray and induced to taking drugs by peers.'

Having looked at the economic change and women's work in Nohia and Platanos and concentrated on three activities women are involved in – handcrafts in Nohia, market gardening in Platanos and the production of olives and olive oil – and having shown how dominant constructions of gender are both reproduced and contested through everyday discourses and practices in Cretan agriculture, I will now examine the way these changes have influenced marriage and family and women's associations in the two villages and the role of the latter in setting some limits to the emancipatory potential of economic change.

Chapter 6
Marriage and Family in Nohia and Platanos

Introduction

It would be a great omission to try and understand the appearances and realities of women's lives in Nohia and Platanos without having looked at the family structure. This chapter examines one of the most conventional topics in Greek anthropology, that of kinship[1] and family, and the salient role of these in women's construction of their collective and individual selves in the villages under study. It concentrates on ways in which certain changes in the respective localities – discussed in previous chapters – have affected women's lives within the family, an institution through which 'individuals acquire their key statuses in the village and the compelling rights and duties which affect their relations' (Loizos 1975: 63).

Demographic Characteristics: Age and Origin of Spouses

The nuclear family (*ikogenia*) is the prevailing pattern in both villages. Seldom does one come across a bachelor and almost never an unmarried woman living alone, unless both parents have passed away. Irrespective of their age, children tend to live with their parents until they marry.

---

1   Kinship studies have not achieved the same depth of analysis and subtlety in the Mediterranean as they have elsewhere '... [these] have suffered from the all-too-easy assumption that a kinship system so familiar requires no further exploration ...' (Davis 1977: 198). Since the late 1970s, however, 'a steady accumulation of ethnographic data has begun to make it possible more fully to appreciate the degree of variation to be encountered within the seemingly all too familiar cognatic kinship systems of Greece and the Mediterranean' (Just 2000: 96). For example, in the case of Greece, Couroucli (1985: 13–14) and Loizos and Papataxiarchis (1991: 8–10) have suggested a four- and threefold taxonomy respectively; the former takes into account differing forms of subsistence and economic activity, whereas the latter is based on forms of residence, household composition, inheritance and dowry, degrees of gender equality and inequality. Nohia and Platanos fall under Loizos and Papataxiarchis' third type, where residence is patrilocal and married brothers do not cohabitate, and is characterized by full partible inheritance of land and Couroucli's third type, that is, fragmented plot of production and nuclear family organization.

Marital Age

There has been no significant change in the age at which men marry in Nohia and Platanos since the 1930s. In Platanos, the average age of marriage for men slightly increased during the war period (1940s), from around 28 to around 30. The explanation given to me by the elderly of the village was scarcity of food and uncertainty about the future. From then on, the age of marriage has continued to decrease; in the 1980s it was around 27.[2] Evidence presented by Kousis (1984: 145) on the marital age of men in Drethia, a village in eastern Crete, suggests that this has increased there due to the 'courting relationships unmarried local males have with female tourists'. Unlike Drethia, the development of tourism in western Crete after the 1960s has not resulted in such an increase in Platanos. In Nohia, the average age of marriage for men was approximately 29 until the late 1970s, when it fell to 26. When I asked the president of the village why, in his opinion, the marital age in Nohia had not increased as it had in Platanos, he attributed this to the fact that people in Nohia were at that time better off financially than people in Platanos, as before the introduction of greenhouses, Platanos was a very poor village indeed, much poorer than Nohia.

For women, the average age of marriage in Platanos gradually decreased from approximately 24 in the 1930s to 20 in the 1980s. This was attributed by local people to the economic development of the village (see previous chapters) and the subsequent ability of families to raise dowries faster than they did before the introduction of greenhouses. Another reason they gave was the rise of demand for local brides since many men, because of the new economic opportunities that were available to them, especially since the introduction of greenhouses (1968), opted to stay in the village rather than emigrate, whereas females tried to marry outside the village, preferably in cities and thus avoid 'dirtying their hands with soil'. Contrary to what was happening in Platanos, women's marital age in Nohia during the 1930s, 1940s and 1950s kept increasing whereas from the 1960s onwards kept falling and in the 1980s it was around 23. The age increase was explained to me by Stavros, the village president, in terms of the adverse economic conditions which did not enable families to raise the daughter's dowry. In fact, as an older woman explained, some had to remain engaged for two to three years before being able to get married. It must be noted here that because men have to provide the house in Crete and women the dowry (see below), there are economic pressures on both spouses' families, which can play an important role in delaying the marriage. Another factor that may have affected the above mentioned patterns has been migration.

In terms of age difference between men and women, on average men in Platanos tend to be seven or eight years older than their wives whereas in

---

2   To calculate the averages, the trimmed mean has been used, whereby the smallest 5 per cent and the largest 5 per cent of the values are trimmed, whereas the remaining 90 per cent are averaged (Ryan et al. 1985: 39).

Nohia this age difference is smaller, with the exception of the 1970s, when men in Nohia were on average nine years older than their spouses. In general, in most couples men are older than their wives. This is a symbolic manifestation of the ideology that the man must be stronger than the woman and capable of exercising some sort of power over her or protecting her, whereas the woman is weak and dependent on her husband.

However, in the early 1960s, when the OGA (Organization of Agricultural Insurance) started giving pensions to older women, many women reported that they were between one and three years older than they had declared. Between 1963 and 1968 as many as 28 women in Platanos asked for their date of birth to be replaced by the allegedly 'correct' one; in Nohia no such case is evident from the information held in the Community Register, either because it did not exist or because the then secretary in the local government office made sure that no traces were left behind.

Origin of Spouses

From the archives in the local government office in the respective villages, and especially from the marriage books and from the Population Register called *Dimotologio*, which gives information on the geographic origins of the spouses, one can notice changes in the origin of the spouses since 1931. Until the late 1950s most marriages in Platanos were largely between locals. Only a few spouses came from nearby villages, such as Sfinari, Kastelli, Granvousa and even fewer from cities like Heracleon, Athens, etc. The tendency to exogamy began in Platanos in the 1960s, linked with the phenomenon of migration. Furthermore, during the 1970s, when greenhouses were introduced in Platanos, more outsiders (both men and women) entered the village via the marriage institution.[3] In other words, the greenhouse phenomenon contributed to this change in the dynamics between the local males and females. This phenomenon is not unique to Platanos; the same occurrence has been noticed by Kousis (1984) in the village of Drethia in eastern Crete, when tourism started to develop in the area. She writes (ibid.: 139):

> ... as the foundations of the new economic base were laid, more outsiders entered the village's families. The number of locals marrying within the village decreased, while non-Cretans from various parts of Greece married locals and established households in Drethia.

---

3   For example, during the 1930, out of the 116 marriages that took place in Platanos, only 10 men and four women were outsiders. During the 1950s, from the 131 marriages which took place there, 17 men and 28 women came from outside the village. In the 1970s the respective numbers were relatively larger; 139 marriages took place and of these, 38 men and 62 women were outsiders (calculated from Book of Marriages and Community Register).

Unlike Meganisi, an island studied by Just (2000: 234–5) where village endogamy was surviving the effects of urban migration and was regarded as 'the best marriage' (*o kaliteros gamos*), in Nohia and Platanos exogamy is popular. Having said that, exogamy in Nohia is more marked than in Platanos. Unlike Platanos, in Nohia in the majority of marriages only one of the spouses is local. In both villages, exogamy is more marked for men than for women. Moreover, unlike Drethia, a popular village with tourists where many non-Greeks, especially women, marry locals and establish themselves as local residents (Kousis 1984: 141, 143), in Nohia and Platanos this is not common. Although in Platanos there is contact with foreigners all year through, this is mostly with third-country migrants and winter tourists who, for reasons discussed in previous chapters in this book, are seen as *letsotouristes* (vagabonds) and the villagers avoid socializing with them. Female summer tourists are seen as easy or loose women, to have a nice time with but nothing beyond. Parents exercise control over children's liaisons with these people. One can often hear parents and young people saying 'papoutsi ap ton topo sou ki as in ke balomeno', which translates as 'it is better to buy your shoes at home, even if they are mended', which means that it is better to marry someone from your own country or village, even if s/he is not perfect, than a stranger whose customs you hardly know. Therefore, there are only a small number of marriages between tourists and locals in Platanos and none in Nohia.

To what can one attribute this disparity? There are a number of plausible reasons. First, as I was repeatedly told, since the late 1960s women in Platanos have preferred to marry men from other villages or, if possible, from urban centres, and thus avoid working in the greenhouses, being exposed to pesticides and various fertilizers and risking their and their children's health. As a result, men marry women from poorer villages. As for Nohia, a possible reason is a similar preference among young women to that of the women in Platanos, to marry men who are not *agrotes* (agriculturalists) and thus combine what they perceive as an upward mobility in the social scale with their desire to live in the urban centres. Another reason is to do with a demographic imbalance in the village, where there are more men of marriageable age than women. The above mentioned reasons are cited here in order to draw attention to the need for more thorough studies on *nuptiality* combined with demographic imbalances in the whole area of Kisamos.

Residence of the Newly Married

In Nohia and in Platanos, as in some parts of Greece (Kenna 1976a: 22; Hirschon 1989: 119) and Cyprus (Loizos 1975: 64; Arnold 1982: 42) and unlike others (Campbell 1964: 71; Friedl 1964: 59), there is a cultural preference for a nuclear family to have a separate dwelling unit and domestic economy of its own from the first day of marriage. 'Marriage marks the point when a separate household is created' (Lever 1984: 110) and is, alongside the time of death of one or both of the parents, one of the occasions when property is transferred from one generation to the other. The ideal of family independence and self-sufficiency has also been noted by Kenna (1976b: 348), who, when referring to Anafi (the Aegean island she researched), writes that 'the islanders insist that the life and fortunes of each family household are united and cannot include those of other families, however closely related'.

In both villages, a main consideration when a couple gets married is the possession of a dwelling unit – somewhere separate to live – and land. However, in other nearby villages there are odd cases whereby couples rent a place until their own house is ready,[4] or cases of renting property by professional people like doctors, teachers and myself, who came from elsewhere to live in the area for a while. No villager that I know of rents a dwelling in Nohia or Platanos.

In other parts of Greece, as Hirschon (1989: 118, italics mine) writes, '*horis spiti i gynaeka den pandrevete*' (without a house a woman does not marry). Hence, at marriage the new couple goes to live in the dwelling which in the past was a hut or a house and at present an apartment or house (depending on the financial circumstances of the bride's family as well as on the part of Greece in which the newly married will live) given to the bride as a dowry by her parents (Kenna 1976a: 22; Hirschon 1989: 118). Unlike this, the situation in Nohia and Platanos (and in other parts of Greece, such as Glendi [Herzfeld 1985: 72]) resembles that of Vasilika (Friedl 1964) and among Sarakatsani (Campbell 1964), where the bride goes to live with her husband (that is, a *virilocal* residence pattern exists); it differs, however, from the latter in that the newly married couple does not go and live in the groom's parents' house, but both leave their respective parental homes and go to live in the house provided by the husband. This can at times, although not often, be his parental house, in which case the parents move elsewhere, but not far away; sometimes they can be as close as in the same courtyard or even in another part or a horizontal extension of the house. As Gamvrakis, a man in his late 60s, who owns and, with the help of his wife, runs a *cafeneion* (coffee shop) in Nohia, informed me, this situation was more common at times when economic resources were extremely limited throughout the area and the means of livelihood precarious. The latter, according to Gamvrakis, seems to have affected people's attitudes to household ownership both before World War II and after the civil war. He said:

---

4   For example, at the time of fieldwork, a newly married couple were renting a flat in Kamisiana, a village on the coastal line between Kolymbari and Chania, until their own house was ready for them to move in. Both spouses complained about the economic burden of having to pay rent. He regarded this as a *perito exodo*, that is, an unnecessary spending. Her feelings, however, were contradictory in that while she also resented the fact that they were paying rent, on the other hand she mentioned from time to time that she dreaded the moment they would move to their own house, which was close to her in-laws.

Those days, most parents did not have the means to move elsewhere; they, therefore, lived, at least for a while, with the newlyweds, in an extension of the house, or at best, in a separate dwelling in the same yard as the newly weds.

Later on, however, and particularly during the late 1960s and early 1970s, the generally increasing affluence in the area (with the development of infrastructure, the use of new methods and techniques in agriculture, the development of tourism in the island) and the granting of credit by the Junta government for the purchase of houses (previously unavailable) and for landowners who wished to build on their property, that is the famous *stegastika thania* (credits for building or buying a house or apartment), were reflected in the preference of newly married villagers for living in a separate household to that of the parents. But although *neolocal* residence on marriage was accepted, similar to Meganisi studied by Just (2000: 210–11),

> the stress on the solidarity between the generations was all the more important lest a *spiti* [house-household] prematurely divided be thought a family riven by strife. As might be expected the assertion of solidarity was of more concern to the senior generation than to the junior, and old men and women who proudly pointed out the new dwellings constructed by their sons quickly added that they themselves were also respected by their children who never failed to give to them.

Nowadays, when young couples build a new house (always a modern structure), they make provisions so that their children's dwelling can be added vertically to the ground-floor dwelling in which they reside; this is why, if one visits the villages one does not see tiled roofs, but flat roofs covered with cement and at odd places wires emerging which can be said to symbolically represent the 'foundation-stone' for a new flat and by proxy a new household.

Nevertheless, even at times of economic difficulties newly married couples did, whenever possible, try to avoid living with the groom's parents. As Katina, a woman in her late 60s living in Nohia, explained, this could lead to tension between the bride and her mother-in-law:

> Mothers-in-law are mothers-in-law. They are not mothers, they are mothers-in-law! I stayed three and a half years with my mother-in-law … in the same house. We shared the same kitchen! But later, we *had* to part … in order to avoid quarrelling … Well, whether we were living together or not, it didn't make much of a difference since she left this house and went to live in the other house … in the same yard that is, … but had her own household! Yes, every day, she was in my house, interfering … in the middle of everything … may God forgive her, well, she interfered all the time.

And she continued:

My poor mother-in-law was jealous of me because my husband loved me. I'll tell you a story: I stayed in the house and cooked and my mother-in-law popped in on her way back from the fields. She opened the pan and looked at the dish I had prepared – it was ready! And she fills a jar with water – this jar was one of my dowry items, it could hold one kilo of water – and she lifts the lid and pours it in … I saw her doing it with my own eyes … I had the baby in my arms and pretended I didn't see her. At lunch she served the food and we ate. After we had eaten she said to me: 'You over there, the food has a lot of broth today' – this is how she called me. Then my husband, without being aware of what had happened, said: 'No, it doesn't have a lot of broth, its fine'. And I, poor thing, didn't say a thing to her. But I did tell my husband in the evening in bed. She did this many times… She has done many nasty things to me … many … There was a time when I didn't want to cook … Nowadays all mothers have progressed and all grandmothers too; in the past, they didn't know how to behave.

The discomforts experienced by Katina were underplayed both by herself and her husband, in order to avoid showing disrespect to the old woman. Although the latter was perceived as behaving inappropriately, no attempt was made to avert it and thus regulate interpersonal behaviour and minimize conflict between mother-in-law (*pethera*) and daughter-in-law (*nyfi*). As I was informed, such instances were common[5] in both Nohia and Platanos and were often justified by claiming that the actor (Katina's mother-in-law) was 'special' (a euphemism for wicked), or that the conditions were unusual. Katina also added that if she had any daughters-in-law she would treat them and love them as she does her own daughters.

At marriage, when the bride enters the couple's new house for the first time, it is customary that her mother-in-law will be waiting for her with a bowl full of honey and after the bride makes the mark of three crosses at the top and sides of the main door, the two women are expected to eat the honey which symbolizes a harmonious relationship between them. However, from the above interview it is evident that the mother-in-law–daughter-in-law (*pethera–nyfi*) relationship was not always a harmonious one, even when they did not have to share the same kitchen. Sharing the same kitchen was regarded by village women as an important factor for triggering tension and disputes between the women concerned, rather than as a second pair of hands who would share the domestic burden. 'Two women sharing the same kitchen is not good news; they are bound to quarrel at some point in time', said a married woman in her early 30s, who visited Katina while the interview was in progress. Another woman, in her early 40s, who popped in later on and heard our conversation, said: 'I have

---

5 There were of course exceptions; for example, another woman argued that her relationship with her mother-in-law was an ideal one. They were friends; 'the old woman was like a real mother to me' she said. This was confirmed by other villagers who remembered the old woman often giving her blessing (*dini tin efhi tis*) to her daughter-in-law, a thing that Katina's mother-in-law seldom or never did.

a very good relationship with my mother-in-law. My in-laws live in a separate house near to ours. But I am sure that if we shared the same house, we would quarrel every day. My kitchen is my kitchen. I want no one else interfering'. And she added: 'You can't have two heads under the same hat' (*Dyo kefalia kato ap ena kapello then horoun*). The same feelings were expressed by women in Platanos. As Georgia, a woman in her mid-40s, said: 'I work all day in our greenhouses; when I go home in the evening I want no one around me; and the last thing I want is to share my kitchen with the old woman'. This attitude is not surprising since the 'kitchen' in rural Greece is

> pre-eminently a woman's realm and the locus of some of her most important functional and symbolic activities ... [It] is also the locus of the everyday intimate life of family and friends, the area in which the most informal socialising takes place... and... where the tasks of preparing and serving food are carried out. (Dubisch 1986a: 207)

Mutual dislike is likely to develop if one of the two women feels threatened by the other, or believes that the other is not behaving properly. As the interview with Katina shows, in Nohia, as in Ambeli (researched by du Boulay 1974), this situation

> created an obvious fault line between the mother-in-law and the bride ... who came into the house; for while she was happy for her son to marry and to give her grandchildren, and happy also to have a young woman in the house to work under her direction, she was also aware that the incoming woman would be a threat, both through her ability to take over the affection of her son and in the fact that by her youth and strength she was in an ultimately victorious position, waiting for the old woman to die [or to move to another house, as was often the case in Nohia and Platanos] before she would in her turn become the mistress of the house. (du Boulay 1986: 147)

The part played by *territoriality*[6] in maintaining smooth social interaction, is very important. If every woman had her own place, a place clearly acknowledged by other people as being her own territory, then potential conflicts might have been averted. Nevertheless, even when living in separate houses, there were problems arising from the everyday face-to-face contact and the lack of breathing space between the two. As evidenced in Ambeli by du Boulay (1986: 147) and as was said by women in Platanos and Nohia, by grumbling to their sons about their wives' incompetence at cooking or looking after the children,

---

6   'Territoriality refers to behaviour connected with the possession, control, or ownership of a particular geographical space ... [It] involves the marking or personalizing of space in some way to indicate ownership, and usually involves defence of the space against intruders' (Berkowitz 1980: 515).

or about her spending too much time gossiping in the neighbourhood, mothers-in-law did exploit the dominant positions of their sons to achieve their own ends and in this way were instrumental in the wife's 'eating a blow or two' (ibid.), as was the case in Ambeli, or inviting the son to modestly support his wife, as was the case with Katina, without, however, hurting her feelings explicitly and thus showing disrespect to an ageing woman. 'Women begin as daughters, attain adulthood only as daughters-in-law, get no satisfaction until they are mothers of sons, and become powerful only when they are mothers-in-law', says Dimen (1986: 64), thus stressing the increase of respect and power women come to enjoy over the years through motherhood and age.

Attitudes and behaviour have changed since the civil war and especially since the mid-1960s; almost all newly married couples have their own houses. One of the basic things that a woman expects when getting married is to have her own *nikokyrio* (house and household). *Nikokyrio* refers to the house as well as to the movable property within it and to the property that is part of the domestic economy (Papataxiarchis 1988: 46).

With the help of parental encouragement, young men and women tend to look for a spouse with equal inheritance prospects. 'You marry within your *sira* (status group)', a villager from Nohia said when asked why he objected to his child marrying a middle-class person from the nearby town. 'Aftos then ine tis siras mas (He is not from the same status group we are)', he explained. Almost all parents in Nohia and Platanos share the view that marriage is for life. It was and it continues to be, if not the most, then one of the most important turning points in one's life regardless of whether one is a man or a woman. It was not considered to be an optional matter, nor one of choice, but rather *proorismos* (a matter of 'destiny') (Hirschon 1989: 107). Thus, pressures are exercised by the parents to ensure its success.

Attitudes to Marriage and Divorce

Marriages were not always successful and divorce was not unknown. In both villages divorce rates were low (five couples divorced in Nohia and four in Platanos between the early 1930s and the late 1980s). However, low divorce rates do not indicate happily married couples. Divorce was and continues to be seen as something bad, a failure in one's life. As in Nea Ionia (Cavounidis 1985), in Nohia and Platanos, even if the quality of the conjugal relationship is low, people prefer to stay together for the sake of the children. Generally, child-centred goals take precedence over conjugal-centred ones. Also, wives fear that the stigma attached to divorce will result in important social disadvantages for themselves and for their children. Often one can hear people saying 'to milo ap tin milia tha pesi' (the apple will fall from the apple tree) in cases of divorce, meaning that if the parents are divorced, the children are likely to follow their example and have unstable marriages.

Divorced women who live alone are also seen as *efkoles* (of loose morals). This is demonstrated by the following story. When I first arrived in Nohia, one of the women I was advised to see was E. When, after a week I visited the village, I asked someone for the directions to E's house; when a villager saw me approaching the gate, he asked me where I was going ('eh, kopellia, pou pas?'). When I explained, he told me, horrified by what he heard, that this was not the house I was looking for. Then he took me to his house and both he and his wife explained that I should never be seen approaching 'that door'. It turned out that the household consisted of four women; the oldest, a daughter of a villager, married when she was 16 to a man 36 years older than her who, a year later, gave birth to a baby girl. Twenty years later, she got divorced. Her daughter got married at 17 to someone from Chania and left the village, only to return a few years later, when she divorced her husband. She has two daughters. Rumour has it that all four of them have 'boyfriends' in the city and that, at times, men were seen visiting the house. 'You seem to be a nice girl, we advise you to have no dealings with them.' Although it was made explicit to me that this was not a place to be visited by a 'respectable woman', it was never actually compared to a *kakofimo spiti* (a house of low repute). It is worth mentioning here the double meaning of *spiti*, that is a house and a brothel, a place where one can sleep or even have sex (Papataxiarchis 1988: 46). A plausible reason might have been the fact that to admit that there is such a house in the village would harm and pollute the reputation of the village as a whole. Similar to the situation in Sohos, the village studied by Cowan (1990: 203), when a woman is talked about,

> accusations are not voiced to her directly; rather they are made about her to others, through commentary (*skholia*) or gossip (*kotsobilia*). She has no opportunity to reply, whether verbally or nonverbally, to 'what they say'.

Unlike Nohia, in Platanos divorce is nowadays more acceptable as a fact of life. Unlike some rural Catholic communities, for example, Lagartera in rural Spain where those who remarry after divorce were refused sacraments and the children of second marriages were considered illegitimate by the Church (Lever 1984: 113), in both villages I studied, divorced people who remarried were more easily accepted by the community. The Greek Orthodox Church does allow an individual to get married up to three times in his/her lifetime and the children from these marriages are recognized as legitimate ones. To quote Ware (1987: 301–2),

> Orthodoxy regards the marriage bond as in principle lifelong and indissoluble, and it condemns the breakdown of marriage as a sin and an evil. But while condemning the sin, the Church still desires to help the sinners and to allow them a second chance. When, therefore, a marriage has entirely ceased to be a reality, the Orthodox Church does not insist on the preservation of a legal fiction. Divorce is seen as an exceptional

but necessary concession to human sin; it is an act of *ikonomia* ('economy' or dispensation) and of *philanthropia* (loving kindness).

Most second and third marriages, however, are between widowers and a woman from another village. The number of widows who remarry is very small indeed compared to that of widowers. From the early 1930s until the late 1980s for example, eight men in Nohia married twice and one three times, whereas only one woman remarried. In Platanos, 19 men and only three women married for the second time and two men married three times. Most widowers do re-marry and this is accepted and justified by the community in terms of a man's inability to take care of himself, his children, if he has any, and the household in general. On the one hand, men need women to look after them and their children; on the other, many local anecdotes portray marriage for men in contradictory terms: both as a yoke and as sweet as honey (Mavrakis 1983: 330–31).

> Vasilio ne lefteria ke i pandria kathena
> ke dialexe poulaki mou, apou ta dyo to ena.
> [Freedom is wonderful and marriage is a yoke
> You may choose my dear one or the other.]
>
> Stous pandremenous i zoi, glykia ne san to meli,
> Ke heronde, os herete o kotsyfas st ambeli.
> [Life for the married ones is as sweet as honey,
> They enjoy it as the blackbird enjoys being at the vineyard.]

Ways in Which Marriage is Arranged

In the old days, the most preferred way of negotiating a marriage between the households of the bride and the groom was through the channel of *proxenio*. *Proxenio* is roughly equivalent to arranged marriage. In the Greek case, 'varying degrees of pressure may be applied, but there is no question of compulsion' (Hirschon 1989: 110). This might have been the case in Yerania in the 1970s, and perhaps in Nohia and Platanos thereafter, but not in the old days. In one of the interviews below, it is clear that when pressure was applied by other family members to a woman, she accepted the arrangement made on her behalf, either because she felt she had no choice, or because she feared that if she did not, she might have been beaten up by her father and/or older brothers.[7] In other words, the awareness of women of the power relations within the family restrained them from going against their parents' wishes. This was a common phenomenon in other parts of Greece as well (see, for example, Handman 1983:

---

7   It was in the brothers' interest for their sisters to marry, because the norm was that the females should marry first.

84; Just 2000: 230). Furthermore, contrary to what was happening in Eressos from as early as the mid-/end nineteenth century where, although marriage proceedings were settled through *proxenio*, both 'women and men had some input into the choice of their mate' (Pavlides and Hesser 1986: 72), in Nohia and Platanos, with a few exceptions, until the mid-1960s, the majority of women did not have any significant input into the choice of their partner. As Just (2000: 228) points out,

> marriage was a weighty matter with consequences not only for the couple themselves, but for their respective families. As such it was unwise to leave its instigation to the accidents of individual infatuation. Both economic standing and the moral reputation of the families from which the perspective bride and groom came had to be reciprocally considered and judged, as did the personal qualities and social prospects of the bride and groom themselves; they also had to be judged by all those who, as a result of the marriage, would thenceforth find themselves related.

At a women's gathering at Katina's house, with women whose ages varied between 26 and 70, it was pointed out to me that Katina's was a representative case of *proxenio* and hence they asked her to narrate her experience to me. This case illustrates the themes discussed above and shows the kind of pressure exercised on young women to marry the man who chose her and was chosen by her father and/or male siblings.

This is the case of Katina as she narrated it:

> I was young. One of my sisters was already married and the other was still very young. It was my turn.[8] One of my brothers and my husband-to-be were close friends and often used to come home together in the evenings. I didn't like Andonis, my husband-to-be; he was getting on my nerves. Anyway, it didn't occur to me that he might be interested in me. Then, one evening, I saw Michalis (his brother) coming over. I didn't think that the visit meant anything; after all, he was working with my father at the time. However, the purpose of his visit was to convey to my father his brother's, Andonis', wish to marry me and the demand that he be given the olive trees at Lagos and Pigadi together with a small parcel of land at Kambos – 40 roots in total.[9] I was neither asked nor allowed to express my opinion … My father replied that he would have to consult his sons before giving me away, and thanked Michalis for honouring our family by asking to marry me. Although my brothers knew that I did not want to marry Andonis, they consented to me marrying him. Finally, the arrangement was made without my consent and celebrations took place without me knowing or participating in them. I didn't want to marry him, I didn't love him. I wanted to join one of my brothers, who at the time was working in Athens. Many times I prayed to the Holy Mary to either make me love him or to make him change

---

8   As in other parts of Greece (see, for example, the work of Papataxiarchis [1988: 68] on Lesbos), in Crete sisters used to marry in order of birth and before brothers.

9   Lagos, Pigadi and Kambos are areas around the village.

his mind about the marriage. I didn't dare tell my parents that I didn't want him; my father would beat me up ... We got married one and a half years later.

As it was confirmed by other villagers, Katina's case was not an exception, but the norm in those days (1953). The only unusual thing was that she did not participate in the celebrations that followed the marital arrangement.

In those days, only a minority of marriages took place without a third party mediating. *Proxenio* often involved a third party (sometimes a relative) acting as an intermediary between the two families, called *proxenitis* if male and *proxenitra* if female. Unlike in other parts of Greece (for example, Lesbos) where this role can be assumed by either sex (Papataxiarchis 1988: 77, 80–81), in Nohia and Platanos this is a man's role. It can be seen as a manifestation of men's role in the public space. As in other parts of Greece, his task is to introduce and aid negotiations between the families concerned, and provide reliable information about potential spouses and their family's reputation, especially if the latter do not live in the same area and the families do not know each other. For the negotiations to be successful *hriazete maestria* (skill is needed). As Papataxiarchis (1988: 77–8) writes,

> The *proxenitis* is obliged to protect and sanction with his ... authority all the positive attributes of the household and the person he ... speaks for. In mediating between the two households he has to assure them of the viability of their potential marriage and to find solutions to the practical problems that arise ... [He] can 'absorb' potential negotiations without harming the honour of the asking party or can guarantee commitments that the two parties themselves would hesitate to undertake.

A famous matchmaker in Nohia (now in his 80s) attributed his fame to the fact that he travelled a lot and hence could bring into contact people from different villages who would not otherwise have had the chance to meet, as well as to the fact that most of the *proxenia* he made turned out to be successful ones. 'Unsuccessful *proxenia* damages the reputation of the *proxenitis*', he said.

Once the negotiations were completed, the bride's father invited the *proxenitis* for dinner and, as I was told by villagers, offered him a suit for his services. In both Platanos and Nohia there were a couple of men who had the reputation of being successful in this task and they were in great demand at times of demographic imbalance, when shortages of prospective brides or grooms made it necessary for parents to look outside the village for suitable partners for their offspring. (Changes in *proxenio* are discussed below.)

The Dowry

As has already been mentioned in this chapter, although the provision of a dowry has been a matter of corporate familial concern, unlike in other parts of Greece (Kenna 1976a: 22; Pavlides and Hesser 1986: 72; Papataxiarchis 1988: 56; Hirschon 1989: 118), in Nohia and Platanos the house *per se* is not part of the bride's dowry because, according to local norms, its provision is the responsibility of the groom and/or his family.[10] The dowry provided by the girl's family did figure in the *proxenio* negotiations; when the agreement was reached – usually the prospective groom asked for particular things, a specific piece of land or amount of olive oil, the *proxenitis* conveyed the message to the bride's father, who along with his sons decided whether to accept or not – a formal contract was signed called *prikosymfono* (meaning 'dowry agreement'), which gave details on the amount and kind of property to be transferred in the form of a dowry (*prika*) on the day of marriage; this could take the form of land, preferably olive trees, olive oil, or cash (in the form of gold sovereigns called *lires chryses*), or sometimes both.[11] If the bride's family was poor, usually her brothers worked to provide for their sister's dowry. This obligation of brothers towards sisters was not peculiar to western Crete (for Epirus, see Campbell 1964: 85; for Euboea, see du Boulay 1974: 235).

Sometimes men preferred to receive a dowry of moveable goods rather than real estate. This is because alienation of non-moveable dowry required the formal notarized consent statement from the wife and the permission of the court (Civil Code sections 1416 and 1417), which means that the husband would have had no direct control over the wife's land. Women, as wives, do not lose their rights over the land, but remain title holders, which could be very important, especially in cases of divorce and also in the decision making process related to passing property to children or selling the property to finance, for example, children's education (both these issues will be discussed below). Other reasons included the cost related to the need to hire someone to look after the property, which was the case when the man came from another village.

The groom was given his share of his parents' joint estate on the day of marriage; there was usually a balance between the wealth that the bride's family contributed and what the groom was given at marriage. For example, in Katina's case, her family contributed to the marriage around 50 olive trees in total, and the groom's father gave him 30 olive trees. Unlike Vasilika and the Sarakatsani where the division of the patrimony took place long after the father's death (Friedl 1964: 60–64; Campbell 1964: 82), the situation in Nohia and Platanos resembled that found by Bialor (1976: 112) in his study of a village on the Gulf of Corinth. However, in Nohia and Platanos when sons and daughters marry they receive their share not only from the patrimony, but also

---

10   Campbell (1964: 18) has noted that 'between the mainland and some of the islands there are important differences in inheritance practices and residence patterns'. An investigation of possible reasons for this variation is beyond the scope of this book.

11   Unlike women in Nohia and Platanos, women in Amouliani, a village in Chalkidiki (northern Greece) studied by Salamone and Stanton (1986: 108), were never provided with cash dowries.

from the property brought into marriage by their mother. Papataxiarchis (1988: 55) maintains that in Lesbos, sons inherit the paternal property post mortem, whereas daughters inherit the maternal property at marriage. He also claims that this relates to the pattern of name transfer, where the first born grandson is named after his father's father and the first-born daughter after her mother's mother. This pattern has also been noticed by Kenna (1976a: 25) on the island of Anafi. Whether these patterns are true for Nohia and Platanos needs to be researched; at the time of fieldwork it was rather difficult to do so, as the two different *hypothicofilakia* (property registry offices), the one in Kastelli for Platanos and the one in Kolymbari for Nohia, kept the records of land and property sales and transfers of all villages and villagers in the area according to alphabetical order of surname and did not file records separately for each village. So, to trace the history of a piece of land through these records would have been extremely difficult and time consuming, given that many people owning property and land have the same surname and/or forename.

The parents help their son financially – and sometimes contribute personal labour too – to build his house. As already mentioned, it is difficult for newly weds to find a house or flat to rent as there are none in either village. Because building a house often takes a long time, the process usually starts long before the young man decides to get married. For example, Koula and Georgos, who live in Nohia, have helped their eldest son Takis (single in his early 30s at the time of fieldwork) to build a house in the village, whereas their younger son Petros. who now lives with his wife on the island of Chios, received an equivalent amount in the form of education expenses paid by his parents and movable property; both sons have olive trees in the village.

The parents, of course, keep some property to live on, which is divided equally among the children when their father dies. Contrary to the situation on Lesbos (Papataxiarchis 1988: 55), in Nohia and Platanos *primogeniturial* tendencies are rare. Moreover, according to the villagers' accounts, there is a scarcity of brides in the marriage market linked with female exogamy; hence, a situation where brothers will withdraw from their inheritance claims in order for the family to be able to secure a good marriage for the sisters, has not arisen.

In both Nohia and Platanos, it is the responsibility of the girl's family to provide the furnishings of the house and clothes as part of the dowry. This female-produced dowry, called *ta prikia*, is distinguished by the village women from *prika* (that is the land, olive trees, cash, etc.); 'alla ta prikia ke appi i prika' (*prika* and *prikia* are not the same thing), one often hears women saying. The *prikia*[12] consists of pieces of furniture, kitchen utensils, electric appliances, two or three dozen items of white, 'over-embroidered' as some women said, underwear, though 'nowadays, young girls wear them as dresses'. Also, they spend hours and hours embroidering bedsheets and pillowcases – at least a dozen

---

12 The word *rouha*, used in other parts of Greece (for example, in Chalkidiki [Salamone and Stanton 1986 :106–13]), is not used in Nohia and Platanos.

of them were required – a mosquito net and as many tablecloths as possible and weaving various items on the loom. But the women are most proud of the so-called *patanies*; these were old blankets, some inherited from grandmothers and others woven on the loom by the brides themselves or their mothers, which were hung in the house for decoration, in such a way that everyone could see them. So, some of the *prikia* were decorative items. *Prikia* are seen by Salamone and Staton (1986: 107) as a key element in the socialization of young women as future *nikokyres* (housewives, mistresses of the house). They write:

> Mother and daughter enter into a prolonged and intimate relationship through which the required virtues of household management, frugality, technical skills, and proper wifely demeanour are transferred from one generation to the next.

The accumulation of *prikia* has always been an important customary practice in Crete.

Today, although the embroidered and handwoven items produced by women in the past are still highly valued and admired, women's crafts have changed in style in an attempt to be more fashionable and practical. The white cotton cloth (calico) used in the past has been replaced by synthetic multicoloured cloths which require minimal ironing; very few women now weave *patanies* for their daughters. Indeed, most of the embroidered items, whether these are sheets, pillowcases or tablecloths, are bought in the market. For those who can afford it, there are a few women in nearby villages and towns who produce and sell hand-made embroidered items to special customers who place their orders well in advance. For those who cannot afford these prices, machine-made embroideries are offered in the market. A young woman from Platanos has a shop of this kind in Kastelli. She commented on these changes as follows:

> Today most women in Platanos work in the greenhouses; they come home late, tired and have to take care of the children and on top of that iron clothes, clean the house and cook. The hand-make tablecloths and sheets need care; most require to be washed by hand, for example. Nobody has time for such things. We all use modern, practical items which are machine washed and keep one or two hand-made ones for special occasions, like for example my husband's name day, Christmas, Easter and the like.

The changed economic conditions and lifestyles are seen as a reason why hand-made goods have been replaced by machine-made ones, which are of lower quality. This attitude applies to Nohia too, despite the commercial production of handcrafts analysed earlier in this book. For example, Koula, a craftswoman herself, and Georgos have already bought their daughter's *prikia*. Unlike Amouliani in Chalkidiki where men are not involved in the purchase of *prikia* (Salamone and Stanton 1986: 110), in Nohia and Platanos most decisions about these purchases were taken by both parents, regardless of their respective financial contributions. *Prikia* range from electrical appliances, such as a washing machine and a food processor, to numerous kitchen utensils, bath towels, bedsheets and tablecloths. The latter are almost all bought in the big stores in Athens and Chania. When I asked Koula why she is not giving her daughter any hand-made ones, she replied: 'life has changed, young people today prefer to have practical things' and added that her daughter would not have time to look after them properly. 'I have bought many things for her – *horis prikia gamos then ginete* (a marriage cannot take place without *prikia*). I will give her a couple of hand-made items that I have from my wedding; I never use them anymore, and I am sure she won't either, because it's too much work to hand wash and iron them ....' Similar views to the ones held by Koula were expressed by young and older women in the village. However, similar to the situation in Amouliani studied by Salamone and Stanton (1986: 111), the trend towards the accumulation of store-bought *prikia* has not diminished their importance – it has just changed its focus.[13]

Some older women commented that in the past, hand-work and implicitly domestic skills were a status symbol, exhibited when the *prikia* are shown publicly a few days before the marriage at the bride's house. As Archondoula, a woman in her seventies, commented:

> Times have changed. Mothers have no longer the time to embroider items for their daughters' *prikia*. In their spare time, they do make a couple of items, but not the amount of things I prepared for my daughters. My grandaughter Archondoula is engaged to be married sometime next year. Although her mother will give her some of the things I passed on to her, *gia to kalo* (for good luck), most of the things have been purchased in Athens. My grandaughter told her mother that she prefers 'modern things'. When I was young, a 'good exhibition of *prikia*' consisted of many hand made, heavily embroidered items. Today, it has to include as many electrical appliances as possible. This is what is in fashion; this is what young people prefer.

There are still items among the *prikia* which show the skills of the mother of the bride. Whether this will continue to be the case remains to be seen, as girls nowadays, instead of learning technical skills from their mothers, spend their free time socializing with their peers. Attitudes governing social and sexual behaviour (see next chapter) have been undergoing changes which influence the way young women spend their free time.

---

13   The change in the content of *prikia* has also been noticed by Papataxiarchis (1988: 61) in his research on Lesbos.

Further Indications of Change

Since the late 1960s–early 1970s, attitudes towards both the institution of *proxenio* and of dowry have dramatically changed in both villages. The way Katina's two daughters got married illustrates this. One of her daughters did marry through *proxenio*, but the difference between Katina's and her daughter's *proxenio* was, as she said, that in the case of the daughter, the groom himself came and asked the parents' permission to marry the girl. Nor did the groom ask for a dowry as Katina's husband had done.

> The groom, my son-in-law, came and asked for the bride himself. He didn't ask me what I have, what I offer … When Elefteria got married, things had already started to change. At that time, people weren't asking for dowries, estates and olive oil.

Katina's tone of voice and her comments show that she thought positively about these changes. The other women who were present when this conversation took place, during a little gathering for coffee at Katina's house – seven in number, ranging from 26 to 70 years of age – also commented favourably on these changes, as if they brought relief to their lives as parents. Irrespective of age, they regarded these alterations in customs as a 'normal progress', something that has come in the nick of time. Unlike in the past, the bride herself had to decide whether to marry the man or not. Most parents no longer took the risk of imposing spouses of their choice on their children. One might argue that through the *proxenitis* who made the acquaintance, the groom could easily get information about the bride's parents' estate. However, there is always the element of uncertainty and risk, in that the father may decide to pass only a small part of his estate to his daughter at the time of her marriage. After all, it was the parents who now decided what to give to their daughter, as opposed to what was the case in the past (see, for example, in Katina's case which was discussed earlier in this chapter), where the groom and his parents were the ones who asked for a specific amount in cash or in kind (olive oil) or a piece of land to be given to the couple. If the father loses or sells everything he has before he dies, the couple will end up inheriting nothing from the wife's kin. Although this rarely happens, one cannot completely rule the risk out. As for Katina's second daughter, she fell in love with someone from a nearby village and got married.

A similar change in customary practice surrounding marriage was recounted to me by Androniki, a woman in her mid-40s, married with two children, living in Platanos, owner of a grocery shop and of greenhouses. It was in the early 1950s, when her father announced one day that she was to marry Andonis, a man from Platanos who had recently come back from Germany. Although she did not like him at first, she agreed with her father's decision. However, her sister, a few years younger than Androniki, went to Athens to work. There she fell in love with someone and wanted to marry him, which she did, but only after long disputes with the father who had promised her to someone else. The youngest sister of all, Mary, 14 years younger than Androniki, still lives in Platanos. Although in her late 20s during the time of fieldwork, she was still unmarried. She runs the father's kebab taverna (*souvlatsithiko*) which, while I was there, was converted into a modern cafeteria; she is also very active in the local Youth Association, has many friends (men and women), is free to socialize with them and joke with tourists. She is respected by all villagers. 'Mary is a very nice women; she isn't frivolous', I heard people saying. When I visited Platanos in the new millennium I found Mary married; 'we fell in love', she said. So by then, love had become the only acceptable motivation for marriage amongst the young generation. This change in attitudes can be attributed to the economic affluence in the village since the introduction of greenhouses and susceptibility to the new ideas brought to Platanos by the mass media and by seasonal workers, traders, tourists, migrants who come every year to the village to harvest their olives and young villagers who study in the cities and visit their parents during the vacations. The same holds true, to some extent, for Nohia. However, since the latter is an ageing village, less influenced than Platanos by human traffic, ideas about women's role and behaviour in the family and in the community have not changed as much as they have in Platanos. Certainly, a woman like Mary would not have been easily accepted in Nohia. Contrary to the situation in Nohia, the emphasis in Platanos has shifted away from a woman's destiny (*proorismos*) and sole fulfilment being to 'get married so that you can have a family'. Although one might argue that this is always the purpose of marriage, the difference is that being single had, by the mid-1980s, become an acceptable alternative among the young population of Platanos. However, this is not to say the unmarried are not subjected to pressure to marry (mainly psychological) from the older generation. Nevertheless, Nohia is, in this respect, a contrast to Skamnia, a village on the island of Lesbos where Papataxiarchis (1988: 63) reports,

> for a woman to escape her 'destiny' is either a disgrace for the natal household and a mark of low status or is often attributed to some deficiency in the woman.

In Platanos, I never heard anyone criticizing any of the unmarried women who live in the village. They are expected, however, to take upon themselves the responsibility of looking after the elderly if all the other siblings are married (see below). Contrary to what was happening in the past, whereas in Lesbos, women who remained unmarried were stigmatized as insane, hysterical or were labelled as *gerontokores*[14] (spinsters), today, perhaps because most are either actively involved in the greenhouse business and/or are active in the local youth and

---

14   The equivalent term to 'spinster' for a man is *bekiaris*. Although the term is extensively used in other parts of Greece, I have never heard it in western Crete. Instead, the word *gerondopallikaro*, meaning 'old unmarried fellow' – which is a milder term – is used.

women's associations, most speak of them with admiration. Occasionally one can hear people trying to explain the single women's unmarried state using the graphic phrase *then tsi hamogelase i tyhi* (fate didn't smile at her). That is, they attribute the fact that a woman has remained single not to a choice rationally made by the person, but to fate. When asked why they did not get married, they usually reply, *then etyhe* (it didn't happen). During the time of fieldwork, I did not hear anyone say that Mary did not marry because she did not want to. Nevertheless, feelings held in the past that a 'bad husband is better than no husband' are no longer expressed in either village.

In February 1983, under the 1329/1983 law passed when the PASOK party was in government, the institution of dowry was officially abolished. This has lifted the burden placed on male children – especially those from relatively poor households – to provide for the dowries of the females. As mentioned earlier, in the past, some brothers had to work for their sisters' dowries and wait till all sisters got married before marrying themselves. Each sister waited her turn. First, the eldest was promoted (she would appear when guests were around, whereas the others were kept more secluded), then the second, and so on. However, even now that the institution of dowry has officially been abolished, people in Nohia and Platanos still give children property when they marry 'to assist them in their new start in life', as they say. This property is given to them as a 'gift', in the form of the so called, *goniki parohi* (parental allowance); depending on the agreement, the children receive the title-deeds of the property assigned to them either before, or after the parents die. That is, the parents have the option of keeping the right to use the property (for example, either live in or rent a house) until they die, but cannot sell it, since this has been assigned to the children. Under this agreement, the children have *psili kiriotita* (a limited ownership) over this property. This way of passing property from one generation to the other is nowadays preferred because it is the cheapest way of doing this. To be more specific, from the early 1980s onwards, when a new family law was introduced, a new tax scale was introduced, whereby for property transferred to the new generation under the *goniki parohi* system valued up to 5 million drachmas, one pays half of the taxes s/he would have to pay if the property was transferred through inheritance; if the value of the property exceeds the above amount, then for the exceeding amount one pays taxes equal to those of inheritance (law 1473/84). To give an example, in 1987–1988 a child in Nohia inherited an estate the value of which was 5,530,000 drachmas. If the property had not been transferred before the parent's death under the so-called *goniki parohi* to his name, he would have had to pay in tax 866,600 drachmas. But because the parents had transferred the property to the child under the *goniki parohi* system, he paid only around 400,000 drachmas for the initial five million and another 41,200 drachmas for the rest. That is, he saved around 425,000 drachmas. So the *prika* and the necessity to supply it in order to marry a daughter, has lost its rigidity and been replaced by gift-giving in form of *goniki parohi*, where, the motivation lay in the moral and sentimental concern for the newly weds to do well and to be seen to do well. But, as Just (2000: 225) argues the dowry 'has been placed in a morally ambivalent area where it could be both a shame to ask for one, and a shame not to offer one'.

Girls who marry men from Athens or other big cities are likely to bring to marriage a flat, regarded nowadays as an essential precondition for marriage; this is imposed by the current economic concerns (high rents, high unemployment), rather than an institution like the dowry.

Friedl (1986a) has argued that the ability of women to bring land into the household as part of their dowry and to maintain control of this land, which cannot be alienated by their husbands without their consent or, in some areas, the consent of the wife's family, means that women have economic power whose significance cannot be underestimated in a social structure where land is very important for supplying the family with food and cash. A factor which is obscured by Friedl's analysis is the psychological pressure men might exercise over women in order to sell the land or put profits from the annual produce of that land in the family budget. If in practice this does take place, one may wonder what the effects of the abolition of this institution on the women's position might be. However, as Greger (1985: 139–40) points out in her writings on women in a Cretan mountain village Magoulas,

> Marriage and dowry negotiations were never conducted in legal terms, but in honour terms; that is, by oral agreement between groups which were fully conscious of each other's reputation. The commitments would be enforced by the honour ethic and by the need to maintain reputation in the local *kosmos* ... such practical, oral agreements – with no thought of what the law orders, nor of ever needing to turn for help to the law – continue to hold sway ...

Today, in both Nohia and Platanos, parents continue to pass on property to the younger generation after having given their word of honour that they will do so. We now turn our attention to the way and the reasons why this is done.

Goals of Marriage and Family Life

In the past, the goal of marriage was, and in many cases continues to be, to have children and place them successfully in society, rather than romance *per se*. However, this is not to say that romance before marriage was never present; in some cases, as for example in the case of Koula and Georgos mentioned earlier on in this chapter, romance did blossom. This presence of romance today seems to be more common in Platanos, where there seem to be more opportunities for young people to meet socially without the presence of the older generation, than in Nohia, where many (but not all) marriages are arranged ones. As is the case of families amongst artisan and worker families researched by Cavounidis (1985) in the community of Nea Ionia in the Greater Athens area, in Nohia and

Platanos too, 'bearing children does not signify the attainment of a goal; it is the beginning of a long struggle for intergenerational social mobility ...' (ibid.: 79). Companionship in the sense of partnership in generating and allocating household resources is highly valued.

The criteria employed for selecting a spouse are for the latter to be industrious and to have material resources at their command. Having a white-collar job in a state institution in Chania or Kastelli is seen as a great asset. The ultimate wish of parents was to achieve intergenerational social mobility through occupational mobility via education attainment and the provision of residential and other property. Similar parental aspirations seem to have existed in artisan and worker households in the Athenian suburb of Nea Ionia. Cavounidis (ibid.) writes:

> It is with reference to these goals ... that men and women ... shape their strategies of fertility, production and consumption, as well as the strategies they employ in their intergenerational relations – their conjugal relations, parental relations and their relations with kin and others outside the household.

Parents do not want their children to become farmers like them, but aspire for them to have white-collar occupations and a standard of living higher than the one they themselves knew when they were young. As Eftychia said: 'I don't want my daughters to grow up and dirty their hands with soil, as I do. That's why I pay for private tuition of Maths and English.' However, the realization of such aspirations is costly; it means instruction at private institutions, which will help the child improve their marks at school (often this involved travelling daily to Kastelli and/or Chania) and will prepare secondary school students to do well in subjects important for entry into university. If successful, parents finance the child's living expenses, and if they attend a university in a town where the parents have no relatives or friends the child can stay with, accommodation expenses bear heavily on them. If the child is not successful, the parents finance training at a private vocational institute. As Cavounidis (ibid.: 83) argues, 'the dimensions of the psychological injuries caused by the constant parental pressure on Greek youth for upward occupational mobility they cannot always achieve are largely uncharted'. Contrary to Cavounidis' findings regarding children in artisan and working households in Nea Ionia, where children are not encouraged to take on part-time work while studying in order to devote all their energy to study (ibid.: 124), as I have shown earlier on in this book, children in Platanos are expected to help in the greenhouses during weekends and school vacations. If the child (usually a boy) decides to work elsewhere, this is done on his own initiative and the money he earns does not usually go to the general household fund, but is spent as the child pleases. Unlike boys, girls tend to save a fraction of their earnings for their *prikia*.

Parents devote much energy in protecting their children from what they consider to be *kakes parees* (bad companions) who might lead them astray.

They are anxious about what will happen when the child goes to study in a big urban town where, as the local government's secretary in Platanos – whose son went to study in a vocational school in Athens while I was staying in the village – said, 'life is beset with perils'. He added, 'a child from a village can be easily led astray'.

Aspirations are adjusted downwards if and when it becomes apparent that the child will not win a place at university or a private vocational institute; then, agricultural work is seen as a 'fate' for the boy, who will begin work on the family's land or, if the father is also an artisan, in his workshop, which the son will eventually take over. If this happens, families are obliged to invest in the business and render it viable. This is the case with Maria, for example, whose three sons did not get good marks at school. She decided to invest and also hopes that her sons will receive a subsidy geared towards encouraging young people to remain and work in rural areas, which will help them to modernize the existing greenhouses even more, or to erect new ones. Afroditi's son Babis is a similar case: his father is a carpenter and has an artisan workshop in Nohia. When it became obvious that Babis' grades at school were not good enough to secure him a place either at university or in the lower level of public tertiary education (formerly KATEE, now TEI), he joined his father in the workshop, which he is expected to inherit. As Afroditi said, 'since he started working there, we have invested money and tried to expand the business, so as to secure a future for Babis'. So the decision as to whether the child is going into the family business or not has an effect on the developmental cycle of the enterprise. Another example is that of Mary; her parents had a small *souvlatsidiko* (kebab house) in Platanos, which would have closed down. However, as soon as Mary expressed her intention to run the business, they invested in it and transformed it into a modern cafeteria with plastic chairs and tables (see Figures 6.1 and 6.2). It even changed its menu: it no longer serves kebabs but only sweets, sandwiches and soft drinks. There are exceptions of course, as is the case with the *cafeneion* (coffee shop) Lambros' parents have in Nohia. Although his future lies there, they refuse to invest any money, because, as they say, 'the village is nowadays like a geriatric institution; in 20 years time, there will be no one left in the village to use the *cafeneion*'. Girls are encouraged to enter university too. However, if they are unsuccessful, most parents encourage them to stay at home. There are exceptions, of course: one such case is that of Thespina, who became a hairdresser in Kastelli.

The same ideas were shared by some offspring, mainly those who were good students; they made it clear that they did not want to do what their parents did. However, the ones that did not make it to university or any other similar institution pointed to the difficulties that graduates are faced with nowadays, in terms of finding a job. As I was informed by Koula's eldest son,

> my brother Petros, despite his lyceum (secondary school) diploma and additional training in vocational skills and a foreign language, cannot find a white-collar job in

Figure 6.1   Traditional *cafeneion*

Figure 6.2   Modern cafeteria

the public sector; our connections (*mesa*) did not seem to work; he had to temporarily take a job in a private firm, a fact that neither we nor he are happy with, because there is no security in the private sector; they can give him the sack any time they want. In the public sector on the other hand, you have peace of mind (*ehis to kefali sou isycho*) that you won't lose your job.

The successful placement of children means provision of education and of residential property at the time of marriage. To achieve these aims, parents work long hours; rather than this being a source of conflict and complaint, it is accepted and praised by spouses in both handcraft households and in households whose members are involved in the production of olives and in market gardening. Both men and women work towards this goal. As already shown in this book, most women's earnings from handcrafts are not spent so much on clothing or conveniences to aid them in domestic work (although some money has been used to purchase a washing machine, TV or video) as on helping towards the heavy expenditure required to finance children's education, improvements on property held at marriage and the construction of dwellings. Via these activities, consumption is deferred to the next generation. As in Nea Ionia, parents in Nohia and Platanos deny themselves new clothing, eating out etc., so as to conserve resources for the fulfilment of their goals, and so that their children can indulge in the consumption of relatively expensive clothing and footwear bearing on them brand names like Lee, Lacoste, Nike, Fila and Timberland. As Cavounides (1985: 87) writes, '[parents] ... do not want their children to lag behind peers in the contest for status consumption'.

This over-consumption has also been noted by Zaharopoulos (1985: 223–4) in his research on the impact of the penetration of foreign mass communications on the culture of a rural community, Efyra, in western Peloponnesos. He argues that the exposure of people living in rural areas to advertising messages via television, radio, the press, placards and posters in the streets and the fact that 60 per cent of the advertised items on television (and I would add to that the internet) are foreign, indicate the huge pressure exerted on the Greek public to adopt foreign products.[15] He also mentions that Greek products are given foreign names – few use Greek words in Latin characters. He writes (ibid.: 225–6):

> The use of foreign names on products sold in Greece, and particularly of Greek products, is not only a means of identification but also part of a broader marketing system, which attempts to market products and services in a way which their use implies a certain status ... most products advertised on Greek television are portrayed as symbols of status ... Competition has historically been a major part of everyday living between Greek families, and status and prestige is a major part of such competition.

---

15   This information derives from a content analysis of television advertising carried out by Zaharopoulos during a five-week period in Efyra in 1984.

He argues that through advertising, it is not only the product that is promoted, but also a lifestyle.

Another factor encouraging the consumption of such products at the village level is the visits of villagers' relatives from urban areas or from abroad during *inter alia* the olive harvest, Christmas, Easter, summer vacations, or when elections take place. Such visits are a channel for the transmission of certain aspects of metropolitan culture to the villagers. According to Zaharopoulos (ibid.: 135), the younger the villager, the greater this influence seems to be. Visitors show off their acquisitions (clothes, cars and other movable luxury goods, including laptops) which symbolize their wealth in the city or abroad, to local people, who in turn compete for prestige by trying to acquire prestigious goods. Consumption of such products is also encouraged by what summer tourists wear. The latter are often asked by young people in rural areas whom they befriended during their holidays to send them as a 'souvenir' a jumper or a t-shirt with a fancy trademark printed on the front or the back. As Kostis, a young man from Platanos who has two greenhouses and, with the help of his mother runs a small cafeteria near the seaside, said to me, 'I asked a tourist woman to send me a t-shirt from Germany. I like it because it is unique, you'll see no one here wearing the same'. When they do not receive the promised 'gift' they are disappointed. It seems that 'a good time' creates the obligation on behalf of the tourist to send or bring back the following year something that would remind the villagers of the time they spent together.

Both men and women in the villages expressed the importance of the wife's work in income-generating activities and the need to make sacrifices for the accomplishment of the above mentioned aims. The reasons are summed up by Eftychia: 'because we want to, it is our duty as parents to do so and we will continue to work hard as long as this is needed by the family, that is until the children settle down.' And she continued: 'when the children get married and enter the labour force, then we will either stop or continue to work for fewer hours, depending on whether we'll be in good health or not.' So the entry of children in the labour force is not automatically followed by the parents' withdrawal from it. There are also other factors, such as the state of parents' health, the kind of work they do, their age and so on, that seem to influence their decision to quit working.

Similarly to Cavounidis' (1985: 246) findings in relation to the households of artisans and workers in Nea Ionia, in Nohia and Platanos the resources allocated by parents towards the education of children and to provide them with a dwelling appear to play a very important role in securing children's compliance with parental wishes. Restrictions placed on children vary by age and sex as well as by the different economic and social circumstances encountered in different villages. In both Nohia and Platanos, few boys older than 16 are restricted as to their outings. Girls in Nohia tend to be restricted; this is what happens to Koula's daughter who studies in Athens and comes home on vacations. In Platanos most daughters older than 19 are more restricted in their outings than the boys of a similar age; they can socialize with peers, provided that they do not offend the local norms and values. In addition, although in Nohia girls are restricted as far as their association with boys is concerned, in Platanos things are easier; however, this gives rise to girls not informing parents of the presence of boys on outings so that parents will not veto them. Similarly, boys do not inform parents of the presence of foreign women, or about drinking and gambling.

Disagreements and arguments often arise between parents and children about their outings, the people they socialize with, where they go and so on. Children believe that parents do not understand them and that they have different ideas about relations between boys and girls. As Mary, Androniki's daughter, said, 'my parents are not educated. Their ideas about relations between boys and girls are outdated. Things have changed, but they do not seem to understand this. As a result, we always quarrel. All they say to me is "think of the sacrifices we have made for you and your brother" ... this is how they express their love and devotion ...'. According to Cavounidis (1985: 87), this parental sacrifice gives meaning, pride and satisfaction to the lives of the parents. 'We work for our children' (*doulevoume giu ta puedia mas*), parents in Nohia and Platanos used to say to me with *kamari* (pride). So, the family's goals in relation to the children's future served as a goal for hard work. This is evident in the case of Georgos and Koula, for example, where, although their children are now adults and capable of earning a living themselves, both still work for long hours, he in his blacksmith's shop and she producing handcrafts, not because they are facing economic difficulties but, as they both said, 'to assist the kids to settle down' (*gia na taktopoiisoume ta pedia mas*).

Often parents use the sacrifices they make for the children as 'a powerful weapon' to control them. It is not uncommon to hear parents screaming at children: 'how do you dare behave like this when you know the sacrifices we have made for you.' As Cavounidis (1985: 99, 249) mentions, and as has been confirmed to me by many young people in Nohia and Platanos, this inculcates 'a deep sense of obligation in ... children'. This, in turn, makes children comply with parents' wishes, despite the fact that they may disagree. When I asked a young woman, who at the time was spending her summer holidays in her parents' home in Nohia, why, despite her parents' disagreement, she did not go out with friends more often, she replied that she could not act against their wishes, not after all the struggles they had undertaken for her welfare. Another reason she gave was that she did not see it as being worth stirring up gossip among the villagers, a thing that would have hurt her parents deeply. It must be noted here that, although the first reason was often cited by youngsters in Platanos, the second was less often mentioned; one reason for this might be the fact that with few exceptions, going out with friends in Platanos is common and seems to be accepted by the older and the younger generations alike.

One of the 'sacrifices' parents make or strategies they follow in order to be able to fulfil the goals mentioned above, is to limit the family size.

Family Size

The size of the nuclear family in Nohia and Platanos has not undergone significant changes since the 1940s. This is a phenomenon mentioned by Kousis (1984: 157) too, in relation to the development of tourism in Drethia (in north-eastern Crete). From the local archives (and in particular from the Population Register Book) it is evident that prior to 1930, families had more than four or five children. The reason for this was first, the high infant mortality rate due to tuberculosis, typhoid and premature birth and. second, the need for labour hands to help parents in the field and housework.

From the local archives it is evident that after World War II, the average number of children born per nuclear family in Platanos and in Nohia was two, in the 1960s it was two in Platanos and three in Nohia and in the 1970s two in both villages. Migration during this period might have affected the number of children per family. Nowadays it seems that most couples have on average one child. *'Ta paedia simera ehoun apetisis'* (children today are hard to please) parents used to say to me. 'We can't afford more children'.

A number of methods are employed in order to control the family size. Apart from a study by Arnold (1985) on childbirth among rural Cretan women, there are no written records on methods of birth control. In order to analyse this one has to depend on information volunteered by local people. Although abortion was, and still is, one of the most popular methods of birth control in Greece, it was only in 1986 (ten years after it was first demanded by Greek feminist groups) that abortions were legalized[16] and the related expenses covered by national insurance schemes. Up to then, it is estimated that around 300,000 (Avdela undated: 9) were illegally performed every year in Greek hospitals and clinics.[17] Although used as a backup measure, the most commonly used contraceptives, at least in the community studies by Arnold (1985), were coitus interruptus and condoms. She argues that the information women, and sometimes even medical students and midwives, have on birth control methods is scant and inaccurate. She writes (ibid.: 109–12):

---

16   All political parties voted in favour of the pro-abortion law.

17   Abortions were illegal until the early 1980s: Law 1492, passed in 1950, governing abortion stated that unless the woman's life was in danger, or a girl younger than 15 had been seduced, women who had an abortion and those who performed it faced imprisonment. From 1978 onwards it was legal within the first 20 weeks of pregnancy if the foetus was to be born deformed, or in order to preserve the woman's mental health. Despite this, abortions were widely performed. Although one could buy the contraceptive pill from the local chemist without a prescription, doctors, who made money from abortions, saw that modern birth control methods remained almost unknown (Avdela undated: 9). Midwives could be imprisoned for performing abortions but carried on doing them; few physicians were taken to court for the same action and they easily got away with it by paying a relatively small fine (Arnold 1985: 124).

During one informant's third caesarean section, she had her fallopian tubes tied. She explained that this can be done only during a caesarean, and that 'they can open them again'. Prophylactics are put on at the last minute. Diaphragms are rare, but when they are inserted without spermaticide cream ... Medical personnel also are not well-informed. One physician measured a woman who requested a diaphragm by inserting his fingers in the vagina and feeling around; then he guessed the size ... midwives had not heard of the diaphragm or the IUD ... Two women said that one could have a small machine inserted, that runs on batteries which must be replaced every six months. Another woman reported that a tablet could be inserted on the third day after menstruation and that this can stay in for three years ... Several informants gave 'turning the uterus inside out' as a method of birth control ... A number of women stated that there are injections which prevent pregnancy ... The rhythm method of birth control is misunderstood by most rural women ... Thus sexual intercourse is avoided near or during a woman's monthly period and engaged in freely at other times of the monthly cycle ... [which] fits well with their view of menstruation being polluting.

The local doctor and midwife, both in Nohia and in Platanos, stated that the most common method of birth control was condoms, which could be purchased even from kiosks. However, these are used by men and many women complained that their husbands did not want to use them. Some women take the pill, which can be purchased from the local chemist 'for regulation of the cycle', as they said, but most avoided it because they believed it could cause cancer. They added,

few women ask for information about birth control methods. Most are ashamed to talk about these things. Most of the time, they mix them with other pills. Unmarried women never discuss these matters with us. They prefer to go to Chania or even Athens to find out about such things where they can hide in the anonymity that cities provide. But I think that they know more than older women. If these methods fail, and they often do, they have an abortion. They rely heavily on it. Most keep it secret. You know, the Church and everything.

As Ware (1987: 302) argues, although the Greek Orthodox Church discourages the use of contraceptives, and 'some bishops and theologians altogether condemn the employment of such methods', others 'urge that the question is best left to the discretion of each individual couple'.

Many women think of abortion as being a sin. The Church is against abortion, as was the state until 1986 when, as mentioned above, abortion was made legal. Yet physicians performed them and women had them and the Church and the state knew all about it. Why do Greek women rely so heavily on abortions? According to Arnold:

A Greek woman's whole purpose in being is to produce children. The mother is 'idealised and considered holy' ... By asking for birth control information, it is as if the woman is explicitly denigrating the only thing that gives her status and power: motherhood. The necessity to repeatedly seeking abortions, however, appears more as a statement proving a woman's great fertility and therefore her potential motherhood. Getting an abortion is less embarrassing than requesting birth control. Physicians reinforce this attitude. (Arnold 1985: 127–8)

Arnold also argues that the reason is connected, on the one hand, to the 'honour-shame' value system (see Chapter 7 on sex and fun), whereby people may do anything they wish as long as they are discreet and, on the other, the fact that 'the official concept of "sin" (*amartia*) is weak as a means of social control' (ibid.: 125). Using Herzfeld's (1985: 232–58) two concepts of sin, the 'eccleciastical' and the 'social', she explains that, although to have an abortion is an ecclesiastical sin, the social sin of not being able to adequately provide for one's children is of more immediate concern for Cretans.

Some women have stated that abortion may lead to fertility problems. Sterility is viewed as a problem which lies with the woman. To be sterile in Greece is a stigma and is often regarded as a legitimate cause of divorce. Regardless of her financial situation, a woman will seek medical treatment and/or make a pilgrimage to holy places such as the Panayia in Tinos, Agios Gerasimos in Kefallonia, Agios Spyridon in Corfu, to name a few, and make *tamata* – this word refers to 'both the act (the vow and its fulfilment) and to objects that have been vowed (which may also be called offerings – *afyeromata*)' (Dubisch 1990: 138).

As I shall show later on in this book, the women's association in Platanos has invited people to talk about available methods of contraception; as a woman in her late 20s said, 'many young women had problems with abortions and they now can't have any children'.

If a woman decides to have a child, she knows that she will go to Chania or Athens to deliver it. Until the 1960s most women used to deliver their babies at home, with the help of the local *mami* (midwife); as a result many women used to die in childbirth and hence, since the 1960s most babies are born either in private clinics or in maternity hospitals in the city, because 'it is safer this way'. Husbands are, in most cases, not allowed in the labour room and even if they were, many said they would not attend because this would damage the sexual life of the couple. Women in both Nohia and Platanos, as well as in other parts of Crete (Arnold 1985: 76, 78), thought of the idea of men being present when they gave birth as being 'revolting' and many doctors were against husbands being present during birth. As Arnold (ibid.: 160) writes,

birth is ... [seen as] a polluting and dirty experience. One physician was horrified when a young Greek woman from Polis wanted her husband (a foreigner) present during birth. He told her that after her husband saw her in such 'filth', he would never sexually desire her again. The doctor warned her that every time her husband approached her, he will remember the dirtiness of her body and be repulsed.

A woman, who for the first 40 days after the birth is called *lehona*, has to stay at home for this time. It is believed that if she visits a house while she is *lehona*, she brings bad luck to it. She is also seen as polluting, perhaps because she is bleeding after the birth. A *lehona* is not allowed to go out of the house for 40 days, until she and the child go to the church and receive a blessing. A menstruating woman in Greece is seen as polluting and dirty, and is not allowed to attend the church. She is also not allowed to bathe or wash her hair during this time, because this is thought to cause sterility, a belief reinforced by many physicians who advise women not to swim while menstruating. Younger women were trying to break with this tradition and even swam in the summer while they were menstruating. Those who did not, gave as a reason the fact that they would have had to wear a tampon to do so, which might make the mother wonder about her daughter's virginity. However, because of economic necessity, many women broke this tradition and went to the fields, taking the baby with them, because they had no one to leave them with. As Koula, a woman in her early 50s, married in Nohia, said: 'All my children were brought up under the trees; I used to place the cradle underneath a tree; whenever the baby cried, I changed it, swaddled it and breast-fed it.' Babies were swaddled (that is, wrapped in a cloth) for up to five months, because it was believed that this helped the bones to grow straight. It was also believed that in this way, the risks of hurting the baby were minimized and that babies slept better if swaddled (Arnold 1985: 159–61). 'Sometimes, the grandmothers used to look after the babies. But I had no one. My mother had died when I was a child and my mother-in-law was herself at the fields', Koula added. The role of grandparents was very important, especially in Platanos before the child care unit was built. When the elderly helped, they expected the kindness to be reciprocated.

Family Obligations towards the Elderly and the Infirm

Having looked earlier on in this chapter at the types of support given by parents to children, we will now turn our attention to the support given by children to parents, and in particular, personal care.

Kousis (1984: 167) found that in Drethia, a village of eastern Crete, sociability patterns had changed since the development of mass tourism in the area; the dependence on kin for help in economic activities decreased and hence kin ties also weakened. In Platanos and in Nohia, this dependence continues, especially during the tomato and olive harvest period. Moreover, as mentioned earlier in this chapter, and as parents themselves claim, nowadays they make more sacrifices for their children than their parents did in the past, sacrifices which are to be reciprocated when the parents get old and need the kind of care that is not provided by the state in rural Greece. Finch (1989: 53) in her book on family obligations and social change in the UK, argues that 'there are predictable patterns in flows of support between older and younger generations

in which support flows in both directions, but on balance the older generation
are the givers and the younger the receivers'. In Nohia and Platanos it seems
that the order is often reversed during the last years of the old generation, where
women from the younger generation become care givers, whereas young men
concentrate on the financial aspect of care.

The care of the elderly and of dependent people in general falls onto the
children. The prevailing ideology is that caring for them is part of the family's
obligation. Within the family, it is usually the woman (mother, daughter,
daughter-in-law) who is expected to carry this burden on her shoulders. Even
in the case of a disabled wife men in Nohia and Platanos do not provide care,
When, for example, Yannis'[18] mother had a car accident in the early 1980s as a
result of which she was paralysed, it was her daughter (who was already married
and living with her husband), who looked after her and not her husband or
son. As she said,

> I loved my mother. She was a kind woman. She was around 40 when the accident
> happened. I used to go every morning to my parents' house to wash her, do the
> housework and laundry, cook, feed her, and again in the evening, on my way home
> from the fields. It was tiring, but it was my obligation, my duty to do so; she was
> my mother and I was her only daughter. Men never help with this kind of thing.
> These were and will always be women's tasks (*Aften itan ke tha ine pandote gynaekies
> doulies*).

Another example is that of Koula, who some years ago got serious backache
from sitting for endless hours uncomfortably while loom weaving, and had
to go to hospital for treatment. During her stay there, her husband and son
managed to look after themselves and the house, as he proudly said. However,
if it was necessary for her to be looked after when she got back home, it would
have been her daughter who would have had to come from Athens, where she
was studying at university, to provide care. 'But what if you had no daughters,
couldn't one of your two sons or your husband Georgos look after you?', I
asked. She replied that then the next most closely-related woman would have
looked after her, namely her daughter-in-law. She said:

> I looked after my mother-in-law when towards the end of her life she needed care. It
> was my duty to do so. Besides, she was like a mother to me. But even if she wasn't, I
> would have had to look after her just the same. There are no other options available.
> The funny thing is that even mothers-in-law who have mistreated their daughters-
> in –law, expect to be looked after by them. Some, in the cities, put their relatives in
> geriatric institutions and leave them to rot. But this is unacceptable, it is cruel and
> 'shameful'. Only heartless women can do this.

---

18   Yannis is an unmarried young man living with his father in Plaranos. He owns
two greenhouses.

This care is provided on an unpaid basis, although the retirement pension or for those over 68 not entitled to a pension, the meagre economic help (this was in the late 1980s, a mere 8,000 drachmas, that is, around €30) received from the Ministry of Health, Welfare and Social Security, via the Organization of Agricultural Security (KEPE 1989: 202) is a contribution, however small, to the family budget. Such care demands a high level of commitment. If there are other female members in the household, they are likely to share the work. However, in cases where both daughter and daughter-in-law are living nearby but not in the house where the person who needs care lives, there is a possibility that the parties can negotiate and either share the work or decide who is going to be the main carer. This does sometimes result in disagreements and disputes. To give an example, in 1987 M's father-in-law was taken ill. Someone had to look after him, because his wife was also ill at the time and could hardly look after herself. It is important to mention here that daughters-in-law are also seen as potential carers and one often hears old people saying, 'I hope my son marries a good woman who will take care of us when the time comes'. Both M (his daughter-in-law) and one of his daughters lived in the village. In the beginning they decided to share the responsibility but they soon started having disagreements as to who was going to look after the old man. According to M, who at the time had two children under ten, it was the daughter's obligation to look after her father. However, the daughter claimed that M should look after him. The dispute was resolved only when M was publicly beaten up by her husband's sister, who refused even to share the care. In other cases, assistance is negotiated between relatives (for example, if two daughters live in the same village as the parents, they might come to an arrangement as to how the work should be divided between them). In other words, although there is pressure for the sacrifices parents have made to be reciprocated, there is room for manoeuvre, depending on the life style of the families concerned. For example, if one of two daughters has small children to look after, it is more likely that the one who does not will devote more time to caring for the parent/s. M's case is somewhat exceptional: usually it is more predictable that if one has a daughter, she will automatically take the burden of looking after the parent/s. It is expected that she will do so. If she does not, she runs the risk of being severely criticized as *egoistria* (self-interested) and *aharisti* (ungrateful) towards her parents, and consequently developing feelings of guilt which are reinforced by the community's intolerance towards such behaviour. Tensions both in the caring relationship and between family members may also develop, with profound consequences for women; the heavy burden placed on them results in physical and emotional strain. Usually these are the 'women in the middle', as Dalley (1990: 7) calls them – 'women generally of middle age, middle generation, between children and their own parents', who work and at the same time have to look after the children and the elderly, since community care of the type that exists in other European countries (with day-care centres, hostels, home nursing, meals on wheels, etc.), is, for reasons discussed below, virtually nonexistent in

Greece in general and in rural Greece in particular. M is one such example. Fortunately for her, as far as public opinion was concerned, the majority of the villagers were in favour of M, for two reasons: first, the old man had a daughter in the village who could take care of him; second, M had two young children to look after, whereas her sister-in-law's children were grown up and did not need as much care. As Finch (1989: 29) maintains, 'there are limits to what one can reasonably expect relatives to do'. However, contrary to research cited in Finch (ibid.), where elderly people in the UK are reluctant or do not want to impose on relatives, most people in Nohia and Platanos expect, as they said, to be cared for by relatives. They see the support they give as a two-way process: they themselves have made many sacrifices for educating their children and/or providing them with a dwelling, and now the younger generation will reciprocate the sacrifice by providing personal care for the elderly. The person who looks after the elderly is not necessarily the major beneficiary of their will. Parents try to ensure that the division of inheritance between the children remains as even as possible, irrespective of who looked after them in their old age. Nevertheless, some children seem to expect to gain something for the care they provided, since they do occasionally complain that, after years of selfless giving, they ended up with less than they thought they deserved and expressed feelings of bitterness emanating from this injustice. As a woman living in a nearby village, said: 'I have sacrificed my youth for the old man and you know what the outcome was? The property he left me is equivalent to that of my brother, not a single penny more. How unfair. Other parents treat the children who provided care for them in their old age better. They make sure that they give them something more out of gratitude for the sacrifices they have made. Anyway, I have the pleasure of knowing that I have done my duty. Thank God, everyone in the village knows that.' So public opinion matters.

Assistance from relatives is still of considerable importance and in the case of craftswomen like M and Koula in Nohia, because of the way their lives are organized (in that there is no spatial separation between productive and reproductive activities), they seem more available than their men, who most of the time work outside in the fields, to perform the caring. In Platanos on the other hand, because men's and women's lives *vis-à-vis* the greenhouses are organized in a similar way, in that both devote many hours every day to working in the fields, women seem to be less and less available to provide any assistance which involves input of time and domestic labour, especially during particular times of the year, namely during the tomato and olive harvests. This tendency or cultural expectation for caring responsibilities to fall on women was challenged when women saw their role as carers as inhibiting them from working and vice-versa, and they succeeded, through their local association, in persuading the government to build a childcare unit (see Chapter 8 on women's associations). So, since women's involvement in market gardening there has been change in the capacity of these women to provide care for relatives. Simply by looking at their working patterns – discussed earlier on in this book – one realizes that they do not have the time needed to look after the old and/or sick people. Although it seems that the economic behaviour of family members has changed family relationships, this does not seem to mean that these women's sense of obligation has weakened, or that they care less emotionally for their relatives, but that changing economic circumstances are likely to start shaping and/or transforming patterns of support. As Finch (1989: 113) maintains,

> a range of social, economic and demographic factors ... together shape the structural context within which family support is worked out ... these cannot be seen as 'determining' patterns of support in any direct sense, still less directly determining beliefs and values about family responsibility and duty, but ... they set the limits conditions within which individuals work out what they are going to provide for each other ... in the sense that they help to shape both people's needs for support from their relatives and their capacity to provide it.

The issue of who is going to provide care for the elderly in the future is likely to become more pertinent as advances in medical care enable more and more people to survive into very old age despite the various infirmities that come with it. Whereas in 1986 the number of people aged 65 and over in Greece was 1,236,000 – that is, they constituted 12.3 per cent of the total population – it is estimated that by the year 2020 the number will increase to nearly 2,000,000. What are the alternatives in providing care? The answer is not many. As many people said, 'if you haven't got good, caring relatives, you are lost'.

There are a few geriatric hospitals which can act as a safety net if needed, but all old people I asked touched wood, symbolically, saying that they hope they would never need them. A few added that since they have daughters there is nothing to worry about, whereas others added: 'I am fortunate enough to have a good daughter-in-law. I have peace of mind knowing that she'll look after me if the need arises'. State support is seen as the last resort. There are a few examples in both villages of older people whose relatives had either migrated or died or both and who, as a result, had no one to look after them; hence they ended up in geriatric institutions. Most talk about these people now, adding 'o kaimenos' (the poor man), or 'o kakomiris' (the unfortunate man), and ending their sentence with 'ihe kaka geramata' (he had a painful old age).

If a family places its elderly or handicapped in an institution, it is seen by the rest of the villagers as dispensing with its responsibility to care for the dependent members and it is usually the woman who is blamed for this. As Finch (1989: 143) writes, 'rights, duties and obligations work differently for women and men in practice, and this is considered to be quite proper; a woman who tries to contravene this will be regarded as acting scandalously'. This attitude towards institutionalization of the elderly is reinforced by mass media revelations about the appalling conditions in long-stay institutions. For example, many people in both villages were shocked when a documentary about the mental hospital on the island of Leros appeared on television in the early 1980s revealing the appalling conditions in there. Another problem is related to demographic factors; if the elderly leave, some villages will simply disappear. People are more tolerant of the behaviour towards the elderly and/or sick of relatives who live in Athens and where both spouses work.

Community care policies should be developed for the provision of types of care; small-scale 'homes', instead of gigantic institutions, should be established. At the time of writing, the high cost of caring for people is borne by the family. All forms of dependency are regarded as being amenable to care in the family. The institutional and residential care currently provided by the state is regarded as unacceptable. Underlying this there are some fundamental assumptions about the nature and structure of family life and the role of women therein. The state seems to see the care provided by the family as a way of saving on the costs of such care, whether it is institutional or community care. In cases of mental illness, once someone institutionalized, the family does not accept them back, because of the prejudices of other people (personal communication with one of the doctors in the psychiatric hospital in Corfu). In addition, as mentioned earlier, women run the risk of being severely criticized by other villagers (both men and women) for not meeting the needs of dependent family members. The family is believed by both the state and by the people themselves to be the appropriate unit and location for care. Caring for and caring about are believed to be integrated; you cannot have one without the other. The community expects that an elderly or sick relative will be cared for by a female relative and it is regarded as the 'normal' thing to do for a devoted daughter, mother, or wife. Men, on the other hand, are not expected to care for relatives. As Dalley (1990: 12) writes,

> He is expected to provide the setting within which the provision of care may take place (his own home ... with his own wife providing the care. But if he has no wife, it is permissible for him to pay for the care to be brought in, or for the dependent person to be cared for elsewhere and/or to live elsewhere).

In other words, the man sacrifices his purse in that he contributes financially, whereas the woman sacrifices herself, in that she does the physical work; many say 'thysia egine gia ta gerondia' (she sacrificed herself for the old folks), with admiration. This has particular poignancy where, as in these villages, women also in fact contribute economically to the household.

As already mentioned, the sick or elderly who have no daughter to look after them are regarded as unfortunate. This contradicts the preference of Greeks for male children. The altruism of women is taken for granted; it is a societal expectation. This is closely linked to their role as carers of children. Women themselves subscribe to this view of their nature. This altruism is reciprocal, in that there are strong bonds and obligations between parents and children, whether the latter are married or not. This is not so strong among siblings; for example, if a man has a handicapped brother, his wife can refuse to look after her brother-in-law without risk of being severely criticized. Are there any circumstances under which wives and daughters can do this without their attempt to contravene the prevailing customs being regarded as scandalous? As Grenda, a social worker, informed me, there are such circumstance; opinions are fluid and may well depend on a person's reputation in the village. People often say things like, 'She wouldn't have done it without a good reason', or 'she is a nice woman, she would have looked after her mother-in-law, if she was fit herself', or 'she pretended to have a bad pregnancy in order to avoid performing her duties towards her parents; she is the kind of person that would have found an excuse even if she invented one', and so on.

In the early 1980s, the PASOK government introduced day centres (KAPI)[19] which provide the elderly with entertainment and the chance to meet other people, especially in large cities where there is a problem of isolation. This function is performed in the villages by the local café. It is there where older people, mainly men, gather to meet fellow villagers and pass their time. People in Nohia and Platanos found it difficult to go to the KAPI; 'pou na trehoume tora' (where shall we go now), they used to say, because appropriate transport was not available to them. Also the KAPI were not geared toward meeting the requirements of those elderly with special needs and of their families. These remained the duties of the female relative, duties imposed on them by a traditional gender regime.

Under-provision of care services together with publicly endorsed concepts of family obligations by restricting the range of care choices open to individuals, do put pressure upon families to take up care responsibilities as well as on the way people think about these issues. In other words, the family is filling the gaps in the welfare state which in Greece is very inadequately developed. A large amount of work to be done is carried out by women and there is an assumption that there are women at home to do it. In the case of Nohia, and especially Platanos, where women work in the greenhouses, this work is nowadays carried out by strangers (hired help). Third-country migrant women from Eastern and Central Europe, Africa or Asia work as either live-in quasi nurses/maids or as maids working during the day, and are employed to perform a healthcare function (see Lazaridis 2007b). The replacement costs for the care services a woman no longer offers her dependents are high (Katrougalos and Lazaridis 2003: 74) and will remain high, unless the state manages to socialize some form of privatized domestic labour through more publicly provided care for the elderly and other dependants at levels which would meet women's needs.

---

19   At the time of fieldwork there were 17 KAPI in operation in Crete, eight in the prefecture of Heracleon, three in the prefecture of Rethymnon, four in the prefecture of Lasithi and two in the prefecture of Chania (one in the town of Chania and the other one in Kastelli).

Chapter 7
Sex and Fun

Introduction

This chapter focuses on aspects of gender relations and sexuality in Nohia and Platanos. It concentrates on local ideas about the sexuality of men and women and on the way in which a shift of values from the traditional 'honour-shame' ethic to somewhat different values and practices has occurred since the early 1970s. I argue that the economic development of the two villages since then, and the economic opportunities this had, by the mid-1980s, opened up for the women and men who lived there, meant a shift of values and practices regarding sexuality away from the traditional 'honour-shame' ethic.

The Honour and Shame Value System

The way Greek women and men view themselves in relation to issues concerning sex, and the way they are viewed by others in relation to these matters, is closely related to the complementary and sometimes opposed moral values of 'honour and shame', which are used to evaluate social worth and to order social relations between individuals. This value system has been the dominant mode of *social control* characteristic of Mediterranean societies. Some anthropologists – notably British structuralists like Pitt-Rivers (1965) and Peristiany (1965) – used this 'cultural archetype', as Gilmore (1987a; 1987b) calls it, which they perceived as being a relatively ubiquitous and uniform value system, to characterize 'traditional' Mediterranean society. This section briefly looks firstly at some issues in the discussion of 'honour' and 'shame' and secondly, at some arguments put forward by social anthropologists about the power and/or subordination of women in rural Greece.

'Honour' is something men strive for and something they can lose through their women's behaviour if the latter act in a way that is considered shameless. That is, honour is perceived as a male prerogative, associated with action, whereas shame is a female characteristic associated with weakness (Petronoti 1980: 25). This prescribes different kinds of behaviour for men and for women and implies restrictions on women's freedom, since they have to be protected from the sexual advances of men. Their believed capacity to control their sexual urges, and at the same time, the belief that men's sexual drive is 'natural' but 'uncontrollable', renders women responsible for 'maintaining the moral code'. As Hirschon (1989: 149–50) writes:

Since women have the power to control their sexual urges, they are at fault when transgressions occur ... The imperative nature of a man's sexual drive casts the woman as a constant potential threat. Her sexuality, if not properly controlled, might undermine her own honour, that of her family, and destroy a man's integrity, seducing him away from his commitment to his own family ... Women in this view present a potential threat to the whole social order; they are powerful and dangerous.

A woman must preserve her sexual purity/chastity whereas a man must defend his and his family's honour. In other words, men's reputation largely depends on the sexual conduct of their women (wife, daughters, sisters, etc.). As Lever (1984: 359) writes, 'it can [also] be interpreted as an expression of patriarchy which cuts across class divisions'. If they are unsuccessful in protecting or guarding their women's *timi* (honour), men are shamed and thus diminished in the eyes of the society they live in. A man's ability to protect his honour will 'provide a guide to his reliability and effectiveness in the public spheres of economic and political activity' (Goddard 1989: 168). In other words, 'honour' is the value of a man in his own eyes and also in the eyes of the community he lives in (Pitt-Rivers 1965: 21); it involves the evaluation of the community (du Boulay 1974). That is, public opinion is very important for the individual. It legitimizes patriarchal practices or the codes of conduct that men try to reinforce over women. Women's ability to cause trouble by performing actions that are regarded as socially unacceptable, gives them 'latent power' vis-à-vis men. Restrictions are thus placed on the movement of women and their behaviour.

According to Peristiany (1976: 9), all societies may have their own forms of 'honour' and 'shame' in that they all need to 'evaluate conduct by comparing it to ideals of social action'. Gilmore (1987b: 90) adds that this model 'easily leads to distortion, because it excludes a broad range of less contentious male virtues that are also typically Mediterranean'. By this he means economic success, family autonomy and physical powers, hospitality, generosity, integrity. So honour is a more complicated variable than it was initially suggested to be (ibid.: 91).

The presumed uniformity of the honour principle in Mediterranean societies has been criticized by writers like Herzfeld (1980). Such writers opt for ethnographic particularism (ibid.: 149). Others (Davis 1977; Lever 1986) have drawn attention to the fact that a number of other issues should also be taken into account, such as economic resources, class, ways in which values change. Lever (1986: 83, 104) has argued that the 'honour-shame' value system is a red herring in that, in her words 'it distracts attention from divisions based on material considerations and from the values of those not dominant ... by virtue of class and gender'.

In general the emphasis on female chastity might not be peculiar to the Mediterranean, but 'it is associated with institutionalized practices that affect and reflect gender-based relations of authority, dominance and coercion' (Giovannini 1987: 61). In the past these involved 'crimes of honour' and ritual displays of virginity which are now no longer practised, which means that the cultural emphasis on female chastity has been subject to change. It is, however, a key dimension in gender ideology and related social practices.

Those who have stressed an 'honour-shame' value system have not, however, necessarily seen this as an indication of women's social powerlessness; as mentioned above, women are potentially powerful, because of their potential for collective disgrace. To quote Pitt-Rivers (1977: 78), 'women hold in their hands the power not merely to put pressure on their menfolk but actually to "ruin" them'.

Regarding Greece, a number of anthropologists have contributed to a greater understanding of women and gender. They have stressed the particular importance of the dichotomy between private and the public realms for an understanding of the position of rural women. The division between the two realms is demarcated physically (house versus public areas like the square or the shops) and behaviourally (house is associated with women), and represents two sets of values which are significant for both sexes. However, in Greek life private and public are complementary and connected (see also Dubisch 1986a: 12), in that women have important roles in the public realm and men within the house. Two arguments exist. The first attributes women's lower status to their association with the private realm. The other suggests that the domestic space is a source of power for women (Dubisch 1986; Friedl 1986; Hoffman 1976); women influence men by constantly reminding them of the effort they make to enable the men to preserve their public honour and of the fact that men must reciprocate this effort. Other ways of exercising power over men include nagging, withholding sex, or even burning a meal when expecting guests, in other words by exercising *poniria* (cunning, deviousness) and in this way getting their way (Dubisch 1986: 16–17; Hoffman 1976: 338). Nevertheless, that power comes at a price (Cowan 1990: 15), such as the psychological pressure or at times the physical force men can exercise on women in order to maintain their position in the household. Petronoti (1980: 21) has pointed out that 'what has not been seriously considered by ethnographers, is the fact that women may openly express their views and attain goals by direct action and not by a manipulation of males'.

Others (Friedl 1986) have argued that women's possession of property (in the form of dowry, inheritance, etc.) gives them power. Yet others have argued that one should consider the impact of women in terms of their spiritual importance (du Boulay 1986). A factor which gives Greek rural women power is the fulfilment of the maternal ideal. Du Boulay (ibid.) argues that the Orthodox religious value system must be taken into account, according to which women are associated with the morally weak, easily deceived and prone to sin Eve – the woman who supposedly caused the Fall of mankind – and also with the Mother of God – the woman who gave birth to the Redeemer. As a woman grows older and her sexual power decreases, she gradually gains in stature. To quote du Boulay (1986: 159), the conversion of Eve into the Mother of God is ... a process which gathers momentum as time goes on; and the respect accorded the woman by her husband and by society is transformed with it.

Caraveli (1986) on the other hand, argues that women wield power through their performance of laments. In her article, 'The Lament as Social Protest', she shows how laments become instruments for voicing the concerns of the living and how these are transformed by the women who perform them into instruments of protest against the social isolation and loss of social status suffered by widows in Greece, and as instruments for airing their own grievances on an everyday basis. Finally, Hirschon (1984: 19) has suggested that 'the domestic/household sphere has been greatly devalued in the western world ... [and that] our own perceptions regarding power and its proper locus in the public domain hinder us from appreciating its different expressions in other societies'.

To recapitulate, many anthropologists who carried out research in rural Greece commented on women's association with the private realm as an important means by which women can seek to overcome or compensate for their subordination in the public domain. This literature shows that adherence to moral values does not in itself guarantee respect for rural women. As Petronoti (1980: 26) notes, 'behaviour which is normally reprehensible may well be excused if it is undertaken because of family interests'. She also argues that the degree to which rural people adhere to 'ideal behaviour' depends on their material affluence and to their role in vital economic responsibilities and that both the material and moral components of 'honour' must be taken into account. Some data relevant to the issues addressed above are discussed in the sections that follow.

Contrary to Arnold's experience that women in eastern Crete were not reluctant to discuss sex with her (1985), women in Nohia and Platanos as well as in other nearby villages, were very reluctant to discuss the topic with me. A plausible reason may be the fact that, as they said, these intimate areas of life are private and improper for an 'unmarried Greek woman' (that is me) to discuss. I was thus reluctant to persevere with my questions for fear that this might negatively affect my position as *persona grata* and render me the personification of impudence. Therefore, the material which follows is from casual observation and from information which people volunteered rather than from formal interviews. It relies less on personal statements to me and more on information that reached me in the form of gossip as well as on personal observations when I was living there. It is, therefore, a far from perfect and/or complete record of what was going on at the time.

As mentioned in Chapter 6 on marriage and family, in both villages the primary goal of the family is intergenerational social mobility. To achieve this, parents provide their children with property and with education. So, if a girl is a promising student, she is not discouraged from going and studying in Athens or any other major city. In contrast to what was happening in the 1950s and

1960s, where women did not dare to move to another city unless a close relative who could look after them was residing there, by the 1980s women had started enjoying considerably more freedom of movement.

This is even more evident in Platanos where, especially since a Youth Association was established (1981) and a Youth Centre (called, *to steki*, that is 'the meeting place') built, boys and girls meet frequently and establish friendships that may lead to courtship. Although at first the older generation was very sceptical about its functions, nowadays the *steki* is accepted and liaisons between the two sexes are presumed to be sexually innocent.

Moreover, in Platanos one can often see young women eating together in a local taverna or sitting and chatting with local boys on the beach or at the cafeteria. In Nohia, women enjoy much less freedom of movement than the women in Platanos do. Women's movements are more restricted than in Platanos; one rarely sees a woman eating in the company of men who are not members of her family and if they go to town, for example, they must do so for a specific reason, for example, to buy materials for their craft work, or to visit the doctor or a relative. In Platanos, because of the nature of their greenhouse work, women are constantly in the company of non-family men. It seems, therefore, that their reputation is determined by their capacity to work and look after their family, rather than by their potential sexual activities *per se* (although these are, to an extent, important too, especially when it comes to adultery or what are regarded by the locals as 'non-natural' sexual practices). In addition, it seems that virginity is not as crucial as it used to be, let us say in the 1960s and 1970s. For example, in reference to women's modesty in Ambeli, du Boulay (1974: 111–12) writes:

> This is still thought of as an absolute prerequisite for the honourable woman, and involves a conception of purity which places an unalterable value on the virginity of the unmarried girl and the chastity of the married woman... honour is given to an individual by the community, and since feminine honour depends on the possession of shame, it is vital for the possessor of shame that this fact should be demonstrated to the community. It is in fact as important to be seen to be chaste as it is to be chaste.

Although some men in Nohia and in Platanos still say that they would like to marry a virgin, most (young people especially) believe that it is not a great dishonour to marry a non-virgin. As Takis, a man in his early 30s who lives in Nohia, said:

> I do not care whether the woman I marry will be a virgin or not. I am modern, whereas my friend over there, is *paradosiakos* (traditional); he says that he prefers his wife to be a virgin; we will see if he succeeds in finding one ... He should have been born fifty years ago, at a time when if a woman was not virgin, her husband

had the right to send her back to her father. Alas to the woman, who, in those days, was discovered by her relatives to have liaisons with men.

As discovered later on, in 1949, a man who still lives in Nohia killed his sister, who at the time was only 24 years old, because she was going out with men. As Takis' mother, a prominent craftswoman, told me, 'he killed her *gia logous "timis"* (for reasons related to 'honour')'. She then explained that such incidents were common at the time and that the man, after spending 17 years in prison, returned to the village. When he returned to the village he was accepted as his act of so-called revenge had not only given him a way of saving the family's reputation but also of proving his manhood to his co-villagers. The principles of a vendetta are 'negotiated by individual actors, who may choose to interpret them in favour of either restraint or further violence' (Herzfeld 1985: 82). Following Elias' (1978) account of the 'civilizing process', one would expect that the actual incidence of male violence would have waned as the modern state removed the legitimate use of violence from the everyday lives of men. Today men in Crete do live a more self-controlled life. Nevertheless, the continued, however rare, incidence of vendetta killings indicates that many men in Crete have retained a sense of their right to protect their honour in the eyes of the community by the exercise of male violence; violence continues to be an aspect of the most celebrated form of masculinity in Crete.

Nowadays, if a couple is engaged, they are given tacit permission to engage in sexual intercourse. The only pressure that the parents can exert is to press the man to marry her sooner than planned if the daughter falls pregnant. One such incident happened in Nohia in the year before I was there; as some villagers commented when I asked when did so-and-so get married, 'they hastened the marriage', connoting that she was pregnant. Evidence from Platanos suggests that values implied by the honour and shame literature are less adhered to there by the new generation than they are in Nohia. The fact that in Platanos the local women's association (see Chapter 8) organized talks on contraception and their insistence that all young people should attend suggests that physical contact before marriage or engagement is expected in Platanos. In contrast. in Nohia, these things are talked about only after the formal engagement of the couple. Furthermore, a few parents in Platanos (mostly between 40 and 50 years old) influenced through the mass media by feminist ideas, say that 'I timi tis koris mou den ine sto vraki tis', which is translated as 'my daughter's honour/virtue is not in her pants'.

A married woman in her mid-40s with three daughters – all in their late teens – who has a greenhouse in Platanos, said to me:

> What is the point anyway; in the past there were women who used to engage in all sorts of sexual activities but somehow managed to keep their virginity and if they did not they had an operation to re-establish it.

The development of market-gardening in Platanos meant that women's interactions with other individuals (government officials, agricultural scientists, merchants), who brought new ideas to the village, increased and have brought a gradual change to these women's traditional beliefs about their nature and role.

In both villages, when they are engaged, the couple obtains the right to sex. Many parents commented on the fact that their daughters were sleeping with their fiancé but hastily added that they would not permit such an act to take place in their own home. A craftswoman from Nohia, whose son and fianceé were studying in Athens and occasionally visit, said:

> I do not know what they do in Athens, but when they visit, they sleep separately. If during the night they go to each other's bedroom, this is something I do not want to know about.

If the engagement breaks up for any reason, this does not mean that, because the woman is no longer a virgin, she loses her reputation. For example, Niki, a woman in her early 30s, was engaged three times, but for different reasons the engagements broke down. Although there is the impression that women have their first sexual experience at the time of marriage, in reality it seems that many women have their first sexual relationship before marriage. As I heard some years later, this did not decrease Niki's opportunity to marry. So, the notion that sex is only for procreation, which, as Hirschon (1989) commented, is 'bound up with religious notions regarding the purpose of the sexual act[1] and the definition of female sexuality',[2] has started to change in both villages.

However, the emerging trend is neither towards what Giddens (1992:58) calls 'the pure relationship', that is 'a situation where a social relation is entered into for its own sake, for what can be derived by each person from a sustained association with another; and which is continued only in so far as it is thought by both parties to deliver enough satisfaction for each individual to stay within it' nor towards 'plastic sexuality ... freed from the needs of reproduction' (ibid.:28).

Marital infidelity is a serious insult to the man, who is then stigmatized as *keratas* which means 'cuckold'. It threatens family stability and justifies a violent reaction by him. If, for example, he beats his wife up, almost all men and women in the village will think of his act as being justifiable, unless he is not able to

---

1   As Hirschon (1989: 148) maintains, in the Orthodox tradition, the sexual act (which in Yerania was sometimes referred to as the 'evil act'), is considered polluting, requiring abstinence from communion.

2   The destiny of a woman was to bear children. 'In motherhood a woman approaches the ideals represented by the archetypal figure of Mary, the mother of God' (Hirschon 1989: 148). Furthermore, while a man's sexual drive was held to be uncontrollable, the woman's was subject to her conscious control (ibid.: 148–9).

perform, to use the expression many local people use when referring to sex, 'his conjugal duties'. At the time of fieldwork, in one of the villages I studied there was a young woman married to someone who, because of cancer, was said to be unable to have sex with his wife. As a middle-aged woman commented:

> She is a very nice woman, otherwise she would have either left him, or committed adultery and rightly so. This does not mean, however, that no one will condemn her for being 'gyneka tou dromou' (a woman of the road); there are always plotters around.

The infidelity of a husband, on the one hand, is more or less expected and is thought of as enhancing his self-image, provided he does not overdo it; *magia tou* (being a rogue), one hears men and women saying. If he does overdo it – and there is a fine line between the two – then he is criticized by both men and women for not showing the appropriate respect to his wife and family. At the time of fieldwork, for example, the media were full of comments on the affair of the then prime-minister with an air hostess. The attitude of the villagers is depicted in the following comment:

> He is a man, he can do whatever he likes; but his wife shouldn't have left him; she should have turned a blind eye, no doubt he will soon come to his senses.

So, although a double standard seems to be in operation here, its fairness is sometimes questioned. Men provide excuses, saying that their wife's persistence in avoiding sex forces them to find other women for sexual liaisons. Since the early 1990s this includes women trafficked for prostitution, originating from Thailand, the Philippines, Ethiopia, Sri Lanka, Ukraine, Russia, Poland, Romania, etc. (see Lazaridis 2001). Although prostitution *per se* is seen as a threat to societal order and prostitutes as dangerous, unclean vehicles of venereal diseases, there is hardly a moral stigma attached to men for consorting with them. Visiting a prostitute for sexual gratification is a legitimate option and an effective outlet of male sexuality in a society where, until recently, women were excoriated for expressing sexual desires and where men's sexual urges needed to be served by other than their 'honest decent women'. This attitude is reflected in a number of laws which lay down the terms and conditions under which prostitution can be practised (see Lazaridis 2001: 76–80). The man is the 'harpoon', the predator, whereas the woman is the prey or the fish, the corruptible (Zinovieff 1991). She is not allowed to 'wag her tail', to use an expression often used to denote women's ability to sensually and coyly express sexual demands.

Arnold (1985: 262–4) argues that Greek women are 'more free in expressing sexuality than American women', in that they 'openly express affection, physically, among themselves and show no reserve in touching what Americans consider to be "sexual body parts"' and gives some examples, such as where a woman pinched her breasts while sweeping the floor of a shop. She juxtaposes this to the fact that these women viewed themselves as 'dirty and disgusting'. She does not, however, see this as a contradiction. She argues:

> As a woman among women, the world is their own, and it is safe; they control this domain. The women's world is separate from men's. As a woman in the larger society, however, the woman subscribes to the negative view of women held by both males and females in Greece ... In the separate female sphere women can relieve tension about their body openings by touching, joking and making light of these dangerous flaws in their boundaries. But when a woman is alone, she sees herself vis-à-vis her husband as his public sphere. She acknowledges her pollution and avoids contact with her own genitals.

This raises interesting questions about women's views of their own sexuality vis-à-vis both men and women.

A different view is put forward by Loizos and Papataxiarchis (1991: 228), who write that:

> Although men conceptually, and sometimes in practice, engage in forms of sexual expression other than 'normal' heterosexuality, such alternatives seem to be unacknowledged in concept and unattained in practice among women.

They go on to argue that contrary to men, women do not use the term *malaka* – *malaka* is the Greek word for the person who masturbates – (which they categorize as a sexual term of address) when addressing each other, and that they address each other as *kori* (which means daughter, maiden), a term which according to the authors 'suggests a subordinate kinship status' (ibid.: 229). Although it is true that I never heard women addressing each other using the term *malaka* in Nohia, the above statement contradicts what I witnessed in Platanos and in other villages in Crete, where the above mentioned terms are used by men and women alike. In fact, women use both the masculine gender of the noun *malaka*[3] or the feminine one, *malakismeni*, interchangeably, when greeting each other. Although it is still seen by the older generation as a sexual term of address and therefore as improper to be used in public – actually older people condemn the young ones for using 'such language' – it has its meaning among the young and it is now used instead of the word 'imbecile' or 'hey you'. As far as the term *kori* is concerned, I have never heard it in the area; another term is used in western Crete, *kopelli* and *kopellia*, which does suggest that the person is young and probably unmarried, but it is used mainly by older people, for addressing young men and women respectively, or by young people for addressing someone whose name they do not remember.

---

3 Both terms (that is, *malakas* and *malakismeni*) derive from the Greek word for masturbation.

Loizos and Papataxiarchis (1991: 229) go even further, saying that they are aware of 'no commonly used term to suggest the possibility of sexual attraction between women in rural Greece'. They also argue that 'not only is there no counterpart to *poushtis*,[4] but there is no common term for a woman who would wish to take a "male" role, either'. The fact that the authors are unaware of this does not mean that such terms do not exist. At least in Crete, people often talk of *androgynekes*, or *agorokoritso*, which mean a 'manlike woman' or 'butch'. However, Loizos and Papataxiarchis (ibid.) also mention Kennedy's (1986: 135) work on female friendships in western Crete, where she states that although women experience intense friendships:

> Neither adult female homosexuality nor hetero-emotionality were, as far as I could determine, evident.

And they suggest that:

> The possibility of sexual love between rural Greek women is 'unknown' in the sense of unconceptualized, and so unrecognised. Sexual practices that may occur are in some sense unseen, or unperceived. (Loizos and Papataxiarchis 1991: 229)

My observations in Crete show the opposite. But in order to determine whether there are homosexual relationships between women, one should define the terms first. What do we mean by homosexuality? Do we confine it to physical relationships? Can it also apply to couples who have deep, strong feelings for each other, but for one reason or another have not expressed their emotions sexually? To my knowledge, at the time of fieldwork there had been no surveys in Greece dealing with women's views of lesbian sexuality. Furthermore, as Faderman (1985: 18) maintains:

> It is ... difficult to trace sexual patterns of love between women, since lesbian sex leaves no evidence in 'illegitimate' offspring.

So-called 'romantic friendships' (Faderman 1985) are not evident in Nohia. That is to say, they either do not exist, or if they do, they remain undetected due to the nature of the women's work/activities, which, to a large extent, confines them at home. They are, however, evident in Platanos. For example, there were two women in their late 20s, who spent most of their time together, shared most aspects of their lives together, and had little connection with men. What kind of relationship did they have? Faderman (1985: 19) referring to sixteenth-, seventeenth-, eighteenth- and nineteenth-century romantic friendships writes:

---

4 *Poushtis* is the word used for male who assumes the effeminate 'passive' role as a homosexual.

The possible lack of overt sexual expression ... could not discount the seriousness or the intensity of the women's passions toward [each] other – or the fact that if by 'lesbian' we mean an all-consuming emotional relationship in which two women are devoted to each other above anyone else, these ubiquitous ... romantic friendships were 'lesbian'.

Despite the societal taboos related to this, such relationships in rural Greece are ignored, provided that they do not provoke the community. Most would say, 'this is the way they are, what can we do?' In most cases, relationships of the type I described above would go unnoticed and unsuspected, provided that the women kept their feminine appearance and avoided behaving in an unwomanly fashion. As Kennedy (1986: 135–6), in her article on women's friendships in Greece writes:

> Women's descriptions of their friendships – including the initiation, course, and content of the relationship – contain elements of courtship; some friendships seem like a second or shadow marriage. But unlike their marriage, which, regardless of whether it proceeded from amorousness or a matchmaker, seems to have been experienced as a shock, women's friendships have an air of continuity, familiarity, and ease.

So women are allowed to demonstrate the most sensual behaviour towards one another without being stigmatized as lesbians. 'Love without a penis is an impossibility' as many villagers said and 'what would two women do', another villager wondered. Others, mainly men, often make references to unusual anatomy or that their attraction to women is caused by their inability to attract men. A woman cannot 'dishonour' another woman and thus cause irreparable harm to her reputation. As a result, affectionate expressions and demonstrations between women are, to a certain extent, permissible. Women often appear in public places holding hands, for example. So women, free from suspicion, can be intimate, as long as they keep their public life within the realm of what is socially permissible. Most relationships of this kind seem to come to an end when one or both of the women succumb to family pressures to marry and raise a family of their own. On a later visit to Platanos, I found that the women referred to above were engaged to be married. It seems that Loizos and Papataxiarchis (1991) have been the victims of a certain naiveté, which, however, did not extend to male homosexuality.

Some *androgynekes* are admired for being clever and skilful and therefore the moral stigma which applies to the passive homosexual man, does not retrospectively apply to them. As Loizos and Papataxiarchis (1991: 227–8) write in relation to the passive homosexual man:

> He is strongly denigrated as someone who fundamentally lacks full humanity, and his moral weakness exposes him to all sorts of evil dispositions ... *Poushtis* comes

to be a synonym for a liar or a thief, a man without dignity, and it strongly contrasts with the characterisation of the man who adopts the 'male' role and who may claim a 'supermale' reputation, much as he might if he consorted with a prostitute.

As one father told me, he could perhaps tolerate his daughter or wife being *poutana* ('a whore') but if he ever discovered that his son was *poushtis* he would kill him. On the other hand, many men in the villages talked with pride of their liaisons as dominant partners with men during the period when they served in the army, whom they give the impression that they treated merely as sexual objects. The deviation from the heterosexual norm, however, because it is seen by local people as a 'legitimate option and an effective outlet of male sexuality', does not carry for the 'active/masculine' man the heavily negative moral implications that the role of the 'passive/womanlike' does, a role which 'implies a fundamental state of dependence and subordination to fellow men' (Loizos and Papataxiarchis 1991: 228). The Greek societal definitions of homosexuality are similar to those in Turkey, where, as Tapinc (1992: 42) writes:

> The conception of homosexuality originates around the schema of penetration, and in this conceptualisation the label of the *homosexual* is attributed to any individual who is being penetrated or thought to be penetrated, whereas the other one remains free of this label regardless of the fact that he is engaged in homosexual sex as well.

As mentioned earlier on, sexual patterns have altered over the last twenty years; in Platanos especially, premarital sex and hence sexual activity not for the sole purpose of procreation, has become a reality in the lives of many young women and in the consciousness of their parents, who no longer believe that their daughters are necessarily repressing their sexual inclinations. Furthermore, although women were in the past encouraged to force any sexual desire they might have to remain latent, television, pornographic videos and magazines and tourists have brought images of sexual expression to the village, which was up to then discouraged. Heterosexual relationships are socially condoned because they are no longer believed to violate the 'honour and shame' moral code. The same does not apply to homosexual liaisons.

If a woman was labelled as homosexual, this would make them feel under tremendous pressure to 'get cured'; alternatively, they would be ostracized by the community. A patriarchal culture like the one in Crete does not tolerate such activities, which pose a threat to family stability. So it is one of the best-guarded secrets in the village. A couple has to take into account what society thinks of lesbians, the Greek Orthodox church's belief that this is something unnatural, wrong or unhealthy. Even to talk about it is a taboo. So in appearance at least, they continue to fulfil the male image of womanhood, and/or to bow to male supremacy.

Just as the lesbian stereotype is for the woman to be masculine, the male homosexual is thought to be effeminate. He has been described to me as having an effeminate voice and liking to do quasi-feminine tasks, like cooking, for example. A middle-aged man in Nohia was described as being effeminate from childhood. 'This is how the poor man was born', villagers used to say. And they continued, 'he never provoked us by bringing his "friends" over here'. Generally, overstepping gender boundaries entails braving the stigma attached to it.

A new emphasis on the dangers of promiscuity appeared with the advent of HIV/AIDS (acquired immune-deficiency syndrome) which is seen as the outcome of non-natural acts provoking God's retribution and which complicates sexual relations. Fear of contagion has affected the way some people think of tourist women as well as the way parents think of their children's sexual conduct. However, although the government, through the media, has encouraged the use of 'safe sex techniques', many had their own theories; for example, many men said that there is no need for use of condoms when having intercourse with a married woman, because this is not a disease heterosexual, married women are likely to have. As in the west, in Crete too it has been identified as the 'gay plague' (Greenberg 1988: 480). The outcome of this was a moral panic against gays and lesbians. This is graphically represented by the following incident: two gay men came to rent a room in a village near Nohia; when, however, they were 'discovered', the owner of the building asked them to leave, providing the excuse that he had to go to Athens for a family event. The news of the incident immediately reached Nohia and Platanos. Although in Nohia people unanimously congratulated the man for not tolerating such degeneracy, people in Platanos were more tolerant: as two women owning 'rooms to let' in the village as well as near the beach told me, what tourists do is their own business; what worried them most was that they might bring AIDS.

Conclusion

The local meanings of male and female sexuality render certain types of same sex sexual experiences and relations as unacceptable, while at the same time enabling sexual practices which are not seen as a challenge to the institution of heterosexuality, to be defined as 'normal' or 'nonexistent'.

> The social construction of 'sex' as vaginal intercourse affects how other forms of sexual activity are evaluated as sexually satisfying or arousing; in some cases whether an activity is seen as sexual act at all. (Richardson 1992: 189)

Moreover, the notion that sex is only for procreation, which as Hirschon (1989) has suggested is 'bound up with religious notions regarding the purpose of the sexual act and the definition of female sexuality', has started to change in both villages. It must be noted, however, that the different economic development of the two villages has had slightly different effects on the form, content and functioning of female chastity codes. The cultural emphasis on female chastity as an indicator of social worth of individuals and their families and the desirability for premarital virginity for women has declined in Platanos and to a lesser extent in Nohia. This change in gender-related values and behaviour, however, conflicts with first, a new emphasis on promiscuity apparently due to the HIV/AIDS phenomenon, which is seen as the outcome of the risks of 'non-natural acts' provoking God's retribution, and second, with the older generation's subscription to traditional gender-related values and behaviour. Many are 'caught between the two worlds' and this brings tension between the sexes and between generations.

Chapter 8
Women's Associations

Introduction

The study of regional voluntary associations has been developed in anthropology within the context of urbanization and migration. Sutton (1978) and Kenna (1983) focus on migrant associations in Athens within the context of rural-urban migration. Sutton (1978: 242) looked at these associations as an attempt to counteract the politico-economic imbalance between the city and the Greek countryside, while Kenna (1983) looked at the interaction and rivalry between islanders and migrants. Studies on associations declined in the early 1980s, with the change of focus in social anthropology from societies, structures, organizations and typologies to cultures, systems of meaning, symbols and relationships (Marcus and Fischer 1986). The work on associations declined since, until Aspraki's (2004) study of voluntary associations in Karagatsi, a village in central Greece. She shows how intergroup and interpersonal dynamics lead to tensions, crises and ultimately friction.

This chapter looks at the role played by the Greek Orthodox Church in setting up, influencing, guiding and 'limiting' the activities of women's associations in Nohia and Platanos. It will be argued that these associations failed in the long run to address the needs of the rural women for whom they were intended and were 'conservative in their approach' in that they did not attack the local patriarchal regime, thus encouraging the maintenance of existing traditional values and practices, albeit in different degrees in the two villages.

The main interest is focused on the changes in rural women's work outlined in previous chapters and the ways in which these changes may have affected the activities of these associations and vice versa. For example, in Platanos, the local Women's Association became relatively more radical when women became actively involved in greenhouses and, as a result, their domestic responsibilities changed. Furthermore, it will be shown that Women's Associations reproduce certain norms regarding female behaviour and express certain beliefs/ideas about the nature of gender relations through their activities as dispensers of charity. This is traditionally viewed by both sexes and by the Greek Orthodox Church as the province of women. It is based on the idea that such activities would enable women to be 'better wives and mothers' and thus fulfil their roles as reproducers and contribute to the maintenance of existing traditional values, rather than attempt to turn women away from their traditional familial roles.

The Women's Associations: Historical Background

The Women's Associations in the regions of Kisamos and Selinon of western Crete were founded during the late 1950s–early 1960s, and were called *Enoriaki Syllogi Kyrion ke Despinidon tis Metropoleos Kisamou ke Selinou* (Parish Associations of Married and Unmarried Women of the Metropolis of Kisamos and Selinon). 'It was in 1958 that Bishop Irinaeos envisaged a programme for the spiritual development and fulfilment of women', as he called it (Grenda 1984: 109), and started the setting up of associations in the parishes of the above regions. These associations were 'under the spiritual protection' of the Metropolis[1] (ibid.). The local clergyman of each village is the honorary president of the local association. By the early 1980s, 40 associations were formally in operation in these regions, having a total of 5,000 members, most of whom were married women between 35 and 45 years of age.

As Bishop Irinaeos himself wrote, the following thoughts encouraged him to create the associations. Although Cretan women have a central role in the family, women did not, as he wrote, have the opportunity in the village to express their charismatic personality creatively in the public domain. 'Women are sacred and their role is not just to bring life in the world, but also to guide it ...' (interview). These ideals about the nature and role of women continue to be influential in the associations' activities.

In 1968, when the Orthodox Academy of Crete (OAK) was founded, a more systematic attempt to organize the Women's Associations began. However, according to Grenda (1984: 109), the Junta (1967–1974) gradually brought about a crisis in this effort which reached its peak with the departure, for political reasons, of Irinaeos to Germany (1972) and his replacement by Bishop Kyrillos, under whose prelature most associations were left in a dormant state (ibid.). Talking to women who were active in the associations at the time, it became apparent that the basic reason for this state of inactivity of most associations was lack of activity from the grassroots. Another reason was the fact that forces from above (mainly the charismatic [in the Weberian sense], benevolent, paternalistic Bishop Irinaeos who, as mentioned above, was the backbone of the associations) were until then keeping the groups alive by stimulating the members and by giving them strength and vitality. Such powerful charismatic leadership could, unintentionally, have inhibited grassroots collaboration. When he left, the associations failed to generate activity from below and hence gradually ceased to function, resulting in the re-emergence of the institutionalized structures of tradition. This was confirmed by Mrs Constandakaki, a middle-aged woman from Kamisiana (a village near Nohia) who, in the mid-1970s, was general secretary of the associations. She said:

1 A Metropolis in the Orthodox Church is equivalent to a cathedral. The Greeks give the name Metropolitan to every diocesan bishop (Ware 1987: 299–300).

We weren't well organized at the time, and he was no longer there to give an impetus to the women to do something. It was after the fall of the Junta and specifically in the mid-1970s, when the Bishop asked the Orthodox Academy of Crete to reorganize us, and Grenda, a social worker who was at the time working there, was appointed to perform this task, that the Associations became alive again.

In her work on the Women's Movement in Greece, Stamiris (1986) mentions that during the Junta period, even in the urban areas, women's organizations lacked confidence. She writes:

> The discussion of feminist theory in Greece was almost entirely stifled by the dictatorship resting on the cult of the family. When the colonels fell in 1974, the women's movement ... re-emerged ... (ibid.: 105).

When Bishop Irinaeos returned from exile, he entrusted OAK with the responsibility of reorganizing the Associations and developing their work.

Aims of the Associations

Before the involvement of OAK in the Women's Associations, their basic functions, as stated by Bishop Irinaeos himself (1986: 7) included talks on the personality of the Christian woman and her role in the family and the parish, social welfare, philanthropy/charity and entertainment.

OAK put a social worker, Grenda, in charge of the associations. She made an attempt, in collaboration with representatives of the various local associations, to set some general goals and aims (Grenda 1984: 110). She expressed these aims as follows:

a) To educate and encourage the women who live in rural areas so as to become active members of their parish. To cultivate their abilities and talents; to have a clear conception of modern life patterns and the rights granted to women as well as those rights and goals they have to fight for; to take initiatives when necessary, aiming at an active and responsible participation in community life.

b) To develop a cooperative spirit aiming at practising charity and helping those in need, the cultural development of the community, the organization of leisure and educational activities.

c) To contribute to the restoration and development of local handcrafts, so that the Cretan cultural tradition is preserved, household income is increased, and women are able to earn a personal income, which will contribute to their independence. To market the goods produced collectively so as to avoid being exploited by tradesmen/merchants (Grenda 1984: 110).

The language used by Grenda is very different from that used by Bishop Irinaeos. Although both talk about the need for encouraging women's active participation in the local parish and in charity, the Bishop speaks about 'the role of Christian women in the family' and about 'entertainment'. Grenda, on the other hand, also speaks about 'women's rights', 'an active participation of rural women in community life', 'leisure', and 'women's ability and right to earn a personal income from handcrafts, etc., which will contribute to their financial independence'. Nonetheless, it seems that both before and after the involvement of OAK in the Women's Associations, the ideal of womanhood as primarily relating to home and family was maintained. In addition, the emphasis on women as being wives and mothers in Orthodox Christian morality has been a crucial influence on defining what the life-style and self-interest of these women ought to be. As Grenda herself came from a family with strong religious feelings – she used to attend a Sunday school (*katihitiko*), where instruction about religion was given to school-age children – her aims for reform were within the boundaries of public and domestic life set by the Christian Orthodox belief. The associations' aims were also geared towards social welfare activities, that is charitable work – carried out not necessarily for women only – as well as leisure and religious activities, such as organizing excursions, celebrating festivals and fundraising for repairing a local church.

Grenda's importance lies in the mediating role which she was able to play between the Bishop and the village women, by virtue of her sex as well as of her position as a social worker assigned to organize the associations. She was influential in trying to articulate the women's demands with those of the Bishop. But in doing so, the religious principles of the Bishop and also of herself came at times in conflict with the more 'radical' demands of the women (see, for example, the Platanos case outlined below) which came as a response to changing economic and social relations in the villages.

The OAK's cooperation with the associations encouraged local women to have an active role in village social and cultural life. In addition, together with the Organization of Greek Handcrafts (a branch of the then EOMMEX [Hellenic Organization for Small and Medium-size Industries and Handcrafts]), they organized a series of training programmes on handcrafts and marketing. These training sessions helped women to earn money on their own through making handcrafts, embroidering, weaving and so on. As a result, workshops of local handcrafts such as weaving were set up in the regions of Kisamos and Selinon, and exhibitions of craftwork took place in nearby towns, namely Kastelli and Kolymbari. These attracted hundreds of visitors, both from all over Greece and from abroad.

Nevertheless, neither before nor after the involvement of OAK in the Women's Associations did issues like rape, rescue for battered wives, maternity leave, pensions, etc. (which since the early 1980s *inter alia* dominated the agenda of women's organizations in Greek cities), appear on the agenda of these associations. These were issues that the associations did not even talk about.

And why should they concern themselves with such urban metropolitan issues which, even when they occur at the village level, remain well hidden? Such issues are not mentioned in public records of the Associations' activities, which suggests that they were hardly ever raised and discussed in public – this point has also been confirmed by Grenda herself – from fear that they will bring shame to the families of the people concerned. This does not mean, however, that such issues were not discussed behind closed doors. According to village gossip, for example, a young woman in Nohia was often beaten by her husband until she was black and blue. The action was condemned by the women who were present and was attributed to the man's habit of getting drunk – as a local woman, Katina, said, 'when he is in his cups, he doesn't know what he is doing'. Nevertheless, the woman was praised for not dissolving the marriage: 'she is a sensible woman, she stays for the sake of the children', the same woman said. It would have been very radical for the local association's members to engage themselves openly in such discussions and to support actions such as the abandonment of a husband and possibly children by a battered wife. In Cretan society, if the wife endures such actions patiently, she is making a martyr of herself and is praised. If she stands up for herself and leaves her husband, she is stigmatized as self-centred, someone who puts her personal interests above those of her family. The local association might have run the risk of being seen by the rest of the village as encouraging the breaking up of families rather than as an institution protecting women against violence exerted on them by men. An open protest would perhaps have required a change, first in local women's life chances and second in local attitudes regarding gender relations. 'Such incidents were not discussed openly in the community; the women involved are "shamed" and their men "dishonoured"', a woman said. Although some informal discussion did take place within the local association, it did not result in giving support to lone mothers. If it had done so, the association might have been seen as encouraging an act that was and still is against the prevailing morals which the church, as well as the community, adhere to. These things are *amartia* (sin) (Herzfeld 1985: 239). Another woman added; 'but it is not the association's business to get involved in this; such incidents if unravelled can destroy a man's life, can dishonour him in the eyes of the community.' The best they could offer to reduce women's burdens were leisure activities such as excursions, so that women could be released for a while from domestic duties,[2] that is, activities concentrating on helping people to adjust to their traditional position rather than to challenge or change it.

---

2 It should be noted, however, that such activities and/or social occasions do encourage women's mutual supportiveness.

Formal Structure of the Associations

The formal structure of all associations is bureaucratic and hierarchical. The Administrative Council[3] of each association comprises nine members (including the local priest who is the honorary president) and is responsible for administering the property of the association it represents. It decides on issues related to the activities of the group and the realization of its aims; it also submits a report on its activities to the General Board meeting.[4] It has the power to strike someone off the membership list if she does not abide by the regulations of the prescribed constitution, is thought to be acting against its interests or does not pay her membership fee; such a decision has to be approved by the General Board. The powers of the Administrative Council, therefore, are restricted by the General Board. As I shall show, in the case of Platanos, these powers of the General Board over the Administrative Council can sometimes prove to be vital for ensuring that the democratic procedures within the associations function properly.

In addition, there is a three-member Audit Council. Its main task is to oversee the execution of the work of the Administrative Council and report back to the General Board. There is a provision in the constitution of each association for regular biannual elections and for an annual General Board meeting. In practice, however, these provisions are not adhered to (see below).

All members of all associations in the regions of Kisamos and Selinon have the opportunity to meet during the *Vouli Gynaekas* (Woman's Assembly), that is the annual open-air meeting organized by the Bishop (see Figure 8.1). In practice, however, far from being a women's assembly or meeting, this is a meeting of all inhabitants of the regions; women are accompanied by their men,

---

3   The Administrative Council of each association has nine members and its chief officer is referred to as the President. On the hierarchical ladder of the associations' formal structure, however, the President stands below the priest of the local parish, who is the honorary president and holds the office for life. As women are not yet ordained as priests by the Greek Orthodox Church, we have a situation here whereby the 'head' of women's associations, the person who formally represents them in meetings with local organizations (for example, the Youth Association in Platanos), organizations from abroad, the Bishop, the local government and so on, is a man. Although honorary presidents often do not play an active role in the associations they represent, their presence is symbolically similar to that of the head of the family, who is the public representative of the household. In addition, there are two vice-presidents, a general secretary, a treasurer and three councillors in the Administrative Council. According to the constitution of each association, the Administrative Council must hold regular meetings, at least once a month.

4   The General Board meeting is a meeting of the general body of members of the association; this is, at least in theory, supposed to meet at least once a year. In practice, however, these seem to be defunct, in that no General Board meeting took place in either Nohia or Platanos or in any nearby village in the 1980s.

Figure 8.1   Annual gathering of the women's associations

children and other relatives, who see this as an opportunity for a family day out or a feast. An open air mass takes place, in which all priests participate and where the president of each of the 40 associations offers a *prosforon*, consecrated bread presented to the saints as thanksgiving for their protection. The saints are then expected to reciprocate (for a detailed account of these offerings to the saints in Southern Europe see Pina-Cabral 1986: 163–73; Dubisch 1990). This manifestation of religious practice is followed by a picnic[5] where people and the church hierarchy drink and dance and sing, that is, participate in the more profane aspects of the feast.[6] This is approved by the church, which stresses the community-wide expression of religion rather than individual salvation. As

---

5   The picnic was not preceded or followed by an account of the activities of the associations or their plans for the future during the proceedings. Instead the presidents offered a *prosforon* (consecrated bread) to be blessed by the Bishop. Contrary to what one might have expected, the preparation of *prosforon* was not the result of a pool of resources by all village women; it was rather the sole responsibility of the president. This is not surprising, as life in villages has, to a great extent, been privatized; nowadays women hardly cook, wash or even prepare feasts together, as they did in the past (until the late 1960s).

6   Many women claimed that these meetings were 'different' in the past, without however being able to specify, when asked, in what way they differed, apart from being attended by more people (around 5,000 compared to no more than 800 who attended the meetings at which I was present).

Dubisch (1990: 129) maintains, 'It is fair to say that, in general, popular religion in Greece ... is outward looking, more concerned with external images, with the public and communal society than with the interior or the mystic'. Generally, and most importantly, ideas and feelings of women from the grassroots of the associations were not voiced in these meetings.[7] An exception was the few who held positions at the top of the associations' hierarchy, such as Mrs Anastasaki, the president of the Confederacy of Women's Associations.[8]

Despite the highly bureaucratic structure of the Women's Associations just described, this did not rule out the expressions of conflict between different groups of women, at least in Platanos. Given the inexperience of local women in running an association, and the inability or unwillingness of the leadership to address many of the needs of local women, in spite of the lengthy rule-books provided by Grenda, the majority of the associations failed to develop appropriate mechanisms to meet these needs. The conceptual gap between the hierarchical leaders and the grassroots needs was a great problem as the associations failed to continue to attract both the active support of the membership[9] and also the attention of the wider community. As a result, they gradually fell into disuse.

---

7   Two further aspects of the meetings I attended are important in illustrating how they were not organized from a woman's perspective. First, the allocation of space was an interesting one in that most of the priesthood, high-ranking state officials and representatives from the armed forces, and other honorary guests sat at tables for lunch, whereas most members were having their lunch sitting on the ground. The allocation of space was symbolic, a manifestation perhaps of the separation between the ordinary village woman and the local hierarchy; at least this is how the women themselves saw it. As an old woman commented: 'all the people who are seen as important by the Bishop sit beside him at the table, whereas the rest of us sit on the soil; the truth is, however, that we have more fun over here; we are free to eat, drink, talk and laugh.'

8   The Confederacy of Women's Associations was developed by Grenda during her work with the associations and functions as a coordinating body for all the associations of the two regions.

9   The vast majority of members were married women with children. Most worked in agriculture-related household activities and were married to men who earned their living from low status occupations, such as agriculture, renting rooms to tourists, working as manual workers in the construction industry, etc. The reason the associations had become idle relative to the past was, according to Irinaeos (1986: 9), the tendency of young local women to migrate. Many moved to urban areas, either through marriage or for education and later on for employment opportunities. As a result, most of the members of these associations were middle-aged women.

Bishop Irinaeos' Impact on the Associations

The Bishop's impact on the associations can be said to be a contradictory one. On the one hand, as it was frequently said, it was because of him that large numbers of women, despite their husbands' initial reluctance, came out of their homes to participate in these associations and thus become 'emancipated'. The reluctance of the husbands can be attributed to an attitude prevailing in rural Greece on the importance of keeping an eye on women or 'protecting' them. As du Boulay (1974: 118) writes,

> This attitude is ... dominated by the concept of women as weak and sensual such that any possibility of a personal relationship with them which is not physical, or which is not strictly controlled by ideal roles, is completely excluded.

So, the Bishop appeared to be a social reformist who worked for, supported and encouraged women to organize on their behalf. In his own writings on the subject he maintained that women should be equal to men, emphasizing the fact that women's and men's roles are complementary; he justified women's roles in the domestic domain in terms of women's 'special needs and qualities'. In other words, he saw women as equal to men, but equality is defined in terms of complementarity and the special qualities of women, which render them indispensable in the private space, the home. The emphasis is on women's reproductive work and encompasses childbearing, the nurturing of infants, the socialization of children and care and maintenance of the home. The last-mentioned involves a range of tasks from food preparation to housework, care for the sick and the elderly, as well as observance of memorial services, making the remembrance food on the appropriate days and counting the strands in the home-made candles made from thread and wax with which, one by one, the dead in both her own and her husband's kindred are commemorated (ibid.: 131). This work affects and is affected by women's productive work (within the private space of the home and the public space outside), and has an influence on relations of power between men and women in a way that the Bishop does not seem to give full credit to. In fact, he seems to disapprove of those women who in practice do not fit preconceived patterns of what women should do and how. At the twentieth anniversary of the associations, he said:

> Generally, one could characterize the work of the Women's Associations in our regions as a (*feministiko kinima*) 'feminist movement', which reminds us of the emancipation of women during the early Christian era. [It is] a movement that gives women incentives and rights without estranging them from their essential nature and without keeping them away from their mission, as is the case with other similar movements ... The modern women's complaint that the one-sided androcentric civilisation does, in many cases, injustice and is prejudicial to them, is well grounded. Asking, however, for equality in a sense that they become like men

[and are treated like men], are in danger of losing their charismatic personality. Christian anthropology sees the human species as being a unified one ... and beyond and above the 'struggle between the sexes' and the antithesis between Patriarchy and Matriarchy; ... it [views] the roles of men and women as different but complementary ones ... [Women should] remain faithful to our Christian tradition and from within this tradition fight for ... [their] rights ... This is my wish for the women of our Metropolis and country now that the Associations in our parishes are about to celebrated their 20th anniversary. (From OAK local archives)

On the other hand, the Bishop de-radicalized the women's movement by emphasizing 'women's nature', as well as a 'natural' division between the sexes, which stems from a woman's ability to give birth, her qualities as a mother and her capacity to hold the house together ... not only by her physical activity in making the place a sanctuary from the outside world in which food, warmth, and peace are to be found, but also by the ritual activities through which in a

metaphysical sense she guards and protects the family (du Boulay 1974: 131).

So, the Bishop tried to break away from traditional customs in seeking a new social role for women while, at the same time, he held traditional and religious ideals about women's nature and role, which can be contrasted with the rhetoric he used above, when he characterized the associations as being a 'feminist movement'. In order, therefore, to be able to comprehend his position first of all as 'patron' of the associations and second, to analyse the directions in which they have moved, one has to take into account Orthodox religious belief. Dubisch (1986: 23) has described this in the following way:

> Women are associated with Eve and with all the evil and wickedness she represents, thereby justifying male superiority and men's control over women. Yet, at the same time, women also are associated with the Mother of God (the *Panayia*) ... Outside their proper roles as wives and mothers, women are Eves and the root of evil; yet in their fulfilment of these roles, they become reflections of their divine archetype.

So, the apparently equal complementarity between the sexes conceals a basic inequality.

These associations failed to address the needs of the rural women for whom they were intended. The ideas put forward can be said to be 'conservative', in that these did not challenge the patriarchal regime prevalent in Cretan culture.

The Women's Associations in Nohia and Platanos

The Women's Association in Nohia was founded in March 1958. It was initially called the 'Orthodox Sisterhood of Married and Unmarried Women of Nohia –

the Holy Trinity'[10] and in January 1973 was renamed the 'Association of Married and Unmarried Women of Nohia – the Holy Trinity'. Unfortunately no one in the village seemed to remember the reason for this change in name. What one can notice, however, is that the word 'Orthodox' is no longer incorporated into the title, which means that, at least in theory, the explicit identification of the association with the Orthodox church is dropped. However, the significance of this change is obscured by the fact that the Association continues to be associated with the main church in the village, whose name it continues to bear.

According to Article 2 of the charter of the association, the aims of the 'Sisterhood' were: first, the internal and external decoration of the church *Agia Trias* (Holy Trinity); second, the commitment to equip the church with several items that it needed; third, the support of any Christian villager who is in need; and finally, the religious education of its members. These do not depart from the general aims of the wider associations outlined earlier. Later on (1973), when a new charter was drawn up, the aims changed slightly in that under both charters the aims of the association remained geared towards social welfare activities and the support of the church, though the heavy emphasis on the latter was dropped in the second charter.

The Women's Association in Platanos was founded in the early 1960s and was called 'Social Welfare' (*Kinoniki Pronia*). Later on, when a new charter was drawn up (1968), the association was renamed 'The Invigorating Impulse'. It is interesting to note here that both titles have a religious resonance in Greek. As in Nohia, no one in Platanos seemed to know why that charter was replaced and the association renamed. In addition, as Ms Jouganaki, a single woman in her early 30s, who was the President of the Association in Platanos during the late 1980s mentioned, the first charter 'went missing' and therefore one could not compare the two or draw any conclusions about any changes that might have taken place.

The aims of the association in Platanos, according to Article 2 of the charter, are: first, the development of a spiritual movement in the local parish; second, entertainment; third, the moral and economic support of the public works of local government; fourth, charity; and finally, the support of parish work and, in general, of the social work of the Metropolis of Kisamos and Selinon.

All women over 18 who live in the two villages and share the goals of the local associations can become ordinary members. Anyone can become an honorary member of his or her local association, irrespective of place of residence or nationality, provided that he or she has contributed either financially or morally to the progress of the association and the realization of its goals. Men can be and are accepted as honorary members and, even today, women neither complain about it nor try to alter the situation as one might have expected, given their exposure to new urban ideas through the media, migration, education and

---

10   Holy Trinity is the name of one of the several churches of the village.

access to towns and cities due to infrastructural developments which have taken place since the 1960s. When I asked some of the members why men were not excluded, a common reply was: 'Why should they be? It is not important'. The honorary members cannot be elected as members of the Administrative Board,[11] but can participate in general meetings and express their opinion, without having the right to vote.

The associations of Nohia and Platanos used to fund themselves through the members' subscription fees,[12] donations in money and goods (such as a hen, a rabbit, a few eggs, a jar of honey, oil, a cake, an embroidery) which are then sold at auctions organized by the association. Other means of supporting themselves were earnings from collections, raffles, selling calendars and so on.

From the archives of the association in Nohia it is evident that most of the charity was donated to a boarding house situated in the nearby town, Kastelli, and run by the Bishop. This housed children whose families lived in mountainous villages who thus could not travel every day to school. Aid was also given to a handful of people in the village[13] who, as the woman who served as President of the Association in the late 1980s maintained, for one reason or another 'were left destitute'. Most were old men and women, with no land of their own, whose children had migrated and had no other close relatives in the village to look after them. Some were young people whose parents could not afford dowry or education expenses, or sick people who needed money to cover the expenses required for treatment to Athens. Since the welfare state in Greece is in an embryonic state (see Lambropoulou 1990; Katrougalos and Lazaridis 2003), its functions are fulfilled by family members. In a way, therefore, the association tried with its activities to meet unfulfilled needs in cases where there were no close relatives available to do so. It also tried to compensate for a rudimentary welfare state in rural Crete as well as for the existence of the institution of dowry. The latter had to be given irrespective of the economic position of the woman involved and irrespective of the fact that dowry agreements were no longer legal. However, from the association's archives, it is evident that from 1958 to 1972, almost every year more money was donated to the church than was spent on welfare, irrespective of whether the latter was directed through

---

11   The members of the administrative board are elected every two years in the Women's Association in Nohia and every three years in Platanos.

12   Although the membership fee was very low (less than the price of a packet of cigarettes) many did not pay it. As Mrs Farandaki, who was president of the association in Nohia in the mid-1980s explained, 'In the old days, the Treasurer used to make a door-to-door collection. Now we do not do this [any more]. They forget to bring us the money'. This, alongside the fact that, contrary to the regulations that appear on the association's charter, there have been no elections held by the Administrative Council's members since 1979, were two indications that the Women's Association in Nohia had become defunct.

13   Since the association was founded, fewer than ten people received financial help.

church institutions or not.[14] This pattern gradually changed; from the 1970s onwards, more money was spent on charity than on their community church. Only a small amount of the income is spent on the association's members and that in the form of leisure activities such as excursions, *horoesperides* (dancing parties) and exhibitions of local handcrafts.[15] Since the early 1980s, the activities of the association gradually began to thin out and by the late 1980s they ceased. As the President argued, 'nowadays, with the use of fertilizers and the subsidies people received for agricultural production, there are no poor people in the village; everyone has a way to support themselves' (interview). The main reason, however, at least according to most villagers I spoke with, is the local women's involvement in the production of handcrafts. Significantly, the women who took up this craft were those who were active in the association; they maintained that they had little time for leisure now, whereas before they had 'nothing better to do'. As the village priest said, 'every woman shut herself in the house in order to earn money'. By contrast, young married women argued that the reason they do not want to get involved in the running of the association is that they are busy bringing up their children. So, according to the women themselves, the chief factor that seemed to predispose them against becoming active in their association is shortage of time and their traditional reproductive role. Another reason was that they have had a different value system to that of the association. Being run by middle-aged women and remaining still under the influence of the values held by the Greek Orthodox church, it still accommodates many of the traditional, patriarchal rules and values governing relations between men and women in the village (see Lazaridis 1995b). As Dimitra, a married woman in her early 30s, whom the president and the councillors tried to persuade to become involved in the association, said when asked why she refused: 'our beliefs are different'. Another woman said:

> I do not want to get involved in this! The priests always try to impose their opinion ... Irinaeos' achievement is very important; he drove the women out of the house at a time when they didn't dare to go anywhere [unaccompanied]. But new ideas are needed now. A step forward ... The association needs to focus on women's problems and issues.

---

14   For example, in 1958 the association bought a chandelier for the church. In 1961 it bore the cost of building the church's bell-tower. In 1967 it provided the church with a large carpet and 12 chairs. In 1969 it financed the electrification of the church. Moreover, money was spent on the Bishop, either in the form of donations to his institutions or by cooking traditional meals for him and his guests.

15   Although the villagers were proud of this, the women who worked for it – that is the President and the councillors – expressed some resentment at having to do all the preparations for the exhibition and receive the guests. 'They expect everything from us', the vice-president said. 'Other women should help too', one of the councillors added. So there seems to be a gap between the leaders of the association and the lower order membership who lack confidence and remain largely inactive and apathetic.

By the late-1980s, Platanos was different from Nohia. Until the mid-1970s, the activities of the association in Platanos were similar to those in Nohia (for example, helping the local church, providing spiritual and material comfort for those in need) and in line with the direction the Bishop wished them to follow. This was encouraged by the *papadia* (the priest's wife) who was at the time president of the association. Maria, a member of the association, maintained that during the *papadia*'s presidency 'all we did was to clean and paint small country churches and chase out the rats'. Another woman, Eftichia, argued: 'the association was very active, but it was very religious oriented'. Summers (1979: 35), in an article on women's philanthropic work in the nineteenth century, argues: 'those who engaged simply in the relief of poverty and distress did so from a sense of Christian duty.' The case of the women's association in Platanos was similar. As a result, instead of trying to help those in need by exercising political and social pressure on the government to introduce a series of social reforms which would eradicate poverty in rural areas, they tried to implement philanthropy as a remedy for the social ills prevailing in the area of Platanos. It seems that the development of a democratic political awareness was inhibited by hierarchical concepts of power. This is not to say, however, that hierarchical concepts of power are confined to the Orthodox Church. They are much more pervasive; and we find them throughout Greece and well beyond.

As far as gender inequality is concerned, similarly to Nohia, the association in Platanos emphasized women's traditional roles and obligations within the household. However, in the mid-1970s, and in contrast to Nohia, with the economic changes in the area of Platanos, which came about as a result of the development of greenhouses (see Chapter 4 on market gardening), some women began to perceive *their* position as being inferior to that of men. In addition, they began to feel the need to achieve an alternative organization in their work and family, whereby the pressure of working for long hours in the family business and, on top of that, having to look after the children and do all the housework would somehow be alleviated. In other words, although a strong conviction of the 'naturalness' of the prevailing gender order still remained, this was not wholly untroubled (see also Cowan 1990).

The attitude of the association mentioned above brought discontent and divided the members into two groups: the first group were the followers of *papadia*; the second group was formed by some women who wanted change in the association's activities and split from the influence of the church. Their motto was: 'The priest should keep himself busy in his church and we with our association.' In other words, a new level of consciousness, which came about from a new practical problem, resulted in the community bifurcating.[16] So, unlike the women of Nohia, women in Platanos did challenge the position of

---

16   A similar political separating out was witnessed by Greger (1985) in the Lasithi programme; when this took an antagonistic form (related to hierarchical power structures) it became destructive (personal communication with Sonia Greger).

the local priest as honorary president of their association and did not hesitate to express their dissatisfaction with it. A young woman, for example, mentioned that *papadia* wanted the association to keep painting churches and engage in various philanthropic activities, because this was the way the Bishop wanted them to be. Others argued that the association should have 'a greater variety of activities'. So 'a conflict between us and the followers of the *papadia* was inevitable', a woman said. The same woman continued:

> Just before the elections of 1976, the villagers were divided into supporters of the *papadia* and supporters of Anousaki [the woman heading the opposite camp]. It was like a [Greek] political rally; one could see slogans written on the walls of the village praising one of the two candidates.

In the 1976 elections of the Administrative Board, the *papadia* lost and the priest of the local parish reacted by resigning from his position as the honorary president of the association. As Mrs Anousaki, the woman who won the elections maintained,

> The situation was not an easy one. Grenda [who at the time supported the priest's wife] acted against the association's charter in that she brought along women who were not members of the association and, therefore, did not have the right to vote, and asked them to vote. We reacted; so, they left ... and the elections were put off for the following week ... They were calling us *andichristes* (antichrists).

When asked to comment on this incident, Grenda initially refused to do so, but later on attributed the whole thing to the ungratefulness exhibited by Anousaki and her followers towards her and the Bishop's work for the association.

From the files of the association it became apparent that new elections took place three months later, because three members from the Board, including the *papadia*, resigned. These elections were a stepping stone to a new era which saw the development of an alternative hegemony to that of the Orthodox Church, under the leadership of Anousaki and her followers – the hegemony of what Gramsci (1971; 1978) would have referred to as 'organic intellectuals' – who came to embrace 'ideas and social relations that circumscribe their own life possibilities' (Cowan 1990: 13).

The activities of the new Board, according to a report read by the President on 9 December 1979, that is, during the end of its term, were the following: first, the creation of a much needed childcare unit, which accepted children from two and a half to five years old. Second, the replacement of the old transmitter with a new one so that all villagers could watch TV. Third, the repairing of a branch road. Fourth, buying a piece of land for building the childcare unit. Fifth, the creation of the 'tomato feast' (*giorti tis domatas*, as the locals call it), which was one of the biggest festivals of the village in terms of participation and publicity, attended by thousands of people. The feast was a major social event, which was intended to promote the product, build up high spirits (*kefi*) and symbolize solidarity among the villagers. Everybody participated. Unlike *horoesperidhes* (annual balls) in other parts of Greece which 'are organised structurally in response to local ideas about males and females as social actors' (Cowan 1990: 134), the tomato feast was a place of entertainment for men and women, where local ideas about males and females as social actors became blurred. The tomato feast offers many contrasts to the *woman's assembly*; whereas the latter is a celebration organized under the church's auspices, the former is held to promote the product and celebrate solidarity between the producers; it promotes secular alliances based on economic interests. Both events gradually moved from an atmosphere of formality, constraint and hierarchy to an atmosphere of informality; the tomato feast also moved to an atmosphere of orderly disorder (that is, men and women being together in a social situation without becoming disorderly) and lack of hierarchy (see Cowan 1990: 134–70). It also differs from the traditional Cretan *glendi*, the hallmarks of which are gunshots (*baloties*) fired by men, an aggressive expression of having a good time the masculine way. In the tomato feast no gunshots are fired; it is a feast celebrating harvest in the female way. And finally, the new Board tried to bring the members of the association and the other villagers in contact with each other by organizing excursions and meetings, New Year parties, a series of cultural activities where many villagers took part, lectures delivered on a variety of topics (such as the behaviour of parents and its effects on the development of the child, the problems of the woman who works in agriculture and her child, infectious diseases and ways in which one can cope with them, etc.). It was also stated that the goals of the association for the subsequent three years (1980–1983) would be: the creation of a children's library and play ground; a solution to the problems created by the lack of water in the village during the summer months; putting pressure on the local authorities to speed up the asphalting of a road which connects the village with the coast; and finally, organizing excursions and cultural events.

The Board continued to be active and, apart from the water problem, which remained unsolved for years, realized its goals. In addition it organized talks and meetings for discussing the problems encountered by women and children of rural areas. Moreover, due to the development of summer and winter tourism in the area (the latter in the form of seasonal labour), members seemed worried and arranged a series of lectures on drugs, contraceptives and venereal diseases. These were well received by the villagers and especially by the older generation; people felt that village youth should be informed about 'the ills brought by modernization', as they put it, exposure to western values through the mass media and proximity to urban centres and people from abroad (which is facilitated by infrastructural developments) and praised the association for its efforts to do so. Furthermore, the councillors collected money through donations, bought a piece of land for erecting an office and a library for the association and asked the Ministry of Culture to help them financially.

Finally, they invited a theatre company to stage a play in the village. Many villagers gave them credit for bringing 'life to the village'. In a village where, as the President mentioned in a speech at the Administrative Board's meeting on 13 March 1983, 'women spend 15 hours per day in the greenhouses and have no time for leisure', these developments were appreciated and fulfilled important needs that should otherwise have been met by the state.

It is important to mention that in both 1979 and 1983, Mrs Anousaki, the President, in her detailed account of the association's activities during the 1976–1979 and 1980–1983 period, complained that the local government office did not offer any help to the association and abstained from all its activities. Since the local government did not support them, one may wonder whether this had anything to do with the fact that the secretary of the local government office is the brother of the local priest and the brother-in-law of the *papadia*; in Crete, as other parts of Greece, 'marriage relations were ... political, in that ... [they] ... created allies in the alien world of non-kin' (Lineton 1971: 39). If the secretary of the local government office had supported the new Administrative Board, he would have created the possibility of friction between his own and his brother's families. Such an explanation was supported by some women who said: 'He is a good man, but what can he do? He cannot betray his brother and support the *papadia*'s enemy.' When in 1983 Mrs Anousaki was replaced by another woman who was related to the local Member of Parliament, they did start to support the activities of the association again. Furthermore, Mrs Anousaki argued that some villagers (she did not mention who these people were) tried to undermine the association's activities by spreading a rumour that these were political activities serving the interests of a certain political party. As Chrysoula, a woman in her early 30s said, ' Anousaki did a lot of things ... but behind all this there were political motives, that is to say, political parties'. Some members of the Board (less than half), including the president, were indeed politically affiliated with the Greek Communist Party (KKE). This brought strong reactions in the village, despite the fact that the then President made clear in speeches on 9 December 1979 and 13 March 1983 that the association was and would continue to be politically neutral and argued that all women are welcome, irrespective of their political affiliations. This did not persuade those who condemned her for transforming the association 'from a Christian into a Communist one'. So, although the association in Platanos is ostensibly civic, thus not involved in political activities, they did go through a process of politicization (*kommatikopoiimeni*). They became the objects of struggle between political factions. When Anousaki was in power, the association seemed to be in the pocket of the local left-wing women. The latter gradually shifted from using their position for the good of all, to using it for the provision of individual favours to those who lent them their support both within the association and within local party politics (for a discussion of civic associations in a village in Northern Greece and the way they become enmeshed in local party political manoeuvrings, see Cowan 1990).

In the elections of 13 March 1983,[17] Mrs Anousaki lost her seat.[18] The outcome of the 1983 elections was viewed by most villagers as the end of a successful but also troublesome era, the end of a process whereby those who with right-wing or centre positions had been squeezed out. As mentioned in the files of the association in reference to the 1986 elections, 'they were carried out peacefully'. This confirms the point made by some local women, namely that in the past, there were political confrontations between the members of the Administrative Board. As a woman in her mid-50s said:

> when Anousaki was President, the Association was politicized; those affiliated with the government in power did not want a President who was in favour of [another party] the KKE [Greek Communist Party], and therefore reacted strongly ....

The association continued to be active under the new President; for example, they continued to celebrate the tomato feast, this time in cooperation with the local government office, the local cooperative and the Youth Association. They also continued to organize excursions and parties, to invite theatre companies to perform in the village, and took a first step to wider considerations by celebrating International Women's Day. They also asked the local government to do something about collecting garbage (a huge problem in rural areas). But gradually, the local priest was re-established as the honorary president of the association and contact with the Bishop was resumed. Initially, he sent a social worker to give a talk about women, children and the family; later on (1985), he himself visited the village and a year later (1986), the association collected money for the Bishop's institutions.

Nevertheless, the direction in which the women's association in Platanos had moved did shape its future, particularly its relationship with the Bishop. This relationship was never again as close as it was during the *papadia*'s era. Under her presidency, the activities of the association became leisure and religion oriented; a series of talks was delivered by the local priest's son (who is also a priest), money was collected and some members decorated two local churches.

17 The election system was as follows: all women members who wanted to be elected announced their willingness to do so 24 hours prior to the election. The council in Platanos consists of five people. During election day, all members are asked to write on a piece of paper the names of up to five candidates, from the list of all people who had expressed their willingness to be elected. Then, the votes are counted and the person who received the most is nominated as president, the next vice-president, the next, secretary and another two, councillors.

18 Seventy-eight women voted. Mrs Anousaki received 8.04 per cent of the votes whereas her opponent, Mrs Skoulaki, received 12.87 per cent of the votes and became President. It is worth mentioning here that during the 1976 and the 1979 elections she received 14.58 per cent and 14.08 per cent of the votes respectively. The results of the 1986 elections were not available in the association's minute book and the village women could not find or remember the percentage of votes allocated to each candidate.

Little by little, the new leadership managed to 'de-radicalize' the association and also to render it inactive. Many women criticized this inactivity. 'This shouldn't be called an association; it has disintegrated', said one woman. Miss Juganaki, who was elected president in 1986, in an informal conversation we had together, justified this inactivity in terms of local women's indifference. There are, of course, women who claim that they do not have time for anything other than the family and the greenhouse. Nevertheless, there are a few women who believe that the issue is more complicated and the reason for the association's inactivity lies in a tendency of the party members in government to keep organizations such as the Women's Association or the Agricultural Association in a dormant state and thus avoid bringing to the open any dissatisfactions or problems which, once in the public arena, would cause problems for the party/government.[19]

Concluding Remarks

Why did the women in Nohia never challenge the traditional and religious ideals about women's nature and role? Why did women in Platanos, at one stage of their history, move beyond the religious ideals and come to address the secular needs of the rural women for whom the association was intended? The answer to these questions lies, I believe, in the different economic development of the two villages and the different opportunities this has created for the women who live there.

As shown above, these organizations were formed in the late 1950s, when women's roles in rural Crete were defined in reference to the family; as du Boulay (1974: 117) argues, 'the family is the basic unit of society which contains all the primary rights and obligations of the individual'. Moreover, the society's value system and its understanding of the ideals of masculine and feminine behaviour were built on the notion that 'men and women form a complementary opposition according to which men have a natural association with the sacred world, and women with that of the demons'. Women's association with the world of demons is closely related to female sexuality which, according to the 'honour-shame' value system, must be controlled, since by nature women possess the quality of shame (see Chapter 7). A woman who has no sense of shame lacks inner defence against the compulsion of the rest of her nature and will inevitably succumb to it (du Boulay 1974: 107). A man's role is to protect his family from shame, that is, to protect the virginity of the unmarried girls and the chastity of the married women in the family. His inability to do so means that he loses his honour, reputation and respect in the community and can thus be ridiculed. No woman is believed to be beyond temptation; hence a secure way to protect one's family from shame is to keep women at home.

---

19   The party in government at the time was the Panhellenic Socialist Party (PASOK).

Thus, in the late 1950s, women getting out of the house regularly, without the company of menfolk and other women, was regarded in both Nohia and Platanos as unacceptable. Men considered the work of the associations with scepticism. Gradually, however, to quote the Bishop, 'they saw their utility and not only did they allow their wives to participate, they also encouraged them to do so' (Irinaeos 1986: 9). This was confirmed by a woman in Nohia, who said,

> When the association was established in the village, for the first time women came out of the houses and started going to other villages to attend meetings. Initially, men were sceptical and reluctant to allow their wives and daughters to join the Association. Later on, however, when they realized that women's participation did not pose any threat to them, they accepted the situation.

The Bishop's involvement in the associations' activities and his reassurance that these were charitable and religious ones, legitimized women's involvement and hence their occasional absence from home. If, perhaps, the initial role of the associations had not been connected with religious oriented and charitable activities, which are regarded in the respective male-dominated communities as legitimate occupations for women outside the domestic domain, this might have risked alienating both men and women, or at least male support, and thus rendered their existence impossible. So, at least in the beginning, the road of caution rather than confrontation was probably the only option available.

As shown above, the women's association in Nohia continued to operate along the above mentioned lines, until the late 1980s when it gradually became defunct, due to the ex-active members' new interest in the production of handcrafts for cash. Its members saw this association as a way of utilizing free time. Thus, the women failed to create an informal interest group among them, which might have exercised political and social pressure on the local government's policies regarding the infrastructural development of the village, as well as on the male population of the village regarding attitudes concerning the female population of the community. The character and conditions of domestic labour, in association with petty commodity production, contributed to this. In the case of Nohia, it was production within the context of the domestic unit which contributed to women's exclusion from the public domain, even though it also gave women the opportunity to produce on their own account and market their product successfully. Furthermore, production within the domestic unit is individualistic and competitive; this might also be the reason why women in Nohia did not exhibit strong solidarity or try to assert their economic position in relation to their husbands. Neither did they exhibit any interest in improving living conditions within the village via the association, nor did they attempt to raise these issues through other channels, such as political parties, or through other women's groups such as the 'Democratic Women's Group', the 'Union of Greek Women', or the 'Federation of Greek Women'. These are mainly urban groups, which function under the umbrella of major political parties. According to Stamiris (1986: 107),

> Party affiliation ... often provided the broader male legitimisation needed for the women to mobilise throughout the country, since male party members or sympathisers found it difficult to oppose the recruitment of their wives and daughters into what they considered as the party's women's group.

However, contrary to Stamiris' claims, such organizations and their socialist-feminist orientation, which saw women's oppression as deriving from capitalism and also patriarchy, did not reach villages like Nohia.

The Women's Association in Platanos followed a different historical path from that of Nohia. Contrary to the 'tea and Bible' (Summers 1979: 58) women in Nohia, the members of the association in Platanos formed a pressure group which exercised some political and social pressure on the government to bring about changes; from these changes, all villagers did eventually benefit in one way or another. One could argue that this was the outcome of the conflicting demands between home and work in the greenhouses, which made them conscious of their position. The character and conditions of the labour involved, as well as the fact that, due to the nature of the work, women were exposed to ideas and faced problems that women in Nohia did not, encouraged a group of active left-wing women. These women exhibited dedication to political education (which is a characteristic of people who adhere to left-wing ideas in Greece and elsewhere) and were thus exposed to wider views of women's questions. The latter encouraged them to try and engineer a shift in order of priorities of the institution's activities and thus use the association as a vehicle to bring about changes in the village in general and facilitate women's work in particular.

Why did this group of active women who succeeded not only in getting a hearing, but also an enthusiastic support and following from other women in the community in implementing many of their goals, emerge at all in Platanos? These differences cannot be explained solely in terms of particular personalities of women involved. Neither is there any evidence of a long-standing Communist tradition in Platanos. The majority of the villagers voted for centre parties such as *Enosis Kentrou* in the 1964 parliamentary elections, *Enosis Kentrou-Nees Dynamis* in 1974 and since 1977 they have been voting for PASOK (Panhellenic Socialist Party), which was born from the *Enosis Kentrou* in 1974. The case of Nohia is similar; here, too, the majority of people have, since 1964, voted for centre parties and since 1977 for PASOK (this being typical of Crete).[20] The

---

20 Crete has always been a stronghold of the parties of the centre, especially since the prominent Cretan politician Eleftherios Venizelos entered the Greek political scene in the first decade of the twentieth century. He was the Prime Minister throughout the Balkan Wars and the leader of the party which governed Greece in World War I, an initiative that brought a clash with the monarchy in 1917. After he died, his son was an

difference between the two villages can be attributed to the different economic developments that these have gone through and their impact on the lives of women and the perceptions of their position in the public and private realms.

One of the reasons why the Platanos Association stopped being active was because at the grassroots level it saw itself dependent on the centre for resources; also, the changes brought about in the life of women since greenhouses were introduced in the area, must have had an influence on the political attitudes of these women, although this is difficult to assert, without having any information on whether women's voting attitudes have changed through the years.[21] What we know from the association's history, however, is that women became embroiled in party politics. Also, as shown earlier, these women undoubtedly achieved some of the things they came together for. Moreover, in 1981 a Youth Organization emerged in Platanos, which took over some of the activities of the Women's Associations. For example, in 1988 it was the Youth Association which prepared the annual tomato feast, invited prominent intellectuals to talk about environmental protection, tourism and family planning and organized a theatre and parties (*glendia*) in the village.

To sum up, we can see that for all the particular personalities involved and the intricacies of the story, the differences clearly reflect the different economic arrangements as they affect women's lives in the villages. As far as the eventual running down of the association in Platanos is concerned, a broader reason was because of the confrontation which arose between these active women mentioned above and their ideas and some other groups, including men and women who felt threatened by the sudden change of women's role in the public domain and their attack on the traditional value systems mentioned above. As the cases of Nohia and Platanos show, voluntary Associations 'constitute social fields through which individuals and collectivities construct and negotiate their relationships with the village over time .... They provide a resilient cultural form, which different groups employ to pursue their diverging ends... [they] constitute, therefore, complex fields of social interaction, the study of which can

---

important leader of the Venizelos party, which was eventually recognized and in the 1950s became known as *Enosis Kentrou* under the leadership of George Papandreou. As Demathas (1991: 11), in his paper on economic and social development in Crete, writes with regard to election results: 'In 1952 when the Right got its power stabilised, Crete continued ...[to be] the stronghold of the Parties of Centre. In 1964 when *Enosis Kentrou* took power, Crete was one of its Centres. The same is repeated right after stabilisation of the political scene, which followed the Junta period (1967–74). Crete is one of *PASOK* centres ... *New Democracy* (the Conservative Party) appears ... [having] an overall percentage of 37% to 36% (considerably lower than the country average)'.

21   Election results kept in the Ministry of Interior in Athens, in the Prefecture (*Nomarchia*) of Chania as well as in the local government's office in the villages, were not available by sex distribution and so one cannot know the voting behaviour of men and women in Nohia and Platanos.

illuminate a whole host of issues of current anthropological [and sociological] interest' (Aspraki 2004: 140).

Epilogue

I have been concerned in this book with the exploration of the limits and possibilities of economic change in transforming women's lives in two village communities, Nohia and Platanos, both situated in the western part of Crete. In each case, detailed analysis has concentrated on the period between the late sixties and the late eighties, although wherever appropriate, references have been made to the period thereafter. The situation and events I have described in this book are nearly 20 years old. Just (2000: 259) writes:

> What frames a period of time, what gives it coherence, what makes it a unit, is the fact that it was a relatively discrete (and for most ethnographers, extremely important) period of one's own life ... It does not worry me at all that the results of my fieldwork must now be read as history (that is the common fate of ethnography). It would, however, worry me greatly if they were not read historically, as a particular moment in a continual process of change, but as the account of a vanished way of life.

I have tried to evaluate the changing position of these women, taking into account a number of discrete theoretical approaches, namely issues appearing in the literature on women and development, those issues highlighted by social anthropologists who have carried out research in rural Greece, as well as certain contributions on the state of Greek agriculture (namely reasons why small agricultural units based on family labour for survival have persisted to the present day), the role of the European Community (now European Union) in transforming the structure of agriculture in Greece and in Crete, and recent theoretical contributions from the world of sociology and gender studies.

The results of this study do not lead to a simple conclusion about the role of economic development (which has evolved out of a set of historical circumstances described in the introductory chapters of the book) in changing women's lives and about the role of culture and ideology in curtailing the emancipatory potential of economic development. Economic development had neither touched nor affected all women in the same way; the fact that these women are not a homogeneous group (they differ by age, occupation, origin, marital status, etc.) means that they are not uniformly affected by economic and other changes, which renders impossible any efforts to draw a common conclusion regarding all.

Two new forms of cash income (in addition to the cultivation of olive trees for production of olive oil), cocoon handcrafts in Nohia and market gardening in Platanos have particularly influenced the division of labour by sex. In Nohia, before engaging in the production of handcrafts local women were working alongside their husbands (the 'head of the household') in agriculture as part of the family labour force, helping him secure an income for the family's livelihood. The production of handcrafts gave these women the opportunity to earn an income independent of the rest of the household's economic activities and thus have a greater say in the spending of money. However, the non-separation of the site of production from that of reproduction meant that besides the fact that these women define themselves as 'self-employed' and their significant contribution in the household budget is recognized as substantial by the rest of the household members, their work remains a 'hidden' occupation, and hence in their social appearance they are housewives. I have argued that this contradiction has its roots in the fact that the occupational status of the household is defined according to the occupation of the male 'head', thus making these women 'invisible' by not defining them as workers. Their 'semi-domestication' has its roots in the prevalent gender regime which reinforces the hierarchical relationship between men and women. In addition, because the workplace is at home, this does not enable these women to challenge the existent traditional values which inhibit the degree of change in women's position in the way that the women who are involved in market gardening in Platanos do.

Unlike Nohia, in Platanos the ideological domestication of women preached by the Greek Orthodox Church and the 'honour and shame' value system, is discarded in practice if economic necessity arises which forces women to work outside the house in the greenhouses to secure the family's subsistence. In addition, new technology being adopted altered the division of labour in the greenhouses; it has had a differential impact on men and women in that it narrowed the tasks done by men and increased some of the burdens for women, without however discouraging women's involvement in agricultural tasks as was suggested by Boserup (1986) back in the mid-1980s in relation to plough cultivation in Asia. The lack of time spent by these women on 'properly' looking after their house and children has meant that self-esteem and prestige conferred on a woman which stems from being a 'mistress in the house' has been transferred to the 'greenhouse'. Unlike women in Nohia, women in Platanos resent having to carry the burden of work in the domestic site without the help of men. The fact that these women are exposed to different ideas from daily contact with agricultural scientists, government officials, merchants and the like, may have been a contributing factor in shaping their views about gender division of labour and challenging women's 'natural' concentration on domestic work and stressing the fundamental role they play in the production of exchange values in the greenhouse.

Moreover, although it was assumed that the impact of the European Community's (now European Union) regulations and directives would be positive for the women concerned, this assumption turned out to be erroneous, despite the fact that the EC then and the EU now, advocated equality/equity between men and women. Evidence from this study shows that although EC subsidies (in the form of inputs – technological and other) were assumed to affect the whole family equally, they were unequally distributed among family members, since they were geared towards the 'head of the family unit', by officials (men and women) who thus, together with traditional values, beliefs and customs embedded in Greek and Cretan culture (legitimizing the attitudes which perpetuate gender inequality) contributed to the perpetuation of the ideological undervaluation of women's work.

The economic changes that took place have influenced two aspects of the socio-cultural realm, namely marriage and family relations and women's associations. I have shown the role played by the Greek Orthodox Church in setting up, influencing, guiding and perhaps 'limiting' the activities of these associations. I have also argued that these associations failed in the long run to address the needs of the rural women for whom they were intended and were conservative in that they did not challenge the patriarchal basis of the local culture, but encouraged the maintenance of existing traditional values. However, contrary to Nohia (where women never challenged the traditional and religious ideals about women's nature and role), in Platanos the local women's association became relatively more radical when women became actively involved in market gardening and, as a result, their domestic responsibilities changed. At one stage of their history, the women's associations in Platanos moved beyond religious ideals and came to address the secular needs of the rural women for whom they were intended.

In addition, I have looked at the way the economic development of the two villages has affected certain aspects of women's lives in respect to marriage. Since the late 1960s the institution of *proxenio* (arranged marriage) and of dowry have changed in both villages. Grooms now tend to ask permission to marry a woman themselves instead of using a third party as mediator, and the institution of dowry (*prika*) was abolished in the early 1980s. Moreover, the emphasis on *prikia* shifted from detailed handmade items to luxurious manufactured items bought in the market. The goals of marriage and family continue to be intergenerational mobility via education of children and provision of residential property at the time of marriage. To achieve this, parents over-exploit themselves by working long hours. Children are expected to reciprocate this, by looking after their parents when the latter are old and/or sick. However, since women's involvement in market gardening, there has been a change in the capacity of these women to provide care for relatives. This indicated at the time that the changing economic circumstances had started shaping and/or transforming patterns of practical support. Nowadays, although social values and sentiments associated with family life remain strong, patterns of support have changed; elderly and other dependents are looked after by migrant domestic workers, quasi-nurses or *apoklistikes* or 'les infirmières exclusives' (see Lazaridis 2007a, 2007b).

Finally, in Platanos, because of the nature of their work, women are constantly in the company of non-family men. Their reputation is determined by their capacity to work and look after their family, rather than by their potential sexual activities. The fact that the women's associations in Platanos organized talks on contraception that young people were expected to attend, suggests that, at the time fieldwork took place, physical contact before marriage was expected. The notion that sex is only for procreation which, as Hirschon (1989) has suggested, is bound up with religious notions regarding the purpose of the sexual act and the definition of female sexuality, had started to change in both villages. It must be noted here that the different economic development of the two villages has affected the form, content and functioning of female chastity codes differently; the emphasis on female chastity and the desirability for premarital virginity for women had, by the mid-1980s, declined in Platanos and to a lesser extent in Nohia. The cultural emphasis on female chastity as an indication of social worth for individuals and their families had given way to hard work in Platanos. This change in gender-related values and behaviour, however, comes into conflict with an emphasis on the risks of promiscuity due to the AIDS epidemic which was seen in the area as the outcome of the risks of 'non-natural acts' provoking God's retribution and with the older generation's subscription to traditional gender-related values and behaviour. Many are even today caught between two worlds, and this creates tension between the sexes and in particular between generations.

Have women in Nohia and Platanos been empowered? The answer to this question is far from simple. In both villages, women's earnings went into the household budget. In Platanos, work in the greenhouses decreased the time available for 'leisure' but increased women's awareness of the paternalistic attitude of local and regional bureaucrats towards their work and created a feeling of uneasiness about the way they were treated.

Since the mid-1980s, when the fieldwork on which this book is based was carried out, I have visited the villages a couple of times, the last time being in 2003; not everything had changed, but a lot had. There were more houses in the villages and some of the old ones had been renovated. Some of my old friends had died, others were now elderly. Handcraft production in Nohia had ceased to exist. At the same time, the global increase of demand for organic products may mean that the demand of vegetables produced in Platanos' greenhouses, where there is extensive application of chemical fertilizers and sprays, will inevitably result in either a switch to other cultivations or abandonment of these activities in favour of what? Tourism? Maybe, as some tourist developments are noticeable, including two noisy kiosks near the beaches which are now covered with umbrellas and chaise-longues for rent. Nevertheless, it has already been reported that the nearby shore has been polluted due to the fact that pesticides and other chemicals used in the greenhouses, as well as refuse from the nearby tourist development, are dumped into the sea untreated. Since it is the young people who have been engaged in these activities, it is likely that they may switch to *pluriactivity*. One may ask: are the various development programmes imposed from above appropriate to the resolution of the island's problems, and to what extent does their successful implementation depend on the fact that many EU policies are mediated by the filter of Athens-based decision making and hence on the capability of the political pressure being exerted by the region concerned?

There are no simple answers to the questions addressed in this book, because the terms upon which women engage in the public sector are variable and operate differentially among different women. I have looked at two different social constructions and levels of women's dependency and I do not claim that one can generalize from this. Has the position of women in Platanos improved? Yes, but it has also meant more work for these women *vis-à-vis* those who do not work in greenhouses. Accumulation of individual rights guaranteed by the state did not mean that things would change from one day to the next; traditional ways of thinking still exist which inhibit women from breaking free from the patriarchal family and its vestiges, that is an ideology which justifies the dependence of women on male kin for support and the allocation of domestic chores to women, irrespective of their access to material resources, such as an income from selling handcrafts or from their contribution in the family business. In other words, men's and women's roles are constructed in a culturally specific way; it is not possible to predict from the socioeconomic profile of the household, the exact level of control women may have over their lives or their access to freedom over their actions and movement in the public space. Women's capacity to act individually or collectively through their associations to change their conditions has been curtailed by ideological and cultural barriers to emancipation. But more often than not, appearances and realities are not two co-tangent circles. The way we see things and perceive 'realities' is affected by what we know and what we believe at a given time.

References

Akeroyd, A.V. (1990) 'Ethics in Relation to Informants, the Profession and Governments', in R.F. Ellen (ed.) *Ethnographic Research: A Guide to General Conduct*. London: Academic Press.

Allbaugh, L.G. (1953) *Crete: A Case Study of an Underdeveloped Area*. Princeton, NJ: Princeton University Press.

Allen, P.S. (1976) 'Aspida: A Depopulated Maniat Community', in M. Dimen and E. Friedl (eds) *Regional Variation In Modern Greece and Cyprus: towards a Perspective on the Ethnography of Greece*. Annals of the New York Academy of Sciences, Vol. 268. New York: The New York Academy of Sciences. Also translated into Polish and published in *Studia Polonijne*, Vol. 18, pp. 19–38.

Amin, S. and Vergopoulos, K. (1974) *Dysmorfos Kapitalismos*. Athens: Papazisis (in Greek).

Anthias, F. (1998) 'Rethinking Social Divisions: Some Notes towards a Theoretical Framework', *The Sociological Review*, Vol. 46, No. 3, pp. 505–35.

Arnold, M. (1982) 'The Struggle for Feminism in a Traditionally Feministic Society: The Case of Greece', paper presented to the 81st Annual meeting of the American Anthropological Association, 3–7 December, Washington DC.

Arnold, M.S. (1985) 'Childbirth among Rural Greek Women in Crete: Use of Popular, Folk and Cosmopolitan Medical Systems', PhD thesis, University of Pennsylvania.

Aspraki, G. (2004) 'Karagatriot Voluntary Associations: "Out of Love for our Village"', *Journal of Modern Greek Studies*, Vol. 22, pp. 137–72.

Avdela, E. (undated) 'Extrosi', *Dini*, Athens.

Barclay, C.R. and DeCook, P.A. (1988) 'Ordinary Everyday Memories: Some of the Things of which Selves are Made', in U. Neisser and E. Winograd (eds) *Remembering Reconsidered: Ecological and Traditional Approaches to the Study of Memory*. Cambridge: Cambridge University Press.

Barlett, P.F. (1986) 'Part-time Farming: Saving the Farm or Saving the Lifestyle?', *Rural Sociology*, Vol. 51.

Beneria, L. (1982a) 'Accounting for Women's Work', in L. Beneria (ed.) *Women and Development: The Sexual Division of Labor in Rural Societies*. New York: Praeger.

Beneria, L. (1982b) 'Introduction', in L. Beneria (ed.) *Women and Development: The Sexual Division of Labor in Rural Societies*. New York: Praeger.

Berkowitz, L. (1980) *A Survey of Social Psychology*, 2nd edition. London: Holt, Rinehart and Winston.

Bernstein, H. (1985) 'Notes in Capital and Peasantry', in J. Harriss (ed.) *Rural Development: Theories of Peasant Economy and Agrarian Change.* London: Hutchinson.

Bernstein, H. (1988) 'The Subcontracting of Cleaning Work in Israel: A Case in the Casualisation of Labour', in R.E. Paul (ed.) *On Work.* Oxford: Basil Blackwell.

Bialor, P.A. (1976) 'The Northwestern Corner of Peloponnesons: Mavrikion and its Region', in E. Dimen and E. Friedl (eds) *Regional Variation in Modern Greece and Cyprus: Toward a Perspective on the Ethnography of Greece.* Annals of the New York Academy of Sciences, Vol. 268, New York: New York Academy of Sciences.

Boserup, E. (1986) *Women's Role in Economic Development.* Aldershot: Gower.

Boserup, E. (1988) 'Economic Change and the Roles of Women', in I. Tinker (ed.) *Persistent Inequalities: Women and World Development.* Oxford: Oxford University Press.

Bryant, L. (1999a) 'The Detraditionalization of Occupational Identities in Farming in South Australia', *Sociologia Ruralis*, Vol. 39, No.2, pp. 236–65.

Bryant, L. (1999b) 'Body Politics at Work: Exploring Gender and Sexuality in Constructions of Occupation(s) in Agriculture', unpublished paper delivered to Gender and Transformation in Rural Europe, Wageningen, 14–17 October.

Bujra, J.M. (1978) 'Introductory: Female Solidarity and the Sexual Division of Labour', in J. Dubisch (ed.) *Gender and Power in Rural Greece.* Princeton, NJ: Princeton University Press.

Burgel, G. (1965) *Pobia: Etude Geographique d' un Village Cretois.* Athens: Centre des Sciences Sociales d' Athens (in French).

Burgess, R.G. (1989) *In the Field: And Introduction to Field Research.* London: Unwin Hyman.

Campbell, J.K. (1964) *Honour, Family and Patronage: A Study of Institutions and Moral Values in a Greek Mountain Community.* Oxford: Oxford University Press.

Caplan, P. (ed.) (1989) *The Cultural Construction of Sexuality.* London: Routledge.

Caraveli-Ioannides, H. (1985) 'The Greek Farm Income Problem in Light of Accession to the EEC', PhD thesis, Wye College, University of London.

Caravelli, A. (1986) 'The Bitter Wounding: The Lament as Social Protest in Rural Greece', in J. Dubisch (ed.) *Gender and Power in Rural Greece.* Princeton, NJ: Princeton University Press.

Cavounidis, J. (1985) 'Family and Production Relations: Artisan and Worker Househlds in Athens', PhD thesis, London School of Economics, University of London.

Centre for Planning and Economic Research (KEPE) (1979) *Economic and Social Development Plan 1978–1982: Preliminary Guidelines*. Athens: KEPE.

Centre for Planning and Economic Research (KEPE) (1989) *Ekthesis gia to Programma 1988–1992: Kinoniki Pronoia*. Athens: KEPE.

Clark, M.H. (1983) 'Variations on Themes of Male and Female: Reflections on Gender Bias in Fieldwork in Rural Greece', *Women's Studies*, Vol. 10, pp. 117–33.

Cocking, J.M. (1987) 'The Folk Textiles of Crete', PhD thesis, University of Manchester.

Commission of the European Communities (1986) 'Equal Opportunities for Women', *Bulletin of the European Communities*, Vol. 3, No. 86, pp. 2–20.

Couroucli, M. (1985) *Les Oliviers du Lignage*. Paris: Maisonneuve et Larose.

Cowan, J.K. (1990) *Dance and the Body Politic in Northern Greece*. Princeton, NJ: Princeton University Press.

Cowan, J.K. (1991) 'Going Out for Coffee? Contesting the Grounds of Gendered Pleasures in Everyday Sociability', in P. Loizos and E. Papataxiarchis (eds) *Contested Identities: Gender and Kinship in Modern Greece*. Princeton, NJ: Princeton University Press.

Crick, M. (1989) 'Ali and Me: An Essay in Street Corner Anthropology', paper presented at the ASA conference on Autobiography and Anthropology, York, 3–6 April.

Dalley, G. (1990) *Ideologies of Caring*. London: Macmillan.

Das, R. (2004) 'Social Capital and Poverty of the Wage-Labour Class: Problems with the Social Capital Theory', *Transactions*, Vol. 29, pp. 27–45.

Davis, J. (1977) *People of the Mediterranean: An Essay in Comparative Social Anthropology*. London: Routledge and Kegan Paul.

Delaney, C. (1987) 'Seeds of Honor, Fields of Shame', in D.D. Gilmore (ed.) *Honor and Shame and the Unity of the Mediterranean*. A special publication of the American Anthropological Association, No. 22. Washington DC: ASA.

Demathas, Z. (1991) 'Economic, Social and Political Developments 1950–1991', paper presented at the Conference for Mediterranean Islands, University of Bristol, September.

Demoussis, M. (2003) 'Transformations of the CAP and the Need for Reorganizing Agricultural Policy in Greece', in C. Kasimis and G. Stathakis (eds) *The Reform of the CAP and Rural Development in Southern Europe*. Aldershot: Ashgate.

Dimen, M. (1986) 'Servants and Sentries: Women, Power and Social Reproduction in Kriovrisi', in J. Dubisch (ed.) *Gender and Power in Rural Greece*. Princeton, NJ: Princeton University Press.

Donatos, G. et al. (1989) *Research on Investment Prospects in the Cretan Region*. Vol. B. Athens: ETBA (in Greek).

du Boulay, J. (1974) *Portrait of a Greek Mountain Village*. London: Oxford University Press.

du Boulay, J. (1986) 'Women – Images of their Nature and Destiny in Rural Greece', in J. Dubisch (ed.) *Gender and Power in Rural Greece*. Princeton, NJ: Princeton University Press.

Dubisch. J. (ed.) (1986) *Gender and Power in Rural Greece*. Princeton, NJ: Princeton University Press.

Dubisch, J. (1986a) 'Culture Enters through the Kitchen: Women, Food and Social Boundaries in Rural Greece', in J. Dubisch (ed.) *Gender and Power in Rural Greece*. Princeton: Princeton University Press.

Dubisch, J. (1986b) 'Introduction', in J. Dubisch (ed.) *Gender and Power in Rural Greece*. Princeton, NJ: Princeton University Press.

Dubisch, J. (1990) 'Pilgrimage and Popular Religion at a Greek Holy shrine', in E. Badone (ed.) *Religious Orthodoxy and Popular Faith in European Society*. Princeton, NJ: Princeton University Press.

Eikeland, S. (1999) 'New Rural Pluriactivity? Household Strategies and Rural Renewal in Norway', in *Sociologia Ruralis*, Vol. 30, No. 3.

Elefteroudakis (ed.) (1960) *Mega Ellino-Anglikon Lexicon*. Athens: Elefteroudakis.

Elias, N. (1978) *The Civilizing Process, Volume 1: The History of Manners*. Oxford: Basil Blackwell.

Etxezarreta, M. (1985) *La Agricultura Insuficiente. La Agricultura a Tiempo Parcial en Espana*. Madrid: MAPA.

Faderman, L. (1985) *Surpassing the Love of Men*. London: The Women's Press.

Fennell, R. (1987) *The Common Agricultural Policy of the European Community*. Oxford: BSP Professional Books.

Finch, J. (1989) *Family Obligations and Social Change*. Cambridge: Polity Press.

Freris, A.F. (1986) *The Greek Economy in the Twentieth Century*. London: Croom Helm.

Friedl, E. (1964) *Vasilika: A Village in Modern Greece*. New York: Holt, Rinehart and Winston.

Friedl, E. (1986a) 'The Position of Women: Appearance and Reality', in J. Dubisch (ed.) *Gender and Power in Rural Greece*. Princeton, NJ: Princeton University Press.

Friedl, E. (1986b) 'Field Work in a Greek Village', in P. Golde (ed.) *Women in the Field*. Berkeley and Los Angeles: University of California Press.

Giddens, A. (1992) *The Transformation of Intimacy: Sexuality, Love and Eroticism in Modern Societies*. Cambridge: Polity Press.

Gillman (1990) 'A Touch of the Vapours', *Sunday Times Magazine*. September.

Gilmore, D.D. (1987a) 'Introduction: The Same of Dishonour', in D.D. Gilmore (ed.) *Honor and Shame and the Unity of the Mediterranean*. A special publication of the American Anthropological Association, No.22. Washington DC: ASA.

Gilmore, D.D. (ed.) (1987b) *Honor and Shame and the Unity of the Mediterranean*. A special publication of the American Anthropological Association, No.22. Washington DC: ASA.

Giovannini, M.J. (1987) 'Female Chastity Codes in the Circum-Mediterranean: Comparative Perspectives', in D.D. Gilmore (ed.) *Honor and Shame and the Unity of the Mediterranean*. A special publication of the American Anthropological Association, No. 22. Washington DC: ASA.

Girgilakis, G. (1985) *The Cultivation of Early Vegetables in Western Kisamos*. Chania (in Greek).

Goddard, V. (1989) 'Honour and Shame: The Control of Women's Sexuality and Group Identity in Naples', in P. Caplan (ed.) *The Cultural Construction of Sexuality*. London: Routledge.

Gramsci, A. (1971) *Selections from the Prison Notebooks* (ed. and trans. Q. and G. Nowell-Smith). London: Lawrence and Wishart.

Greenberg, D.F. (1988) *The Construction of Homosexuality*. Chicago: The University of Chicago Press.

Greger, S. (1985) 'Village on a Plateau: Cretan Mountain Women in a Changing Economy', PhD thesis, University of Manchester.

Grenda, K. (1984) 'Women's Associations of the Metropolis of Kisamos and Selinon: An Educational Programme of the Orthodox Academy of Crete', *Eklogi*, Vol. 64, pp. 109–14 (in Greek).

Halliday, J. and Little, J. (2001) 'Amongst Women: Exploring the Reality of Rural Childcare', *Sociologia Ruralis*, Vol. 41, No. 4, pp. 423–37.

Hammersely, M. and Atkinson, P. (1990) *Ethnography: Principles in Practice*. London: Routledge.

Handman, M.E. (1983) *La Violence et la Ruse. Hommes et Femmes dans un Village Grec*. La Calade, Aix-en-Provenve: Edisud.

Herzfeld, M. (1980) 'Honour and Shame: Problems in the Comparative Analysis of Moral Systems', *Man* (n.s.), Vol. 15, pp. 339–51.

Herzfeld, M. (1985) *The Poetics of Manhood: Contest and Identity in a Cretan Mountain Village*. Princeton, NJ: Princeton University Press.

Herzfeld, M. (1991) 'Silence, Submission and Subversion: Towards a Poetics of Womanhood', in P. Loizos and E. Papataxiarchis (eds) *Contested Identities: Gender and Kinship in Modern Greece*. Princeton, NJ: Princeton University Press.

Herzfeld, M. (2004) *The Body Impolitic: Artisans and Artifice in the Global Hierarchy of Value*. Chicago: The University of Chicago Press.

Hirschon, R. (1978) 'Open Body/Closed Space: The Transformation of Female Sexuality', in S. Ardener (ed.) *Defining Females*. New York: John Wiley and Sons.

Hirschon, R. (ed.) (1984) *Women and Property – Women as Property*. Kent: Croom Helm.

Hirschon, R. (1989) *Heirs of the Greek Catastrophe: The Social Life of Asia Minor Refugees in Piraeus*. Oxford: Oxford University Press.

Hitiris, T. (1988) *European Community Economics*. London: Harvester Wheatsheaf.

Hoffman, S.M. (1976) 'The Ethnography of Islands: Thera', in M. Dimen and E. Friedl (eds) *Regional Variations in Modern Greece and Cyprus: towards a Perspective on the Ethnography of Greece. Annals of the New York Academy of Sciences*, Vol. 268, pp. 328–40.

Hornby, A.S. (1974) *Oxford Advanced Learner's Dictionary of Current English*. Oxford: Oxford University Press.

Hubbard, L.J. and Harvey, D.R. (1986) 'Greece and the Common Agricultural Policy', in G.N. Yannopoulos (ed.) *Greece and the EEC*. London: Macmillan.

Inalcik, H. (1985) *Studies in Ottoman Social and Economic History*. London: Variorum.

Ioakimidis, P.C. (1984) 'Greece: From Military Dictatorship to Socialism', in A. Williams (ed.) *Southern Europe Transformed*. London: Harper and Row.

Irinaeos (1986) 'Emancipation of Women within the Greek-Orthodox Tradition'. Chania (unpublished pamphlet).

Joekes, P. (1989) *Women in the World Economy*. An INSTRAW study. Oxford: Oxford University Press.

Jones, A.R. (1984) 'Agriculture: Organisation, Reform and the EEC', in A. Williams (ed.) *Southern Europe Transformed*. London: Harper and Row.

Just, R. (1978) 'Some Problems for Mediterranean Anthropology', *Journal of the Anthropological Society of Oxford*, Vol. 9, pp. 81–95.

Just, R. (2000) *A Greek Island Cosmos: Kinship and Community in Meganisi*. Oxford: James Currey.

Kasaba, R. (1988) *The Ottoman Empire and the World Economy*. New York: State University of New York Press.

Kasimis, C. (1983) 'Socio-economic Change in Two Greek Peasant Communities, 1949–1981', PhD thesis, University of Bradford.

Kasimis, C. and Stathakis, G. (2003) 'Introduction and Overview of the Volume', in C. Kasimis and G. Stathakis (eds) *The Reform of the CAP and Rural Development in Southern Europe*. Aldershot: Ashgate.

Kasimis, C., Papadopoulos, A.G. and Zacopoulou, E. (2003) 'Migrants in Rural Greece', *Sociologia Ruralis*, Vol. 43, No. 2, pp. 167–84.

Katakis, M. (1987) *Green-house Cultivation in the Region under the Responsibility of the 21st Geotechnical Review*. Kisamos: ATE (in Greek).

Katrougalos, G. and Lazaridis, G. (2003) *Southern European Welfare States: Problems, Challenges and Prospects*. Basingstoke: Palgrave.

Kenna, (1976a) 'Houses, Fields and Graves: Property and Ritual Obligation on a Greek Island', *Ethnology*, Vol. 15, pp. 21–34.

Kenna (1976b) 'The Idiom of the Family', in J.G. Peristiany (ed.) *Mediterranean Family Structures*. Cambridge: Cambridge University Press.

Kenna, M. (1983) 'Institutional and Transformational Migration and the Politics of Community: Greek Internal Migrants and their Migrant's Association', *European Journal of Sociology*, Vol. 24, pp. 263–287.

Kenna, M. (1985) 'Icons in Theory and Practice: An Orthodox Christian Example', *History of Religions*, Vol. 24, pp. 345–68.

Kenna, M. (1986) 'Twenty Years After: Gender, Property and Ritual Relations on Nisos and the Effects of Migration and Tourism', paper presented at the inaugural symposium, University of the Aegean, Mytilene, Greece, September.

Kenna, M. (1989) 'Changing Places and Altered Perspectives: Research on a Greek Island in the '60s and in the '80s', paper presented at the ASA conference on 'Autobiography and Anthropology', University of York, York, April.

Kennedy, R. (1986) 'Women's Friendships on Crete: A Psychological Perspective', in J. Dubisch (ed.) *Gender and Power in Rural Greece*. Princeton, NJ: Princeton University Press.

Kinsella, J., Wilson, S., de Jong, F. and Renting, H. (2000) 'Pluriactivity as a Livelihood Strategy in Irish Farm Households and its Role in Rural Development', *Sociologia Ruralis*, Vol. 40, No.4, pp. 481–96.

Kloosterman, R. and Rath, J. (2001) 'Immigrant Entrepreneurs in Advanced Economies: Mixed Embeddedness', *Journal of Ethnic and Migration Studies*, Vol. 27, No. 2, pp. 189–201.

Kordatos, G. (1973) *Istoria tou Agrotikou Kimimatos ston Ellada*. Athens: Boukoumanis. (in Greek).

Kousis, M. (1984) 'Tourism as an Agent of Social Change in a Rural Cretan Community', PhD thesis, Univerisity of Michigan.

Lambropoulou, K. (1990) 'The Relationship between the Welfare State and the Family: Selective Theoretical Perspectives with Particular Reference to Greece', MSc thesis, University of Bristol.

Lazaridis, G. (1995a) 'Aspects of Greek and Cretan Rural Development', *Journal of Mediterranean Studies* Vol. 5, No.1, pp. 108–28.

Lazaridis, G. (1995b) 'Market Gardening and Women's Work in Platanos, Greece', *European Journal of Women's Studies*, Vol. 2, pp. 441–67.

Lazaridis, G. (1999) 'The Helots of the New Millenium', in F. Anthias and G. Lazaridis (eds) *Into the Margins: Migration and Exclusion in Southern Europe*. Avebury: Ashgate.

Lazaridis, G. (2001) 'Trafficking and Prostitution: The Growing Exploitation of Migrant Women in Greece', *European Journal of Women's Studies*, Vol. 8, No. 1, pp. 67–102.

Lazaridis, G. (2003) 'From Maids to Entrepreneurs: Immigrant Women in Greece', Freedman, J. (ed.) *Gender and Insecurity: Migrant women in Europe*. Avebury: Ashgate.

Lazaridis, G. (2007a) 'Irregular Migration and the Trampoline Effect: "Les Infirmières Exclusives", "Quasi-nurses", Nannies, Maids and Sex Workers in Greece', in E. Bergrren, B. Likic-Brboric, G. Toksöz, N. Trimikliniotis and S. Durgun (eds) *Irregular Migration, Informal Labour and Community in Europe*. Denmark: Shaker Verlag.

Lazaridis, G. (2007b) 'Les Infirmieres Exclusives and Quasi-nurses in Greece', *European Journal of Women's Studies*, Vol. 14, No. 3, pp. 227–45.

Lazaridis, G. (2008) ' Highly Educated and/or Skilled Migrants from Third Countries and Self-employment in Greece: A Comparison between Men's and Women's Experiences', in U. Apitzsch and M. Kontos (eds) *Self-Employment Activities of Women and Minorities. Their Success or Failure in Relation to Social Citizenship Policies in Europe*. Wiesbaden: VS Verlag Fur Sozialwissenschaften.

Lazaridis, G. and Koumandraki, M. (2007a) 'Networks and Migration: The case of Third Country Migrants in Greece', in IMEPO (ed.) *Capturing the Benefits of Migration in Southeastern Europe*. Washington DC: The Hellenic Migration Policy Institute.

Lazaridis, G. and Koumandraki, M. (2007b) 'Albanian Migration to Greece: Patterns and Processes of Inclusion and Exclusion in the Labor Market', *European Societies*, Vol. 9, No. 1, pp. 91–111.

Lazaridis, G. and Psimmenos, I. (1999) 'Albanians in Greece: Social, Spatial and Economic Exclusion', in R. King, G. Lazaridis and C. Tsardanidis (eds) *Eldorado or Fortress? Migration in Southern Europe*. Basingstoke: Macmillan.

Lazaridis, G. and Romaniszyn, K. (1998) 'Inflow of Undocumented Polish and Albanian Migrants in Greece', *Journal of European Social Policy*, Vol. 8, No. 1, pp. 1–22.

Lazaridis, G. and Wickens, E. (1999) '"Us" and the "Others": The Experiences of Different Ethnic Minorities in the Greek Cities of Athens and Thessaloniki', *Annals of Tourism Research*, Vol. 26, No. 3, pp. 632–55.

Lever, A. (1984) 'Agriculture, Handicrafts and Migration in Rural Spain', PhD thesis, University of Bristol.

Lever, A. (1986) 'Honour as a Red Herring', *Critique of Anthropology*, Vol. 6, No. 3, pp. 83–106.

Lever, A. (1988) 'Capital, Gender and Skill: Women Homeworkers in Rural Spain', *Feminist Review*, Vol. 30, pp. 3–24.

Lineton, M. (1971) 'Mina Present and Past – Depopulation in a Village in Mani, Southern Greece', PhD thesis, University of Kent, Canterbury.

Loizos, P. (1975) *The Greek Gift*. Oxford: Blackwell.

Loizos, P. and Papataxiarchis, E. (eds) (1991) *Contested Identities: Gender and Kinship in Modern Greece*. Princeton, NJ: Princeton University Press.

Luhmann, N. (1968) *Trust and Power.* Chichester: John Wiley and Sons.

Maravegias, N. (1989) *I Entaxi tis Elladas stin Evropaiki Kinotita: Epiptosis ston Agrotiko Tomea*. Athens: Idrima Mesogeakon Meleton.

Marcus, G. and Fischer, M. (1986) *Anthropology and Cultural Critique*. Chicago: University of Chicago Press.

Marsh, J. (1979) 'Agriculture', in L. Tsoukalis (ed.) *Greece and the European Community*. Westmead, Farnborough: Saxon House.

Mauss, M. (1935) 'Les Techniques du Corps', in *Journal de Psychologie Normale et Pathologique*, Vol. 35, pp. 271–93.

Mavrakis, Y. (1983) *Laografika Kritis*. Athens: Historikes Edthosis S. Vasilopoulos.

Mies, M. (1982) *The Lace Makers of Narsapur: Indian Housewives Produce for the World Market*. London: Zed Press.

Misztal, B.A. (1996) *Trust in Modern Societies*. Oxford: Polity Press.

Momsen, J.H. (1991) *Women and Development in the Third World*. London: Routledge.

Mouzelis, N. (1976) 'Capitalism and the Development of Agriculture', *Journal of Peasant Studies*, Vol. 3, pp. 483–92.

Mouzelis, N. (1978) *Modern Greece: Facets of Underdevelopment*. London: Macmillan.

Mouzelis, N. (1979) 'Peasant Agriculture, Productivity and the Laws of the Capitalist Development: A Reply to Vergopoulos', *Journal of Peasant Studies*, Vol. 6, pp. 351–57.

Moysides, A. (1986) *I Agrotiki Kinotita sti* Synhroni *Ellada*. Athens: Idryma Mesogeakon Meleton.

Nelson, N. (1989) 'Selling her Kiosk: Kikuju Notions of Sexuality and Sex for Sale in Mathare Valley, Kenya', in P. Caplan (ed.) *The Cultural Construction of Sexuality*. London: Routledge.

Niotakis, I.G. (1958) *Oikonomiki Erevna tis Kritis*. Heracleon: Promiteus.

Oakley, A. (1985) *The Sociology of Housework*, 2nd edition. Oxford: Blackwell.

OECD (1973) *Greece: Economic Survey*. Paris: OECD.

Papataxiarchis, E. (1988) 'Kinship, Friendship and Gender Relations in two east Aegean Village Communities, Lesbos, Greece', PhD thesis, London School of Economics.

Papataxiarchis, E. (1991) 'Friends of the Heart: Male Commensal Solidarity, Gender and Kinship in Aegean Greece', in P. Loizos and E. Papataxiarchis (eds) (1991) *Contested Identities: Gender and Kinship in Modern Greece*. Princeton, NJ: Princeton University Press.

Pavlides, E. and Hesser, J. (1986) 'Women's Roles and House Form and Decoration in Eressos, Greece', in J. Dubisch (ed.) *Gender and Power in Rural Greece*. Princeton, NJ: Princeton University Press.

Peristiany, J.G. (ed.) (1965) *Honour and Shame: The Values of Mediterranean Society*. London: Weidenfeld and Nicholson.

Peristiany, J.G. (ed.) (1976) *Mediterranean Family Structures*. Cambridge: Cambridge University Press.

Petronoti, M. (1980) 'The Economic Autonomy of Rural Women: A Survey of the Mediterranean with Specific Reference to Three Greek Islands', MPhil thesis, University of Kent, Canterbury.

Petronoti, M. (1980) 'The Economic Autonomy of Rural Women: A Survey of the Mediterranean with Specific Reference to Three Greek Islands', MPhil thesis, University of Kent at Canterbury.

Pini, B. (2002) 'The Exclusion of Women from Agri-Political Leadership: A Case Study of the Australian Sugar Industry', *Sociologia Ruralis*, Vol. 42, No. 1, pp. 65–76.

Pini-Cabral, J. de (1986) *Sons of Adam, Daughters of Eve: The Peasant Worldview of the Alto Minho*. Oxford: Clarendon Press.

Pitt-Rivers, J. (1965) 'Honour and Social Status', in J.G. Peristiany (ed.) *Honour and Shame: The Values of Mediterranean Society*. London: Weidenfeld and Nicholson.

Pitt-Rivers, J. (1977) *The Fate of Shechem or the Politics of Sex: Essays in the Anthropology of the Mediterranean*. Cambridge: Cambridge University Press.

Plascasovitis, I. (1986) 'A Regional Context for Assessing the Impact of the CAP on Greek Agricultural Revenue', PhD thesis, University of Reading.

Powell, P. (1970) 'Peasant Society and Clientelistic Politics', *American Political Science Review*, Vol. 64.

Putnam, R. (1993) *Making Democracy Work*. Princeton NJ: Princeton University Press.

Richardson, D. (1992) 'Constructing Lesbian Sexualities', in K. Plummer (ed.) *Modern Homosexualities: Fragments of Lesbian and Gay Experience*. London: Routledge.

Rogers, B. (1986) *The Domestication of Women: Discrimination in Developing Societies*. London: Tavistock.

Rogers, R. (1970) *The Domestication of Women: Discrimination in Developing Societies*. London: Tavistock.

Rushdie, S. (1980) *Midnight's Children*. New York: Penguin.

Ryan, B.F. et al. (1985) *Minitab Handbook*. Boston: PWS-Kent.

Salamone, S.D. and Stanton, J.B. (1986) 'Introducing the Nikokyra: Ideality and Reality in Social Process', in J. Dubisch (ed.) *Gender and Power in Rural Greece*. Princeton, NJ: Princeton University Press.

Salomon, S.D. and Stanton, J.B. (1986) 'Introducing the Nikokyra: Ideality and Reality in Social Process', in J. Dubisch (ed.) *Gender and Power in Rural Greece*. Princeton, NJ: Princeton University Press.

Saugeres, L. (2002) 'Of Tractors and Men: Masculinity, Technology and Power in a French Farming Community', *Sociologia Ruralis*, Vol. 42, No. 2. pp. 143–59.

Settas, N. (1963) *I Agrotiki Anaptixis tis Kritis*. Athens: n.p.

Shortall, S. (2002) 'Gendered Agricultural and Rural Restructuring: A Case Study of Northern Ireland', *Sociologia Ruralis*, Vol. 42, No. 2, pp. 160–75.

Silvasti, T. (2003) 'Bending Borders of Gendered Labour Division on Farms: The Case of Finland', *Sociologia Ruralis*, Vol. 43, No.2, pp. 154–65.

Simmel, G. (1971) 'The Stranger', in D.N. Levine (ed.) *On Individuality and Social Forms*. Chicago: University of Chicago Press.

Stamiris, E. (1986) 'The Women's Movement in Greece', *New Left Review*, Vol. 158, pp. 98–111.

Stathatos, H.E.S. (1979) 'From Association to Full Membership', in L. Tsoukalis (ed.) *Greece and the European Community*. Westmead, Farnborough: Saxon House.

Summers, A. (1979) 'A Home from Home – Women's Philanthropic Work in the Nineteenth Century', in S. Burman (ed.) *Fit Work for Women*. London: Croom Helm.

Sutton, S. (1978) 'Migrant Regional Associations: An Athenian Example and its Implications', unpublished PhD thesis, University of North Carolina.

Swindell, K. (1985) *Farm Labour*. Cambridge: Cambridge University Press.

Tapinc, H. (1992) 'Masculinity, Femininity and Turkish Male Homosexuality', in K. Plummer (ed.) *Modern Homosexualities: Fragments of Lesbian and Gay Experience*. London: Routledge.

Tsoukalis, L. (ed.) (1979) *Greece and the European Community*. Westmead, Farnborough: Saxon House.

Vergopoulos, K. (1975) *To Agrotiko Zitima stin Ellada – I Kinotiki Ensomatosi tis Georgias*. Athens: Exantas.

Vergopoulos, K. (1978) 'Capitalism and Peasant Productivity', *Journal of Peasant Studies*, Vol. 5, pp. 446–65.

Walby, S. (1997) *Gender Transformations*. London: Routledge.

Ware, T. (1987) *The Orthodox Church*. London: Penguin.

Williams, A. (ed.) *Southern Europe Transformed*. London: Harper and Row.

Woolcock, M. (2000) 'Social Capital in Theory and Practice: Where Do We Stand', paper presented at the 21st Annual Conference on Economic Issues (http//www.world-bank.org/poverty/scapital/index.htm).

Yannopoulos, G.N. (ed.) *Greece and the EEC*. London: Macmillan.

Zaharopoulos, E.D. (1985) 'Foreign Mass Communication in Greece: its Impact on Greek Culture and influence on Greek Society', PhD thesis, Southern Illinois University.

Zinovieff, S. (1991) 'Hunters and Hunted: *Kamaki* and the Ambiguities of Sexual Predation in a Greek Town', in P. Loizos and E. Papataxiarchis (eds) *Contested Identities: Gender and Kinship in Modern Greece*. Princeton, NJ: Princeton University Press.

Zolotas, X. (1976) *Greece in the European Community*. London: Macmillan.

Zolotas, X. (1978) *The Positive Contribution of Greece to the European Community*. Athens: Bank of Greece.

Index

Greek terms and acronyms are indicated by *italics*. 'f' (e.g. '154f') indicates reference exclusively to a figure, and 'n' (e.g. '88n') indicates reference exclusively to a note.

Confederacy of Women's Associations
190
conflict within families 45, 163–4
inter-generational 136–9, 210
consumption, status 155–6
contraception 158–60, 174, 210
cooperative
labour 102–105
production 73–76
producers' 109
cooperatives, women's (*synetaerismos*) 73
cooperatives' associations 109, 129–30
councils, village 35
courtship 173
credit, financial 16
house purchase 136
men favoured 112, 113
Crete: geography 11
CSFs (Community Support
Frameworks) 33
cultural awareness (author's) 4

data, official: inaccuracies 6–8
daughters-in-law: relationships with
mothers-in-law 136–9
day-wage labour 126
dealers: *koukoulia* 71–2
debt 13, 16, 91, 129–30
derogatory connotations 73
interest rates 16
dependency: men's on women 111
dependents: responsibility for 43–4, 56,
76, 78, 92, 101
development, regional programmes 73,
210–11
women disadvantaged 112, 114
differentiation: of agriculturalists 102
divorce 139–41, 160
domestic animals: as pets 42
domestic work (*ikiaka*) *see* work,
domestic (*ikiaka*)
dowries (*prika*) 77, 132, 135, 143–7, 209
abolition, official 150
alternatives 151
assistance from women's associations
194
brothers' responsibilities 144, 150
decline 148

female-produced (*prikia*) 145–147,
153, 209
olive trees 124

EC *see* European Community
Economic and Social Development
Plans 23n, 24–5
economic dependency of women:
challenged 57
economic development: impact on
women 207
education: parental involvement 78, 89
effeminacy 178n, 179–81
elderly
care 161–7, 209
financial assistance 163
number (population) 165
eleotrivio (olive press) 128n
eleourgio (olive press) 128n
emborikos tropos (commercial way of
marketing) 106
embroidering
dowries 145–6
koukoulia 57, 63
employment rate: agriculture 19
endogamy 134
engagement 174, 175
environment, care for 29
EOMMEX 73, 186
European Community
agricultural policy
viability of farms 25–6
developmental assistance 32–3
Directive 85/148/EC 118
equality, promotion of 114
Greek membership 19–20
Regulation no. 355/77 31
Regulation no. 797/85 20–21n, 31
subsidies 17, 82, 118, 208–9
given to men 124, 126
Eve 171–2, 192
exogamy 133, 134, 145
exports, agricultural 25

families
conflict within 45, 136–9, 163–4, 210
mutual support within 93, 102–5
care for elders 163

For Product Safety Concerns and Information please contact our
EU representative GPSR@taylorandfrancis.com, Taylor & Francis
Verlag GmbH, Kaufingerstraße 24, 80331 München, Germany.